Marginalized Groups, Inequalities and the Post-War Welfare State

Examining the ways in which societies treat their most vulnerable members has long been regarded as revealing of the bedrock beliefs and values that guide the social order. However, academic research about the post-war welfare state is often focused on mainstream arrangements or on one social group. With its focus on different marginalized groups: migrants and people with disabilities, this volume offers novel perspectives on the national and international dimensions of the post-war welfare state in Western Europe and North America.

Monika Baár is Professor by Special Appointment of Central European Studies at Leiden University, the Netherlands. She is principal investigator of the ERC-funded research project Rethinking Disability: the Global Impact of the International Year of Disabled Persons (1981) in Historical Perspective.

Paul van Trigt is Postdoctoral Researcher with the ERC-funded research project Rethinking Disability: the Global Impact of the International Year of Disabled Persons (1981) in Historical Perspective at the Institute of History, Leiden University, the Netherlands.

Routledge Studies in Modern History

55 Transatlantic Trade and Global Cultural Transfers Since 1492
More Than Commodities
Edited by Martina Kaller and Frank Jacob

56 Contesting the Origins of the First World War
An Historiographical Argument
Troy R E Paddock

57 India at 70
Multidisciplinary Approaches
Edited by Ruth Maxey and Paul McGarr

58 1917 and the Consequences
Edited by Gerhard Besier and Katarzyna Stoklosa

59 Reforming Senates
Upper Legislative Houses in North Atlantic Small Powers 1800-present
*Edited by Nikolaj Bijleveld, Colin Grittner, David E. Smith
and Wybren Verstegen*

60 Unsettled 1968 in the Troubled Present
Revisiting the 50 Years of Discussions from East and Central Europe
Edited by Aleksandra Konarzewska, Anna Nakai and Michał Przeperski

60 Unsettled 1968 in the Troubled Present
Revisiting the 50 Years of Discussions from East and Central Europe
Edited by Aleksandra Konarzewska, Anna Nakai and Michał Przeperski

61 Marginalized Groups, Inequalities and the Post-War Welfare State
Whose Welfare?
Edited by Monika Baár and Paul van Trigt

62 Union and Disunion in the Nineteenth Century
Edited by James Gregory and Daniel J. R. Grey

63 Intellectuals in the Latin Space during the Era of Fascism
Crossing Borders
Edited by Valeria Galimi and Annarita Gori

64 The Co-opting of Education by Extremist Factions
Professing Hate
Sarah Gendron

65 Alcohol Flows across Cultures
Drinking Cultures in Transnational and Comparative Perspective

For a full list of titles, please visit: https://www.routledge.com/history/series/MODHIST

Marginalized Groups, Inequalities and the Post-War Welfare State
Whose Welfare?

Edited by Monika Baár
and Paul van Trigt

LONDON AND NEW YORK

First published 2020
by Routledge
2 Park Square, Milton Park, Abingdon, Oxon OX14 4RN

and by Routledge
52 Vanderbilt Avenue, New York, NY 10017

Routledge is an imprint of the Taylor & Francis Group, an informa business

© 2020 selection and editorial matter, Monika Baár and Paul van Trigt; individual chapters, the contributors

The right of the editor to be identified as the author of the editorial material, and of the authors for their individual chapters, has been asserted in accordance with sections 77 and 78 of the Copyright, Designs and Patents Act 1988.

All rights reserved. No part of this book may be reprinted or reproduced or utilised in any form or by any electronic, mechanical, or other means, now known or hereafter invented, including photocopying and recording, or in any information storage or retrieval system, without permission in writing from the publishers.

Trademark notice: Product or corporate names may be trademarks or registered trademarks, and are used only for identification and explanation without intent to infringe.

British Library Cataloguing-in-Publication Data
A catalogue record for this book is available from the British Library

Library of Congress Cataloging-in-Publication Data
A catalog record has been requested for this book

ISBN: 978-1-138-38882-6 (hbk)
ISBN: 978-0-429-42435-9 (ebk)

Typeset in Times
by Deanta Global Publishing Services, Chennai, India

Contents

List of illustrations	vii
List of contributors	viii
Introduction MONIKA BAÁR AND PAUL VAN TRIGT	1
1 **Rescuing the European welfare state: the Social Affairs Committee of the early European Communities, 1953–1962** BRIAN SHAEV	9
2 **From territorialized rights to personalized international social rights? The making of the European Convention on the Social Security of Migrant Workers (1957)** KARIM FERTIKH	29
3 **The ILO and the shift towards economic liberalization in the international professional rehabilitation policies of people with disabilities after World War II** GILDAS BRÉGAIN	49
4 **Farewell to social Europe? An entangled perspective on European disability policies in the 1980s and 1990s** PAUL VAN TRIGT	69
5 **The history of a phantom welfare state: the United States** ROSE ERNST	81
6 **Managing the transition from war to peace: post-war citizenship-based welfare in Italy and France, 1944–1947** GIACOMO CANEPA	101

7 **Disabled citizens and the neoliberal turn in Britain: whose rights and whose responsibilities?** 119
MONIKA BAÁR

8 **Welfare: defended, questioned, complemented? Belgian welfare arrangements in the 1970s–1980s from the perspective of disability organizations** 137
ANAÏS VAN ERTVELDE

9 **A new inequality in the Danish welfare state: the development of immigration and integration policy in post-war Denmark** 155
HEIDI VAD JØNSSON

Conclusion: beyond citizenship and "responsibilization" in the exclusionary welfare state: realizing universal human rights through social resilience-building and interactional justice? 173
VERONIKA FLEGAR

Index 191

Illustrations

Figures

5.1 Percentage of FDR speeches including the word "welfare"   83
5.2 Comparison of "general welfare" versus social insurance/relief mentions in FDR speeches   84

Table

5.1 Comparison of state-administered "social service" programmes, Washington State   90

Contributors

Monika Baár is Professor by Special Appointment of Central European Studies at Leiden University, the Netherlands. She is the principal investigator of the ERC-funded research project Rethinking Disability: the Global Impact of the International Year of Disabled Persons (1981) in Historical Perspective. She is the author of the monograph *Historians and Nationalism: East Central Europe in the Nineteenth Century* (2010), co-author of the two-volume *Negotiating Modernity: A History of Modern Political Thought in East Central Europe* (2016 and 2018), and her articles have appeared in journals including *Past & Present* and *First World War Studies*.

Gildas Brégain is a researcher with the National Center for Scientific Research, specializing in transnational disability history at the High School of Public Health in Rennes, France. He is the author of two books: *Syriens et Libanais d'Amérique du Sud* (1918–1945) (L'Harmattan, Paris, 2008) and *Pour une histoire du handicap au XXe siècle: Approches transnationales* (Europe et Amériques) (2018). In addition he has published numerous articles which appeared in journals such as ALTER and in the prize-winning volume *The Imperfect Historian* (2013).

Giacomo Canepa is a PhD candidate in contemporary history at Scuola Normale Superiore (Pisa, Italy) and the Centre d'histoire de Sciences Po (Paris, France). He is currently working on the transformations of social assistance systems in Italy and France between the end of Second World War and the 1970s. He has published several articles on refugees, welfare and the construction of democracy in post-war Italy in journals such as *Meridiana: Rivista di storia e scienze sociali* and *Contemporanea*.

Rose Ernst is Associate Professor of political science at Seattle University, United States. Her teaching and research interests include welfare politics, critical race theory, politics of intersectionality and social movements in the United States. She is the author of *The Price of Progressive Politics: The Welfare Rights Movement in an Era of Colorblind Racism* (2010). Her current book project is titled *Colonial Moods: Administrative Violence and Welfare State Development*.

Contributors ix

Anaïs Van Ertvelde is a PhD candidate at the Institute for History, Leiden, the Netherlands. Her thesis intends to track the ways in which the International Year of Disabled Persons (1981) and the subsequent International Decade of Disabled Persons (1982–1993) influenced government agencies on the international and national level (Belgium, Poland, Canada), disability organisations and people with disabilities themselves in conceiving of and dealing with disability. In 2017 she edited, together with S. Bracke and L. Lefranc, a special issue of the journal *Digest*. She also co-authored the book *Vuile Lakens* (2017), which presents a historically informed perspective on sexuality.

Karim Fertikh is Associate Professor of political science at the University of Strasbourg, France. He is a researcher at the CNRS–Center Sociétés, acteurs et gouvernement en Europe (SAGE) and is member of the Academic Institute of France. His current research focuses on the Europeanization and internationalization of social rights. He is the author of the monograph *Le Bad Godesberg de la social-démocratie allemande. Une histoire sociale des idées politiques* (2019), edited a volume on Social Europe (2018) and his articles have appeared in journals including the *Revue française de science politique, Genèses* and the *Austrian Journal of Historical Studies*.

Veronika Flegar is a PhD researcher in public administration at the University of Groningen, the Netherlands, where she conducts research on administrative justice and vulnerability in social and humanitarian policies. In addition, she is an affiliated researcher in the ERC-funded research project 'Rethinking Disability' at the Institute for History, Leiden University, the Netherlands. She has conducted extensive fieldwork with the United Nations High Commissioner for Refugees (UNHCR) and the International Organization for Migration (IOM) in Sudan and published on the administrative, legal and policy dimensions of assessing and addressing vulnerability in several edited volumes and international peer-reviewed journals.

Brian Shaev is University Lecturer at the Institute for History, Leiden University, the Netherlands. His publications include a comparative history of the Schuman Plan in *International Review of Social History* (2016); the Algerian war and European integration in French Historical Studies (2018); socialist policies on trade liberalization, customs unions and the Treaties of Rome in *Contemporary European History* (2018); and a co-edited book under contract, *Social Democracy and the History of European Competition Policy: Politics, Law and Regulation*. Currently he is co-leader of a grant project financed by the Jan Wallanders och Tom Hedelius Stiftelse on municipal policies on migrant integration in post-war Europe.

Paul van Trigt is a Postdoctoral Researcher with the ERC-funded project Rethinking Disability: the Global Impact of the International Year of Disabled Persons (1981) in Historical Perspective at the Institute of History, Leiden University, the Netherlands. He has published about the modern history of the welfare state, human rights, disability and religion. His monograph *Blind in* *een gidsland* (*Blind in a Guiding Country*) was published in 2013. Currently, he is writing a genealogy of the United Nations Convention on the Rights of Persons with Disabilities.

Heidi Vad Jønsson is Associate Professor at Institute of History/Danish Centre for Welfare Studies (DaWS), University of Southern Denmark (SDU). She has a proven record of active participation in interdisciplinary research and teaching in Scandinavian welfare and immigration policy. She has published in journals such as the *Scandinavian Journal of History* and edited the volume *Migrations and Welfare States*. Her recent publications include two books *Fra lige muligheder til ret og pligt: Socialdemokratiets integrationspolitik* (2018) and *Indvandring i velfærdsstaten* (2018).

Introduction

Monika Baár and Paul van Trigt

Whose welfare?[1]

In 2015 Jeroen Dijsselbloem, at that time chair of the Eurogroup, framed the so-called refugee crisis as a threat for well-developed welfare states in Europe. In his view, external borders must be guarded because otherwise "loads of people will come to demand support and they blow up the system."[2] Dijsselbloem's statement raises the question of how welfare has been used by policymakers to govern, coerce, mobilize and pacify their citizens and whether welfare has always been framed in such exclusive terms. Moreover, his unreserved approval of the welfare state may provoke reflection at a time of constant criticism when its bitter death is being forecast by many. In light of these constantly changing, intense and often controversial engagements with the welfare state in both academic and public debates, it appears to be timely to question whose welfare is precisely at stake in those discussions and to seek answers from a historical perspective.

This volume contributes to filling the lacuna that exists between the omnipresent and often unqualified references to the welfare state, on the one hand, and our insufficient knowledge about the precise contours and dynamics of its history in Western Europe, on the other. The enhancement to the existing literature that this volume offers lies in the combination of three ambitions: its focus on marginalized groups, its engagement with the problem of inequality and its critical scrutiny of the dominant narrative of the post-war welfare state.

Marginal groups

Despite omnipresent claims that examining the ways in which societies treat their most vulnerable members reveals the bedrock beliefs and values that guide the social order, academic research about the post-war welfare state has remained focused on mainstream arrangements. At the centre of this volume are people with disabilities, migrants and refugees, while certain aspects of the welfare of workers in precarious situations and the racialized aspects of the welfare state also receive attention. The common denominator among these groups is that their status does not align with the ideotype that is often implicitly assumed to represent the "mainstream" societal group in Western societies: the white, heterosexual, able-bodied, middle-class man whose life is typically considered normative for welfare arrangements. Analyses from a gender and critical-race perspective have demonstrated how exclusive these arrangements could be – even despite inclusive intentions.[3] This volume builds further on this scholarship: the majority of contributions undertake an empirical analysis of how policymakers and representatives of these marginalized groups have dealt with the welfare state mechanisms of inclusion and exclusion, whereas some contributions employ a critical conceptual perspective.

Even in those instances when this subject features in the welfare state literature, the focus typically lies on one specific group.[4] We have sought to push forward those debates by diversifying this standard singular range in the hope that this enables us to articulate the perspective of the margins more forcefully in the welfare state historiography. At the same time, we also hope to contribute to the separate historiographies of these groups, particularly to the relatively well-researched subject of migrants and to the much less studied subject of disabled people. With regard to the latter, as editors specializing in the history of disability, we seek to stimulate intersectional research. In particular we hope to meet the ambition to add the concept of disability to the toolbox of historians "both as a subject worth studying in its own right and as one that will provide scholars with a new analytic tool for exploring power itself" because disability is "crucial for understanding how Western cultures determine hierarchies and maintain social order as well as how they define progress."[5]

Bringing these groups together in one volume helps us to reveal commonalities between their welfare trajectories, whereas it also reminds us that these "groups" are far from homogeneous entities. Moreover, we gain a better impression of how welfare categories become instrumentalized by the state in order to regulate and/or restrict access to welfare services. Politicians and policymakers often find themselves confronted with a "distributive dilemma": how to cater for the needs of those who have no access to the labour market without damaging the societal work ethic.[6] As they constantly navigate between the competing ideals of offering protection and reducing expenditure, the old binary between the "deserving" and "undeserving" poor may be reiterated: those who maintain employment have different citizenship entitlements from those who are unemployed. In times of labour shortages, marginalized groups may be perceived as a potential resource, while in times of austerity and labour surplus they may be viewed as a burden on the welfare state or even a threat to national values – a phenomenon that can be observed during migration crises. The focus on marginalized groups exposes such dynamics.

The lens of inequality

The second historiographical challenge that this volume takes up is related to a pivotal concept which has been brought into the limelight due to the contemporary awareness of increasing (global) inequality. The lens of (in)equality renders it easier to place the welfare state on a longer timeline of the ordering "the social" in modern societies and to undertake comparisons with societies and thinkers who did not support the welfare state. It also helps to contemplate the ways in which welfare states create (in)equalities and how welfare states are restructured to prevent inequalities.[7]

Both in public and scholarly debates, the welfare state is, in its incarnation in the decades after the Second World War, frequently viewed as a model that has created a higher degree of (material) equality between citizens. In addition, the existing literature typically implies that the development of the post-war welfare state went along with attempts to foster a greater degree of equality between countries. Interrogating how the welfare state and the related ideals of equality have become fiercely contested since the 1970s, journalists and scholars often point to the end of the post-war consensus following the breakthrough of neoliberalism after the economic crisis in the 1970s.[8] In these debates, the relationship of the welfare state to marginalized groups and the critique on welfare arrangements by policymakers and by representatives of those groups themselves have hitherto received insufficient attention.

This engagement with inequality enables us to establish connections between the historiography of the welfare state and other branches of history-writing, in particular conceptual and international history. As the existing literature increasingly suggests, the historical investigation of equality benefits from an approach in which the interconnection of national and international dimensions is taken into account. Scholars such as Sandrine Kott, Julia Moses and Klaus Petersen – to mention just a few – have made interventions that prove crucial for the specialized welfare state literature, which is often characterized by methodological nationalism and fixed typologies.[9] Inspired by and building on this recent body of literature, the various chapters in the volume unravel the entanglement of domestic welfare policies with international social strategies and the considerable global transformations in those policies over time. Nevertheless, it is not only that the national context needs to be enriched with inter- and transnational aspects; the same holds true for the opposite direction. All too frequently, the "international is approached in an internalist way, which leads to a neglect of national developments. In his book about the European Convention and Court of Human Rights, Marco Duranti demonstrated that only by taking into account the domestic context of the founders the coming into being of the convention can be properly understood.[10] This approach is not yet self-evident: in recent literature on global inequality, sometimes regrets are expressed about the downfall of the welfare state without paying attention to how the national context could serve as an explanation for why people became critics of the welfare state. The local case studies in our volume therefore bring the national dimension into international history.

New (dis)continuities

In the third place this volume poses a historiographical challenge to the dominant narrative of the post-war welfare state. The qualitative historical analyses of the inclusion and exclusion of marginalized groups demonstrate that social policies addressing the most precarious societal groups have often deviated, sometimes significantly, from dominant welfare trajectories. The literature on these trajectories is dominated by quantitative approaches. Since the publication of Gøsta Esping-Andersen's extremely influential *Three Worlds of Welfare* (1990), typologies of welfare regimes have been refined and expanded. Today there exists consensus that welfare states are and were never "pure" types, but always hybrids.[11] Yet quantitative typologies continue to dominate the field, and these rely heavily on static models, which make it difficult to capture the specific dynamics of social policies directed at citizens in marginal positions. National typologies often obscure the highly comparable issues with which marginalized groups were confronted in their specific context.

Moreover, these typologies tend to float above history and can hardly be integrated into a historical timeline. In our volume we pay extended attention to certain intensified periods, such as the "post-war moment" and the period of economic crisis in the 1970s and 1980s, without suggesting that no welfare state existed before the Second World War and that the welfare state disappeared as a consequence of the emerging neoliberal consensus since the 1970s. On the contrary, the contributions in this volume challenge the dominant narrative about the existence of a post-war Western welfare state consensus that aimed at equal social citizenship, but became contested in the 1970s and since then made way for neoliberalism. Building on literature that has questioned this periodization, our volume shows the ambivalent nature of transitional moments such as the war and the economic crisis.[12] It reveals that from the vantage point of marginalized groups, both the welfare state consensus and the subsequent neoliberal consensus fostered unexpected inequalities.

This volume

The volume contains ten chapters that address diverse themes and historical periods, which take as their point of departure the fundamental experience of limited participation in society. There is no pretence here of a systematic or comprehensive analysis; rather, the contributions seek to highlight the potentials of this subject and invite further research.

The book first investigates how marginalized groups and the welfare state were addressed in welfare practices of international and in particular European institutions in the half century after the war. In his chapter on the Social Affairs Committee of the European Communities (Chapter 1), Brian Shaev discusses how this international group of politicians conceptualized welfare in the transition from a coal and steel community to a general common market. He shows how the committee during the 1950s promoted pro-active supranational social policies and how the discussions gradually shifted from welfare policies targeted at coal and steel workers (traditional subjects of welfare state policies in Europe) to the broader workforce and to migrants – which indicates an increasing awareness of the inequalities that arose during the development of post-war welfare states. In Chapter 2 about the making of the European Convention on the Social

Security of Migrant Workers (1957), Karim Fertikh further underlines the importance of coordination and internationalization of welfare provision after the war, as it was given shape by a transnational network of social reformers through bilateral agreements on social security concerning migrants. Fertikh addresses the dichotomy between the principles of territorialization and individualization. He demonstrates how in the framing of social insurances the personalization of social rights replaced the territoriality principle. This entailed the idea that social rights had to be attached to individuals independently of the territory where they lived or worked.

People with disabilities constituted another important target group of international social policies. In Chapter 3 about vocational rehabilitation policies of the International Labour Organization in the 1950s and 1960s, Gildas Brégain demonstrates that those policies could often be controversial and contradict the taken-for-granted post-war consensus about the welfare state. In the context of the Cold War, these debates were characterized by opposing stances between the government representatives of capitalist countries and those of socialist countries, while the views of employers' representatives clashed with the workers' representatives. A change in these debates took place when disabled people raised their voices, as becomes evident in Paul van Trigt's chapter about European disability policies in the 1980s and 1990s (Chapter 4). In this period of austerity politics, the internationalization of welfare remained a significant desideratum, but besides welfare equality accorded by the state, people started to make claims for other forms of equality. For European disability self-advocates, these demands entailed status equality.

The next half of the volume presents five case studies on national welfare state practices concerning marginalized groups in an international context. Rose Ernst (Chapter 5) offers a fundamental rethinking of the concept of the welfare state in the United States. Against the backdrop of its European counterparts, she interprets it as a phantom welfare state, a collective sensation containing a fictional element. The analysis, drawing on sources from the Washington State archives, demonstrates that welfare as an ideological construct plays a pivotal role in maintaining systems of social control and racialization.

In Chapter 6 Giacomo Canepa adopts an alternative approach by focusing on marginalized groups' position within the welfare state during the "post-war moment": he compares Italy and France during the years 1944–1947. In his analysis, Canepa shows how marginalized war-torn groups challenged the existing welfare categories in these years. Poverty and displacement affected all social strata, and their needs could not be met by the existing welfare system that drew on contributions and previous work activities. The chapter explains how these post-war emergencies stimulated the expansion of the welfare state and how social welfare was used to pacify citizens.

The next three chapters deal with a period in which welfare states became subject to austerity policies. Monika Baár (Chapter 7) investigates the impact of the "neoliberal turn" on disabled citizens in Britain, which coincided with the coming to the power of Margaret Thatcher's Tory government. Taking as its lens the repercussions of the International Year of Disabled Persons in Britain (1981), she demonstrates that disabled people, who had been neglected in the post-war welfare settlement, experienced a further deterioration of their status in this period. The chapter illuminates how the disability movement's desire for independence – including the principle of independent living and the right to work – was co-opted by the neoliberal state as a pretext for reducing welfare services and the "responsibilization" of citizens. In her chapter on the Belgian welfare state (Chapter 8), Anaïs van Ertvelde shows how the neoliberal reshaping of the welfare landscape towards more autonomy, personal responsibility and individualized approaches took place with the active involvement of disabled people and their grassroots organizations. This involvement was two-pronged: disabled people protested the rollback of the welfare state, while they developed complementary alternative frameworks based on a human-rights perspective. This notion that disabled people may not only be entitled to welfare, but also to unalienable rights – including the right to work and health – was a novel development.

The neoliberal restructuring of welfare states became, in the case of migrants, often entangled with a revival of welfare nationalism. In Chapter 9 about the Danish welfare state, Heidi Vad Jønsson explains how the Danes turned their immigration policy from one that could be characterized as liberal to one of the most restrictive ones, and she also situates this transformation within a broader international pattern. She shows how immigrants' access to social security became politicized as the question arose to what extent newly arrived migrants should gain access to welfare. As the population became more diverse, emphasis was increasingly placed on the duties of migrants, which included participation in integration programmes with the aim of reinforcing national norms and values.

In the concluding chapter, Veronika Flegar takes as her starting point two mechanisms that continue to determine whether marginalized groups are eligible for welfare benefits: legal citizenship and migration status and "responsibilization" policies with conditionality-based provisions. These mechanisms, which we often see at work in national welfare practices, appear to contradict international norms such as human rights. Utilizing the concepts of vulnerability and resilience, Flegar undertakes a normative-theoretical inquiry with the aim to instigate novel frameworks for reconciling universal human rights with everyday political and economic realities in a way that can be serviceable for persons commonly marginalized in the welfare state debate.

While Flegar's approach represents one of the several ways to deal with the challenges of the welfare state, her chapter convincingly underlines this volume's assumption that bringing the "national" and "international" together is highly relevant for both historical investigations and the drawing of future policies. Last but not least, it invites us to contemplate the desired nature and extent of those policies. Minimum levels of protection might ensure survival on the margins of the existing social order, but if the aims of the welfare state include the facilitation of social mobility, then its policies should also allow for leaving behind the marginalized status. This volume explores how in different contexts the welfare state was utilized to meet these challenges and how arrangements could both include groups in welfare provision and exclude them from it. "Whose welfare?" therefore deserves a multi-layered answer, and this is why not only Jeroen Dijsselbloem should be confronted with this question.

Notes

1 The authors acknowledge the support of the ERC Consolidator Grant Rethinking Disability under grant agreement number 648115. This volume is the outcome of a workshop held in Leiden in January 2017, organized by the Rethinking Disability team. The authors wish to thank Marieke Dwarswaard and Yoram Carboex for their assistance with editing and reviewing literature.
2 "Dijsselbloem: Refugee Crisis Could Trigger 'Mini-Schengen'," Reuters, 27 November 2015, accessed 10 June 2019, www.reuters.com/article/us-europe-migrants-dijsselbloem-schengen/dijsselbloem-refugee-crisis-could-trigger-mini-schengen-idUSKBN0TG0VX20151127. The Eurogroup is the collective of finance ministers of states that have adopted the Euro as their official currency.
3 Ann Shola Orloff, "Gendering the Comparative Analysis of Welfare States: An Unfinished Agenda," *Sociological Theory* 27, no. 3 (2009): 317–343; Melinda Cooper, *Family Values: Between Neoliberalism and the New Social Conservatism* (New York: Zone Books 2017); Roberta Bivins, "Picturing race in the British National Health Service, 1948–1988," *Twentieth Century British History* 28, 1 (2017): 83–109; Stephen Castles and Carl-Ulrik Schierup, "Migration and Ethnic Minorities," in *The Oxford Handbook of the Welfare State*, ed. Francis G. Castles, Stephan Leibfried, Jane Lewis, Herbert Obinger, and Christopher Pierson (Oxford: Oxford University Press, 2010), 278–291; Paul van Trigt, "Human Rights and the Welfare State: An Exploratory History of Social Rights in the Post-war Netherlands," *Zapruder World: An International Journal for the History of Social Conflict* 3 (2016); Jennifer L. Hook, "Incorporating 'Class' into Work–Family Arrangements: Insights from and for Three Worlds," *Journal of European Social Policy* 25, no. 1 (2015): 14–31; Robbie Shilliam, *Race and the Undeserving Poor: From Abolition to Brexit* (Newcastle upon Tyne: Agenda Publishing, 2018).
4 An exception: Beate Althammer, Lutz Raphael, and Tamara Stazic-Wendt, eds., *Rescuing the Vulnerable: Poverty, Welfare and Social Ties in Modern Europe* (Oxford: Berghahn Books, 2016).
5 Catherine J. Kudlick, "Disability History: Why We Need Another 'Other'," *The American Historical Review* 108, no. 3 (2003): 763–793.
6 Deborah Stone, *The Disabled State* (Philadelphia: Temple University Press, 1984).
7 Pierre Rosanvallon, *The Society of Equals* (Cambridge: Harvard University Press, 2013); Frederick Cooper, *Citizenship, Inequality, and Difference: Historical Perspectives* (Princeton: Princeton University Press, 2018); Siep Stuurman, *The Invention of Humanity: Equality and Cultural Difference in World History* (Cambridge: Harvard University Press).
8 For recent overviews: Samuel Moyn, *Not Enough: Human Rights in an Unequal World* (Cambridge: Belknap Press of Harvard University Press, 2018); Christian O. Christiansen and Steven L.B. Jensen, eds., *Histories of Global Inequality: New Perspectives* (in press).
9 Sandrine Kott and Kiran Klaus Patel, eds., *Nazism across Borders: The Social Policies of the Third Reich and Their Global Appeal* (Oxford: Oxford University Press, 2018); Julia Moses and Martin J. Daunton, "Editorial – Border Crossings: Global Dynamics of Social Policies and Problems," *Journal of Global History* 9 (2014): 177–188; Pauli Kettunen and Klaus Petersen, eds., *Beyond Welfare State Models: Transnational Historical Perspectives on Social Policy* (Cheltenham: Edward Elgar Publishers, 2011).

10 Marco Duranti, *The Conservative Human Rights Revolution: European Identity, Transnational Politics, and the Origins of the European Convention* (New York: Oxford University Press, 2017).
11 Gøsta Esping-Anderson, *The Three Worlds of Welfare Capitalism* (Cambridge, UK: Polity Press, 1990); Wil Arts and John Gelissen, "Three Worlds of Welfare Capitalism or More? A State-of-the-Art Report," *Journal of European Social Policy* 12, no. 2 (2002): 137–158.
12 Frank Nullmeier and Franz-Xaver Kaufmann, "Post-War Welfare State Development," in *The Oxford Handbook of the Welfare State*, ed. Francis G. Castles, Stephan Leibfried, Jane Lewis, Herbert Obinger, and Christopher Pierson (Oxford: Oxford University Press, 2010), 81–102; Anton Hemerijck, "Two or Three Waves of Welfare State Transformation?" in *Towards a Social Investment Welfare State? Ideas, Policies and Challenges*, ed. Nathalie Morel, Bruno Palier, and Joakim Palme (Brison: Policy Press, 2015), 33–60; Johannes Kananen, *The Nordic Welfare State in Three Eras: From Emancipation to Discipline* (London: Routledge, 2016); Peter Abrahamson, "European Welfare States beyond Neoliberalism: Toward the Social Investment State," *Development and Society* 39, no. 1 (2010): 61–95.

1 Rescuing the European welfare state

The Social Affairs Committee of the early European Communities, 1953–1962

Brian Shaev

Introduction[1]

Welfare and European integration are emblematic of Western Europe's revival after the tumult of economic depression, social dislocation, mass population movements, genocide and war that marked the first half of the twentieth century. They were children of the post-war era, though they drew and built upon pre-war models. Several decades ago, Charles Maier famously employed the phrase "the politics of productivity" to analyse the nexus of domestic and international socio-economic policies that shaped the "post-war consensus" from the Marshall Plan to the early European communities.[2] Maier's formulation fits well with John Ruggie's concept of "embedded liberalism," in which international institutions provided an anchor of stability and a propitious setting around which national governments constructed welfare states.[3] In these accounts, the philosophy that guided the hands of the architects of Western Europe's revival was that a stable institutional foundation for economic growth would in itself engender an improvement in living standards and welfare, a view shared as well by the International Labour Organization.[4] The European communities, which later became the European Union (EU), were among the most important products of this context of designing institutions to manage the economics and politics of inter-state bargaining. For his part, historian Alan Milward took a different approach to Maier and Ruggie, famously arguing that the European communities were designed to "rescue" national welfare systems, in particular by passing the costs of welfare in troubled economic sectors (Belgian coal and European agriculture) to the European level.[5]

Though social rights have found piecemeal recognition in European conventions and treaties in the last sixty years, they have generally been subordinated to internal market issues in European law. The second-tier position of social rights in the European communities mirrors their marginalization in Western conceptions of international human rights law established in the 1940s–1950s. The 1948 United Nations Declaration of Human Rights embodied "a dominant Western paradigm of individual rights" in which "economic, social, and cultural rights were included ... but in a secondary position" that was further degraded when debates shifted to negotiating a legally binding human rights convention.[6]

Despite the UN General Assembly voting multiple times for the inclusion of economic and social rights in a single covenant with civil and political rights, the "human rights convention ... was further fragmented into two treaties – civil and political rights, championed by Western states, and economic, social, and cultural rights, supported, albeit less forcefully, by Third World states and the communist bloc and therefore given an inferior legal and political status in the UN system."[7] The 1950 European Convention on Human Rights (ECHR), described by one scholar as "the crown jewel of the Council of Europe and more generally postwar Europe," also excluded social rights; it contained instead only "a select number of civil and political rights."[8] According to Marco Duranti's influential study, the ECHR must "be understood as a product of its free-market and social conservative origins" in which a coalition of conservatives and Christian Democrats defeated centre-left concepts of social rights as human rights in the 1949–1950 debates in the Council of Europe.[9] Nonetheless, the ECHR remained largely a dead letter until the end of the 1950s, whereas a supranational European community opened in 1952–1953. The Treaties of Rome (1957) that established the European Economic Community (EEC) largely omitted social policy, though it figured more prominently in the Treaty of Paris (1951) that created the European Coal and Steel Community (ECSC).

Social policy in the European communities, the subject of this chapter, was contentious from the start. In the spirit of Roger Normand and Sarah Zaidi's work on the UN and of Duranti's book on the Council of Europe, this chapter does not view "the denigration of economic and social rights" within the European communities as "inevitable nor inescapable" but rather as "closely contested and historically contingent."[10] Historians have investigated the intergovernmental negotiations that led to the (limited) social provisions of the EEC Treaty, the role of member states and the European Commission in setting up the European Social Fund and the European Investment Bank, the collaboration of the International Labour Organization in the social policy of the ECSC/EEC, and the consultative Economic and Social Committee that brought together employer, trade union and consumer organizations.[11] This contribution is among the first to analyse in its own right the early years of the Social Affairs Committee of the Common Assembly, from 1958 the Social Committee of the European Parliamentary Assembly, the predecessor of today's European Parliament.[12] European deputies were national parliamentarians delegated by their parliaments to oversee community activities and ensure the democratic accountability of the High Authority and European Commission, the communities' executive bodies. The assembly held few formal powers and its claims of democratic representation were undermined by the exclusion of communist and far-right deputies. Nonetheless, the deputies' positions were strengthened by their dual mandates in national and European assemblies and their persistence in treating the Common Assembly as a formidable European parliament in the making. The initiative for the creation of the Social Affairs Committee came from community socialists, who argued for a robust and expansive mandate for the assembly during its inaugural sessions. Dissatisfied with the proposal for a committee mandate limited to "housing issues," they proposed a committee "on work and social questions" in September 1952 that would deal with "questions concerning workers' policies, freedom of migration, living standards, and social affairs and benefits." The Social Affairs Committee was inaugurated in January 1953 as one of four large committees (along with common market, investment and external relations) that would conduct the lion's share of the assembly's day-to-day work overseeing ECSC policy.[13] It is worthwhile examining how this international group of politicians conceptualized welfare in the move from a coal and steel common market to a general common market in the 1950s–1960s. Doing so brings to the fore the contested nature of early European social policy. In this committee, moderate socialists, centre-left Christian Democrats and socially minded liberals held a majority that supported social rights and distrusted aspects of the "politics of productivity." The chapter covers a timeframe from the opening of the coal and steel market in 1953 to the move from the first to second transitional stage of the EEC customs union in 1962. It begins by considering how committee members conceptualized the impact that a coal and steel common market would have on the working conditions, (un)employment, and social rights of coal and steel workers in 1953–1955. It then examines their attempts to influence and revise the social clauses of European treaties in communication with the High Authority and the intergovernmental team negotiating the Treaties of Rome in 1955–1957. Finally, it analyses their efforts to build supranational welfare policies in and beyond heavy industry during the first years of the EEC in 1958–1962. Through an examination of committee minutes, resolutions and communications the analysis demonstrates (1) how committee members claimed to speak for workers in their repeated criticisms of the inadequacy of European social policy, (2) how they differentiated between groups of workers as they campaigned for supranational social rights, and (3) how the focus on employment as the basis for social rights as well as their acceptance of contemporary social and gender norms constricted their otherwise large ambitions to build legitimacy for the European project by means of a pro-active and interventionist European social policy.

Building legitimacy for European integration by promoting workers' welfare, 1953–1955

Jean Monnet, president of the supranational ECSC High Authority, spoke of the "tight interdependence" between economics and social policy in his first appearance in April 1953 before the Social Affairs Committee of the ECSC Common Assembly. In preparation for this meeting, Monnet wrote, "I believe that it is no exaggeration to say that all of the High Authority's activities have a social character."[14] Despite Monnet's gloss, the ECSC treaty's philosophy is better summed up by Albert Coppé, a High Authority commissioner, who told the first meeting of the Common Market Committee that "it is essentially by means of a rise in productivity, the principal task of the Community, that we will arrive at an improvement in the living and working conditions of workers."[15]

This interpretation of the treaty as an embodiment of the "politics of productivity" found a cold welcome in the new Social Affairs Committee. From its inception, committee members were at odds with core aspects of this governing philosophy of the European Community. The elected chair, Gerard Nederhorst of the Dutch Labour Party, opened the committee's second meeting in March 1953 by stating, "When we examined the report of the High Authority" in January, "I had the impression that our committee did not fully approve the method employed by the High Authority to develop projects in the social domain." He complained that the High Authority "has given the wrong impression that social policy is of secondary importance" and that "compared to the constant movement in the economic field, the major lines of policy that the Coal and Steel Community intends to practice in the social field remain vague and poorly defined."[16] He suggested a formal protest to Monnet, a request his colleagues unanimously approved. It was this protest that prompted Monnet to respond with the assurances quoted earlier.

In the first committee meetings, members expressed concern that a neglect of social policy could gravely damage the legitimacy of the European project. The committee attempted to add weight to social policy by strengthening its own position vis-à-vis the High Authority and the other Common Assembly committees. Nederhorst and his colleagues insisted that the High Authority consult the committee before making major decisions on issues like pricing and cartel policy, core fields of community activity. In these early years, comments such as this were common: "It is [unacceptable] that a decision has been taken in the economic or financial domain without having first examined the social consequences of these decisions."[17] In addition, committee members emphasized the importance of expanding units of the High Authority bureaucracy devoted to employment and social issues that were understaffed compared to their economic counterparts.

Most glaring were the apprehensive remarks committee members repeatedly made about how people in their countries perceived the newly founded community. Italian member Italo Mario Sacco said during Monnet's appearance that

> the creation of the International Labour Organization in the Treaty of Versailles gave birth to great hopes of the improvement of working conditions but these hopes were in large part disappointed. The reason was that certain countries, fearing competition, adopted an overly restricted or prudent social legislation and were forced to do so by their neighbouring countries. It is necessary not to fall into the same error.[18]

Sacco emphasized the "psychological problem" that "workers have the impression that the interest in the social aspect of problems is somewhat neglected," pointing to employers using "the pretext of the uncertainty born of the creation of the common market ... to delay accepting workers' demands that certainly would have been accepted at other moments." Nederhorst, for his part, relayed to his colleagues, "In the Netherlands we are witnessing a weakening of interest of the population" in the ECSC.[19]

Especially prominent in committee debates were members' claims that the community was damaging the interests of miners and steel workers in their countries. Often forgotten in European integration history is that many coal and steel workers and their trade unions reacted with considerable misgivings or strong opposition to the original ECSC proposal. This was so in the Nord/Pas-de-Calais and the Ruhr, the main coal-producing regions of France and Germany, as I have analysed elsewhere, and in the Borinage, Belgium's troubled mining area.[20] A central purpose of the ECSC was to lower the costs of energy to fuel the economic modernization needed to fund reconstruction and the emergence of modern welfare states, but, somewhat perversely, this goal had the potential to harm the workers for whose benefit the rudimentary welfare systems of the eighteenth and nineteenth centuries had first emerged: coal miners and raw steel producers. Furthermore, coal and steel workers tended to be the largest reservoir of support for communist parties in Western Europe during the early Cold War, presenting a toxic cocktail for the ECSC if not handled carefully. Nederhorst warned the High Authority in January 1954 that, "public opinion often attributes unemployment to the existence of the High Authority and the Common Market."[21] Willi Birkelbach, a German Social Democrat, repeatedly invoked the situation of steel industries in Salzgitter, near the border of East Germany, for which "the establishment of the Common Market has accentuated the deleterious effects" of the region's structural difficulties. "Without the Common Market," which banned state subsidies, "Germany would have taken vast measures on the national scale to stimulate steel production." Most concerning, for Birkelbach, was that "the Government of the Soviet Zone has exploited this situation in its propaganda against the ECSC."[22]

Discussions on welfare focused on the two industrial sectors that fell under the ECSC treaty. On this basis, Nederhorst explicitly defined whose welfare fell within the purview of the committee and whose welfare did not. This came out clearly in an April 1953 exchange between Alfred Bertrand, the committee's Christian Democratic vice president, and Nederhorst in which Nederhorst stated that the committee's work would focus only on coal and steel workers and not on consumers as Bertrand had suggested. In January 1956, Nederhorst said that "he is of the opinion ... that the Treaty authorises isolating in a way the two industries that fall under the Treaty from other branches of the economy," and he sought to further define its focus, suggesting that "under these conditions, would it not be possible to separate the working conditions of underground miners from those of [surface] workers?"[23]

Despite its focus on a traditional welfare constituency, the committee did more than replicate national discussions on coal and steel: it spent a large proportion of its time discussing the living, employment and housing conditions of migrant workers in these industries whose conditions had typically been neglected by national governments as well as trade unions.[24] The perennial problem of the transferability of welfare benefits across borders was of particular concern.[25] This interest was soon channelled into support for the international negotiations that began in 1954 to create a framework for non-discrimination and the portability of social benefits for all migrant workers (of signatory states) and then into support for the resulting 1957 European Convention on Social Security of Migrant Workers, the history and importance of which Karim Fertikh discusses in Chapter 2 of this volume.[26] Further, there were discussions of the welfare of migrant workers' families, in particular the children of Italian miners who had migrated to the coalfields of Belgium, France and Germany.

In its first three years, the committee emphasized the concerns of coal and steel workers largely to the exclusion of workers in other fields as well as people outside of the labour force. A number of members urged the committee to consider any potentially negative impact that its proposals might have on workers in other sectors, but these comments did not go much beyond statements of principle.[27] Underlying the committee's agenda was a recognition of the traditionally privileged status of coal and steel workers relative to other "blue-collar" occupations. One member, for instance, recalled, "the numerous privileges (exemption from military service, the highest salaries) that compensated for the inconveniences of the profession" and regretted that, "the current levelling of working conditions for all has brought disadvantages to the miners."[28] Another stated that "the committee does not hesitate to conclude that it is necessary to grant miners a privileged situation," and "[t]he working conditions in the mines are such that it would not be necessary to extend the advantages conceded to miners to workers in other sectors...."[29] This commitment to miners' welfare manifested itself in a continuous dialogue with High Authority officials in which committee members urged the community's executive to interpret its legal powers as widely as possible. ECSC social policy was almost entirely devoted to the well-being of coal and steel workers. It included a re-adaptation programme in which community funds matched national government investment in the retraining of workers laid off due to competition in the common market; a reinstallation programme to fund the resettlement of unemployed coal and steel workers to other sectors; a housing investment programme in mining and steel regions; investigations into the living and working conditions of migrant workers in coal and steel; and study commissions focused on workplace safety and occupational hazards and diseases.[30]

Committee members quickly concluded that the ECSC treaty did not provide sufficient supranational powers to combat the negative social repercussions that might befall certain workers during the opening of the common market. As early as April 1953, Belgian Socialist Max Buset stated, "The Treaty [only] grant[ed] the possibility of indirect actions, [and therefore] it is necessary to entirely exhaust [the legal possibilities] until a supranational authority [invested with appropriate powers] is created."[31] Disappointment with community social policy combined with a critique of the limitations imposed by the ECSC treaty. By 1954, the committee was discussing a treaty revision that would expand the powers of the High Authority and the Common Assembly. In advocating a pro-active community social policy, committee members demanded that the High Authority gain the legal right to initiate aid to workers when national governments failed to do so. Nederhorst lamented that "the procedure foreseen in social affairs by the authors of the Treaty has not led to the favourable results expected," and "[t] herefore we must foresee a new manner of acting in the future, especially in the area of a generalised common market."[32] Such was the general thrust of discussions within the committee, though there were divisions over what policies should move from national to supranational levels as well as disagreements concerning the leeway available within the existing treaty to expand the community's role in social affairs.

When the six ECSC member-state governments began negotiations to extend the common market to their entire economies in the aftermath of the June 1955 Messina conference, committee members ratcheted up their criticisms of the meagre role assigned to social policy in the community. Bertrand noted that "the economic evolution ... following the establishment of the Common Market has been favourable, but the owners have been the primary beneficiaries while labour should also share in the benefits obtained."[33] A trade unionist deputy agreed, telling the committee that "the results of three years of the common market have frankly disappointed the workers who had a right to expect more tangible benefits."[34] An Italian member said that "at the moment of the 'European relaunch'... it is more important than ever to create, by means of tangible benefits for the working class, this European consciousness without which the treaties will have little success."[35] Bertrand summed up the committee's assessment of the first years of ECSC social policy by stating that "it has generally been admitted that the economic improvements due to the common market would automatically bring with it social improvements" but "three years of experience have demonstrated that this is not the case."[36]

Lobbying for supranational social policies during the European "relaunch," 1955–1957

The year 1955 was a bustling time in European integration history. The question of West German rearmament, which had paralysed integration initiatives beyond coal and steel in 1952–1954, fell from the supranational agenda and a path opened for Dutch Foreign Minister Johan Beyen's proposal for a European common market. The Dutch initiative was the basis for a June 1955 Messina summit in which the six governments established a working group, the Spaak Committee, to prepare a new treaty. This committee, after intense negotiations, issued a report in favour of the common market, laying the groundwork for the hard-nosed intergovernmental negotiations that unfolded from October 1956 to March 1957. The result was the Treaties of Rome for a supranational atomic energy community and, most important, a European Economic Community. Beyen's 1955 proposal came at a time when the ECSC was nearing full operation. The growth in community activity on all fronts is evidenced by the rising number of committee meetings and by the increased length of committee protocols.

The Social Affairs Committee was no exception, and, in addition to the quantitative increase in committee records, there was a qualitative burst in enthusiasm, as Nederhorst welcomed that, for the first time, "social problems are situated at the heart of [the community's] concerns."[37] The European "relaunch" came as the committee was preparing proposals to expand the ECSC's authority in social policy. The ECSC Treaty allowed revision at the end of a transition period in 1957. In preparation, the Common Assembly formed a working group to coordinate the views of the various committees. In a June 1955 letter, the president of the Working Group, Roger Motz, instructed Nederhorst to indicate, first, "the measures that would permit the full application of the treaty without modifying the text" and, second, to lay out "what extension will be necessary to give the Community powers in social affairs necessary to fulfil the objectives fixed in the Treaty."[38] Herein lay the crux for the discussions in the Social Affairs Committee.

In its reply, the committee presented its case for a pro-active community policy. First drafted in June 1955, the month of the Messina conference, it claimed that "in the current system, the Community cannot sufficiently protect workers' interests" because it "leaves to governments the initiative in the area of social legislation" while "experience shows us that governments hesitate to grant workers in the coal and steel industries the social advantages they could obtain." This state of affairs "creates obstacles to the realisation of the social objectives of the Treaty," and it was therefore necessary to grant the community the right to initiate supranational social policies. The note supported expanding supranational powers (but to varying degrees) over working conditions, salaries, housing construction, re-adaptation and migration. The text was an internal compromise, especially on the issue of the "harmonization" of member-state social policies that was a constant source of dispute in other international fora like the International Labour Organization. The committee would only support weak supranational powers over salaries, calling instead for the High Authority to promote community-wide collective bargaining between trade unions and employer organizations. This contrasted with the stronger supranational powers the committee promoted for other policy fields. The overall intention was to "permit the Community to directly realise social improvements and influence living standards."[39]

The note signalled the committee's dissatisfaction with ECSC social policy. It described the community's efforts in the field of re-adaptation as "completely deficient," regretted that national governments left many laid-off coal and steel workers in the lurch by not requesting community funds to assist them, and objected that the treaty's provision to facilitate the migration of coal and steel workers was being interpreted in such a way as to "inevitably restrain free movement." The discontent continued during the following years. In June 1957, the committee expressed its "regret that the period of economic growth has not been utilised sufficiently to put in place the necessary measures for reconversion and re-adaptation" and demanded an action programme that would lay out community objectives "to achieve social improvements for the next 15 years." Further, it stated that it could not "formulate a judgement concerning whether integration has granted particular advantages to workers of the coal and steel industries" because the High Authority had not provided it with adequate information.[40] In the meantime, a mining disaster in Belgium re-focused the committee's attention on a policy field that had been the heart of nineteenth-century social reforms in European industry: occupational safety. In 1956, over two hundred miners died when a fire broke out in an underground mine in Marcinelle, near Charleroi. The catastrophe sparked an ECSC crisis when the Italian government responded by forbidding further recruitment of Italian workers, who made up approximately half of the casualties in Marcinelle, until the Belgian government addressed safety concerns. The Common Assembly established a new committee on mine safety to monitor and advise an ad hoc intergovernmental conference on safety held in 1957. Working closely with the Social Affairs Committee, whose members took most of the seats on the new committee, the deputies lobbied for a powerful mine-safety body that would be independent of national governments and invested with powers to fine businesses that failed to meet safety standards.[41] The committee called for inserting supranational powers in matters of occupational safety into the ECSC treaty and demanded that governments follow up with a second conference on safety issues in the iron and steel industries.[42] There was a clear public relations component to the discussions: ECSC commissioners noted that the Soviet Union would emphasize mine safety at the 1957 Universal Exposition, with the implicit intention of embarrassing the community.[43] Committee members urged the High Authority to counter the Soviet tactic by dedicating a significant portion of the ECSC's display at the exposition to the mine-safety programme. Under pressure from multiple directions, ECSC member states agreed to establish a permanent intergovernmental body to monitor and assess mine-safety issues, which began operation in autumn 1957.

In this as in other policy fields, the standard by which the committee measured the success of the community's social policy remained their perception of the well-being of coal and steel workers. The coal industry was generally performing well at this time, but storm clouds were gathering. High welfare expenditures, lower transatlantic freight rates and a growing abundance of increasingly cheap petroleum foretold the severe displacement that the coal industry would experience in just a few years' time. At the dawn of this wrenching transformation, committee members remained committed to preserving coal miners' privileged status. Birkelbach, for instance, said that "the disaffection of workers towards work in the mines confers responsibilities to the Community" that "requires common measures to avoid irreparable harm to the Community."[44] The committee faced a conundrum because the modernization programmes underway were unable to sustain coal's long-term competitiveness. In October 1957, Bertrand expressed his "fear that soon miners' salaries will be lower than those in other branches of industry" while "the High Authority should remind governments that miners' salaries should at whatever price be at the summit of the salary pyramid."[45] Despite isolated comments against creating "'economic oases,'" the committee began a long struggle in association with a number of trade unions for a "Miners' Statute" to protect coal workers from the whims of market forces.[46] Social Affairs Commissioner Paul Finet acknowledged the "open question of justification of the state, of society, [favouring] an industry compared to other industries with lower burdens of social costs."[47] However, this concern was brushed aside. Finet spoke of his desire to "restore the honour of the mining profession" and "ask[ed] himself whether the miners' profession ought to be considered a service for the collectivity and escape the laws of the market." It would be "difficult to accomplish" but "worth the effort to try ... so that miners eventually enjoy a privileged position thanks to the creation of a European Miners' Statute."[48]

We pick up the story of the Miners' Statute in the next section, but the point here is that the context of disappointment and the perceived failure of community social policy directly informed committee attempts to influence the common market negotiations in 1956–1957. Birkelbach criticized ECSC policy in a November 1956 committee report that laid out recommendations for the ongoing negotiations. It stated that "your committee ... has repeatedly concluded that [the ECSC Treaty] has provided far fewer powers in the social field than in the economic field." This, in turn, "often led in practice to unsatisfactory, unamenable and even ineffective solutions to the provisions and mechanisms provided in the Treaty." The report then demanded protection and re-training of unemployed workers regardless of whether their termination was caused by the opening of the common market, "a programme for the elimination of structural unemployment," and an "initiative right for the European Commission in questions of the raising of living and working conditions." Further, it included a moderate call for social harmonization, a promotion of community-wide collective bargaining, permission for state aid in cases of emergency, a Keynesian-style community macroeconomic expansionary programme, complete and equal social security protection for migrant workers, and an expansion of the powers of the Social Affairs Committee to propose social legislation.[49] The Common Assembly approved Birkelbach's resolution on 30 November.

As national governments hammered out remaining areas of disagreement over the winter of 1956–1957, the Social Affairs Committee designated members to lobby for its design. Nederhorst summarized the committee's perspective in a letter to Hans von der Groeben, chair of the common market committee of the intergovernmental conference negotiating the Treaties of Rome. The letter repeated the key points of Birkelbach's report, adding the goal of "full employment," and called attention to the necessity "of finding a means to guarantee a better situation for workers."[50] The intergovernmental committee received the committee's delegation in December 1956, politely listened to its concerns and then in large part ignored its conclusions. The Treaties of Rome that emerged in spring 1957 reinforced the philosophy underpinning the Treaty of Paris that welfare gains would follow economic growth engendered by the common market. They did not include the more extensive supranational social policies demanded by the Social Affairs Committee. In October, Nederhorst told the committee that, "The ECSC Treaty seems to be better than the [EEC Treaty]" because the economic powers of the European Commission were weaker than those of the High Authority and, therefore, "the ECSC Treaty should be retained in all areas in which it gives more power than the EEC Treaty."[51] Though there were divisions within the committee, liberals like French deputy André Mutter shared this view, which accorded with French governmental policy, stating that "it seems that the High Authority is practicing a general policy in which social policy is subordinated to economic policy whereas it should normally precede it."[52] He put his view in stark terms: "man should constitute an end in himself and not a means to reach an end," a comment that elicited general approval.

The expansion and limitations of the Social Affairs Committee's welfare vision, 1958–1962

After the European Parliamentary Assembly opened in 1958, the reconstituted Social Committee struggled to adapt to its increased mandate of overseeing the social conditions of all community workers under the EEC Treaty, in addition to those of coal and steel workers under the ECSC Treaty. The continuity in the committee's leadership and membership encouraged it to approach the common market in light of the work that it had accomplished in 1953–1957. The EEC Treaty created a special status for agriculture, which developed into the Common Agricultural Policy (CAP), a controversial and expensive supranational protectionist policy set up in the 1960s. Historian Ann-Christina L. Knudsen titled her history of the CAP's early years "Farmers on Welfare," adding her piece of the puzzle to Alan Milward's framework of the "European rescue" of post-war welfare states.[53] The challenge for the Social Committee was that agriculture had a history and culture different from those of heavy industry. Many committee members were trade unionists from the coal and steel industries and, regardless of their political background, generally had little experience in agricultural matters. A comparative framework was therefore implicit from the start, as committee members sought to conceptualize welfare in farming by considering the sector's similarities and differences to coal and steel. This work is the subject of this section, which also touches upon how the committee approached the welfare of other disadvantaged groups, in particular women and people with disabilities.

First, we pick up here where we left off with the welfare of coal and steel workers, which remained a primordial concern of the committee, especially during the "coal crisis" of 1958 that hit Belgium hard and other countries to differing degrees. In 1958–1959, Bertrand and Nederhorst, the committee's Christian Democratic and Socialist leaders, respectively, repeatedly raised the alarm over the social consequences of the crisis, while trade union deputy Arthur Gailly stated that, if left unaddressed, "the workers ... may turn their back on the Community."[54] The committee also expressed concern about the impact of the crisis on migrant workers, demanding statistics from the High Authority to determine whether they were being laid off at greater rates than native workers, insisting on proactive measures to prevent discrimination on the basis of nationality, and calling on governments to accord equal benefits for re-training and unemployment to laid-off migrants.[55]

As the European communities began implementing the first transitional stage of the common market, the committee persisted in demanding a privileged status for coal and steel workers, which took the form of a European Miners' Statute to secure minimal benefits for all community miners. Gailly, who was charged with formulating a parliamentary proposal, promoted "a social policy that guarantees a privileged situation to the miner in relation to his dangerous profession."[56] Other committee members expressed similar views. A differentiation was made, as Gailly, Nederhorst and others called for targeting benefits towards underground miners rather than to surface workers.[57] This was in part for financial reasons, as the High Authority worried that "extending the statute to other categories risks aggravating the financial situation of the mining industry."[58] Yet the problem remained, as a liberal member pointed out, that "[i]t will not be easy to grant further financial benefits to miners without finding a way to permanently lower the price of coal."[59]

Nicolas Verschueren argues in his history of the European Miners' Statute that the Social Committee and the High Authority were allies in the ultimately unsuccessful effort to persuade member-state governments to agree to a special statute for community miners.[60] This is surely true, yet it is worth emphasizing that the committee was also quite critical of the High Authority. Nederhorst deplored its "overly passive" attitude in October 1958 and later questioned whether it "was aware of the gravity of the problem."[61] In 1962, Gailly's replacement, Antoine Krier, said that he "could not hide [his] profound disappointment" at the stagnation of "the miners' statute that [should] constitute the first example of a social achievement at the European level." Another committee member commented that "it unfortunately seems that public officials only remember miners during the dark days of catastrophes."[62] To the committee's chagrin, the Miners' Statute failed, despite the first mass protest of community workers in 1964, when miners gathered in Dortmund with the president of the High Authority to demand a "Social Europe." Though the Miners' Statute was not successful, it did point the way towards regional structural funds, which became the most direct means of alleviating inequalities within the European communities (in addition to the CAP) after they were established in 1975. The idea for regional funds was already present in the committee's prolonged discussions of how to deal with declining industrial regions in the 1950s. In 1959 Anton Storch, formerly German Labour Minister (1949–1957), demanded the implementation of regional funds "as proof of European solidarity that demands that richer countries (*pays*) aid poor countries (*pays*)."[63] The ambiguous French word *pays* refers here not only to countries in the national sense but also to regions. In September, another member said that "... if we cannot always eliminate all the inconveniences of unfavourable economic positioning, we should correct as much as possible the differentiation in social conditions resulting from this situation ... [by] develop[ing] a plan to develop the less developed regions...."[64] The next month Nederhorst said, "In almost all countries there exist disadvantaged regions in which factories close their doors, leading to structural unemployment ... the EEC Commission would be a pioneer if it adopted [...] at the European level, practical measures in favour of these areas."[65] A December 1958 resolution made this official committee policy: "The Treaty instituting the EEC allows us to more harmoniously develop certain disadvantaged regions" by classifying at the supranational level their needs and preparing applications for funding from the newly created European Social Fund, charged with retraining and reinstallation of workers on the ECSC model, and the European Investment Bank, responsible for directing capital investment to disadvantaged areas and to projects of common interest.[66]

Agriculture presented a new set of challenges to the formulation of the committee's social policy when committee members began to lay the groundwork for their discussions on welfare in rural communities in 1958. The committee charged

Nederhorst with contacting the president of the new Agricultural Committee. Nederhorst suggested that the two committees exchange transcripts of their sessions, organize joint meetings on issues of mutual concern and invite each other's presidents to participate in their meetings. His intention was "to coordinat[e] rather than delimit somehow the mandates of the two committees."[67] The Agricultural Committee designated a Dutch Labour deputy, Henk Vredeling, to collaborate with Nederhorst. Vredeling was a regular presence at the Social Committee and authored reports on agricultural social policy. On this basis, a lasting collaboration was constructed that benefited the committee because its members were mostly novices when it came to agriculture. Though some members contested the need for the committee to deal with agriculture and suggested leaving the field entirely to the Agricultural Committee, the prevalent view was expressed by Maria Probst when she said that "this category of workers also has the right to demand security in social affairs."[68]

The philosophy behind EEC agricultural policy was "farm-income parity" in which farmers' incomes were supposed to rise as fast as those in industry. In his first appearance before the committee, EEC Agricultural Commissioner Sicco Mansholt said that the goal as laid out at the recent Stresa Conference was "that the position of agricultural workers should be totally equivalent to that of workers in other industrial sectors."[69] One committee member pointed out that this was a "delicate" problem because "it is not possible to apply to agricultural workers the social provisions planned for miners," a point shared by representatives of the EEC Commission.[70] In these first years, the committee immersed itself in designing a survey questionnaire to identify the social problems facing agriculture. The impetus came early in April 1958, when Probst suggested that the committee "establish a catalogue of the different problems that are unique to agriculture" because "she thinks that social problems in industry areas are not comparable to those that arise in agricultural areas."[71] In January 1959, she mentioned in this regard the need to "examine all the social problems of farmers: accidents, insurance, retirement, family benefits."[72] There followed extensive discussions about social conditions in the countryside that culminated in a joint questionnaire agreed by the Agricultural and Social Committees in May 1959.[73] Discussions on how agriculture differed from heavy industry encouraged committee members to conceptualize welfare in a more expansive manner. There had been only passing references to women, children and families in discussions on coal and steel, but these social categories gained new prominence when members' gaze turned to agriculture. In November 1958, Birkelbach said that investigating employment in family farms "is extremely important if we are to establish a fertile social policy for rural populations."[74] Several months later, Nederhorst agreed with Bertrand and others that families should be included in committee investigations.[75] The questionnaire explicitly enquired into the social conditions of rural women and children with regard to pensions, employment, sickness and accidents. Also, it posed questions that took each family as a unit. This was in line with the romantic ideal of the "family farm" that EEC agricultural policy purported to protect, though the reality in agriculture was, of course, often rather different.[76]

There was another manner in which committee discussions on agriculture expanded its vision of social policy: a new concern arose for the welfare of the self-employed. This corresponded to a general context in the late 1950–1960s in which self-employed workers were demanding access to national welfare systems in Europe, often for the first time. In discussions on social policy in the coal and steel industries there was no concern expressed about the social conditions of employers, who were presumed to be able to care for themselves. Committee members realized that agriculture was a completely different story, yet some resisted extending social policy beyond salaried agricultural labourers to include self-employed farmers. Nederhorst noted, however, that he "thinks that it is very difficult to distinguish clearly between employers and workers in agriculture."[77] The self-employed category became particularly relevant in debates about who would be eligible for assistance from the European Social Fund as unemployment assistance at national and European levels was generally set up in such a way that it was difficult for non-salaried workers to access such funds. A number of members demanded that the fund reach into the countryside and that potential beneficiaries not have to register at unemployment offices, which were generally located in cities and recourse to which was often alien to the culture of rural areas as well as inconvenient.[78] By summer 1959, committee members "recommend[ed] that we speak about independent workers and that in the future we deal equally in social affairs reports with the social security of self-employed workers, for example, old-age insurance of artisans and in agriculture."[79] The November 1959 committee resolution explicitly included "family" and "independent workers" as targets of community social policy.[80] By the time that committee members debated a resolution on the formation of the European Social Fund, it is clear that a learning process had taken place: the committee considered what it had learned to be relevant beyond the sphere of agriculture. The resolution stated: "Your committee emphasises once again the specific character of agriculture; it has nonetheless asked itself whether other categories of independent workers find themselves in an analogous situation." It concluded, "Your committee is of the opinion that it is necessary to examine the possibility of a generalisation of the system of family benefits in favour of all independent workers and of independent workers in agriculture in particular."[81]

Finally, the committee discussed improving the conditions of disadvantaged social groups, in particular of women and people with disabilities, but it must be emphasized that these discussions were brief, largely preliminary in nature, and focused on employment and labour-market issues. At the demand of the French government, a clause requiring equal pay for men and women was inserted into the EEC Treaty, but it had little impact until landmark decisions of the European Court of Justice in the 1970s breathed life into this dormant piece of European social law. Women had a largely marginal presence in the coal and steel industries, particularly in the former, as revealed by enquiries that the committee requested from the High Authority.[82] The aforementioned emphasis about privileging underground mine workers, where women were totally or almost totally absent, over "surface workers" had an implicit discriminatory gender dimension as women were largely employed as office workers and support staff in these industrial sectors. Gailly, a driving force behind the Miners' Statute, said, for instance, "the coal and steel industries do not employ female laborers in the proper sense of the term."[83] Nederhorst repeatedly called for an active community policy to implement the equal-wages clause, but a number of the (male) committee members sought to limit its reach. The general reluctance of the committee to promote and protect female employment is evident in its discussions on vocational training. Vredeling's social policy proposal of December 1961 reads, "young female workers [should] be equally prepared for their tasks, not less important from an economic and social point of view, that awaits them in a majority of their cases as manager and mother of the family."[84] Storch, for his part, wanted to tie equal pay to equal productivity, arguing perhaps facetiously that otherwise women would be the first laid off during crises.[85] At a later session he said, "It is desirable to aim for an economic order in which a married women is not obligated to work," continuing that "there are essentially feminine professions like stenographer and secretary" and it would "be a mistake to insist too much on professional training for women in all fields."[86] Another member stated that "we must avoid demanding of female labour tasks above their [sic] abilities."[87] No one (according to the minutes) contradicted such statements, but Probst, for instance, called attention to the damaging impact of employment law and practice in Germany where part-time workers, disproportionately female, did not receive benefits.[88] She also encouraged the committee to focus on the professional training of disabled workers. A European Commission official promised that it would examine the employment conditions of "handicapped persons, women, youth, and old workers."[89] The welfare focus for these disadvantaged groups, which are mentioned a number of times, was overwhelmingly focused on promoting labour-market integration. When Probst, for instance, asked for a discussion of International Labour Organization (ILO) negotiations calling for social assistance for mothers without an explicit link to employment, Nederhorst responded that he agreed with her but that this lay outside of the committee's mandate.[90]

Conclusion

The erosive impact that European integration is alleged to have had on some welfare states from the 1980s to the present has raised the stakes in debates about the place of welfare in the early European communities. The topic's contemporary relevance has inspired scholars to return to the 1950–1960s to investigate what legal scholar Stefano Giubonni has called Europe's "original constitutional compromise."[91] This compromise defined a national and international division of labour that shielded most national social policies from the reach of supranational authority, an argument that intersects well with Milward's contention that the European communities originated as a "rescue of the nation-state" and, in particular, a rescue of national welfare states during their glory days of growth and expansion.[92] From this perspective, the marginalization of social rights in the ECHR had little direct impact, as national governments reserved for themselves authority over most aspects of their welfare states. However, starting in the 1970s, this division broke down, in Giubonni's view, due to a supranational "infiltration" of economics into the sphere of social affairs. A particularly influential account of this transformation is that of Fritz Scharpf, who argues that "the EU cannot be a 'social market economy'" because its institutional "asymmetry" undermines national welfare states while preventing their reconstitution at a supranational level.[93]

This chapter has sought to restore the contested nature of social policy in the early European communities by rescuing ideas of a European-level welfare state from contemporary oblivion. The debates, communications and resolutions of the Social Affairs Committee/Social Committee of the European assembly demonstrate that the "politics of productivity" were far from having unanimous support among politicians tasked with overseeing community social policy. For at least a decade, committee members criticized the capacity of such politics to ensure social welfare, insisting instead that regional organization harness economic integration in the service of social objectives. Though the committee criticized High Authority and commission officials, it also found support among Social Affairs commissioners, for instance when Commissioner Giuseppe Petrilli issued a report in 1959 asserting that economic integration was not an end in itself but should rather be subordinated to social needs.[94] This vision of a post-war European social order lived on, first, in the tireless efforts of Petrilli's replacement, Lionello Levi Sandri, to place social welfare at the centre of European integration in the 1960s; second, in fleeting efforts to build "Social Europe" in the 1970s, followed by Commission President Jacques Delors's initiatives for a supranational social policy that would keep pace with the European economic "relaunch" of the 1980s; third, in efforts to strengthen the EU's social components in the Amsterdam, Nice and Lisbon Treaties in the 1990s–2000s; and, finally, in contemporary critiques of the EU's response to the financial and sovereign debt crises and the straightjacket imposed by Eurozone debt and deficit rules on social policies. That these efforts have been at most partial successes comes out clearly in the EU's decision in 2017 to declare a new European Pillar of Social Rights, the core achievement of a European Social Summit recently held in Gothenburg, Sweden, the results of which remain to be seen.[95]

In addition to restoring the extended critique the Social Affairs Committee offered to the post-war paradigm of national welfare and European integration, the chapter demonstrates how European parliamentary records can be used to trace growing ambitions to expand the target beneficiaries of welfare policies, and to identify the gender norms and employment-based framing that constrained such visions in the 1950s–early 1960s. The committee supported extensive community measures to guarantee the welfare of those working in sectors in decline, first in coal, then in agriculture and later in steel, in line with Milward's argument. Coupled with proposals to aid disadvantaged regions, which reached fruition in the regional funds set up in 1975, these measures have together consumed a large majority of the European community budget from the 1960s to the present day. European initiatives and programmes in the social sphere remain focused on employment and labour-market issues. EU migrant workers and, to a lesser extent Third Country Nationals, are protected by European law from discrimination in welfare and employment, the grounds for which were prepared during the 1950–1960s. Shifts have also occurred within this social framework. From the mid-1970s the European Social Fund began prioritizing the labour-market integration of people with disabilities, and new community vocational programmes were created to focus on youth employment. Gender inequality remained by and large tolerated and sometimes even embraced in the early 1960s, but in the 1970s the European Court of Justice took the lead in enforcing the equal rights protections of the Treaties of Rome. In this period, the European Community's first Social Action Programme promoted employee protection during the economic downturn of the 1970s. Besides isolated measures like the Working Time Directive, by the 1990s EU employment policy focused on making labour markets more flexible, which in contrast to earlier policies usually meant removing employment protections within an economic frame of increasing competitiveness and a welfare frame of making labour markets more accessible to marginalized social groups under the banner of "social inclusion."

After a lost decade of widespread unemployment in Southern Europe and austerity in the EU, an ILO-sponsored report on the European social model in times of crisis bore the subtitle "Is Europe Losing Its Soul?"[96] The past ten years have been marked by narratives of welfare state retrenchment as well as popular anger at free movement, the "posting" of workers and ECJ decisions opening national welfare services to citizens of other member states. Accompanying this has been a rise in "welfare chauvinism" and Euroscepticism. In this context, the warnings of the Social Affairs Committee in the 1950s–1960s that the legitimacy of European integration rests on proving its success in expanding social welfare in Europe appear more pertinent than ever.

Notes

1 The author acknowledges the support of the Economic History Unit and the Centre for European Research at the University of Gothenburg (CERGU) and the Riksbankens Jubileumsfond'—The economic history unit is not part of the Centre for European Research (so not 'of')—it was a dual post for the postdoc, also the funder Riksbankens Jubileumsfond is misspelled—so NOT 'The author acknowledges the support of the Economic History Unit of the Centre for European Research at the University of Gothenburg (CERGU) and the Rijkbanken Jubileumsfonds.
2 Charles Maier, "The Politics of Productivity: Foundations of American International Economic Policy after World War II," *International Organization* 31, no. 4 (October 1977): 607–633.
3 John Gerard Ruggie, "International Regimes, Transactions, and Change: Embedded Liberalism in the Postwar Economic Order," *International Organization* 36, no. 2 (April 1982): 379–415.
4 Lorenzo Mechi, "Economic Regionalism and Social Stabilisation: The International Labour Organization and Western Europe in the Early Post-War Years," *The International History Review* 35, no. 4 (2013): 844–862.
5 Alan Milward, *The European Rescue of the Nation-State* (London: Routledge, 2000).
6 Roger Normand and Sarah Zaidi, *Human Rights at the UN: The Political History of Universal Justice* (Bloomington: Indiana University Press, 2008), 177, 194.
7 Ibid., 204–206.

8 Mikael Rask Madsen, "From Cold War Instrument to Supreme European Court: The European Court of Human Rights at the Crossroads of International and National Law and Politics," *Law & Social Inquiry* 32, no. 1 (2007): 137–159, here 148; Ed Bates, *The Evolution of the European Convention on Human Rights: From Its Inception to the Creation of a Permanent Court of Human Rights* (Oxford: Oxford University Press, 2010), 2.
9 Marco Duranti, *The Conservative Human Rights Revolution: European Identity, Transnational Politics, and the Origins of the European Convention* (Oxford: Oxford University Press, 2017), 304–308, 391.
10 Normand and Zaidi, *Human Rights at the UN*, 212.
11 Lucia Coppolaro, "Setting Up the Financing Institution of the European Economic Community: The Creation of the European Investment Bank (1955–1957)," *Journal of European Integration History* (2009): 87–104; Lise Rye Svartvatn, "In Quest of Time, Protection, and Approval: France and the Claims for Social Harmonization in the European Economic Community, 1955–56," *Journal of European Integration History* (2002): 85–102; Lorenzo Mechi, "Les États membres, les institutions et les débuts du Fonds Social Européen," in *Inside the European Community. Actors and Policies in the European Integration 1957–1972*, ed. Antonio Varsori (Nomos: Baden-Baden, 2006), 95–115; Cédric Guinand, "A Pillar of Economic Integration: The ILO and the Development of Social Security in Western Europe," in *Networks of Global Governance: International Organisations and European Integration in a Historical Perspective*, ed. Lorenzo Mechi et al. (Newcastle: Cambridge Scholars, 2014), 111–133; Lorenzo Mechi, "Between Community Building and External Relations: ILO-EEC Cooperation from the Treaty of Rome to the Charter of Social Rights (1958–1989)," in *Networks of Global Governance, International Organisations and European Integration in a Historical Perspective*, ed. Lorenzo Mechi et al. (Newcastle: Cambridge Scholars, 2014), 205–228; Lorenzo Mechi, "Du BIT à la politique européenne: les origines d'un modèle," *Le Mouvement social* 3 (2013): 17–30; Antonio Varsori, ed., *Il Comitato economico e sociale nella costruzione europea* (Venice: Marsilio, 2000).
12 The only existing account known to the author is Mario Taccolini, *La costruzione di un'Europa del lavoro: La Commissione per gli affari sociali dalle origini all'applicazione del Trattato di Rome (1953–1960)* (Milan: FrancoAngeli, 2006).
13 Débats de l'Assemblée Commune. Compte Rendu in Extenso des Séances, Herbert Wehner's comments, 12 September 1952 and plenary debate 10–11 January 1953, Archive of European Integration (AEI), Pittsburgh.
14 14 April 1953, AC AP PV ASOC-195304140010FR, Historical Archives of the European Parliament (HAEP).
15 12 January 1953, AC AP PV MACO-195301120010FR, HAEP.
16 11 March 1953, AC AP PV ASOC-195303110010FR, HAEP.
17 Nicolas Margue, AC AP PV ASOC-195304140010FR, HAEP.
18 14 April 1953, AC AP PV ASOC-195304140010FR, HAEP.
19 Ibid.
20 Brian Shaev, "Workers' Politics, the Communist Challenge, and the Schuman Plan: A Comparative History of the French Socialist and German Social Democratic Parties and the First Treaty for European Integration," *International Review of Social History* 61, no. 2 (August 2016): 251–281; Milward, *The European Rescue*, 77–84.
21 7 January 1954, AC AP PV ASOC-195401070010FR, HAEP.
22 28 April 1954, AC AP PV ASOC-195404280010FR, HAEP.
23 12 January 1956, AC AP PV ASOC-195601120010FR, HAEP.
24 For a more extended treatment of European parliamentary discussions on migration, see Brian Shaev, "I Socialisti europei, la libera circolazione dei lavoratori e i flussi migratori dall'estero nelle prime comunità europee," in Giuliana Laschi et al., *Europa in movimento: mobilità e migrazioni tra integrazione europea e decolonizzazione, 1945–1992* (Bologna: Il Mulino, 2018), 101–135.

25 Note relative à l'application de l'article 69 du traité, présentée au nom de la commission des Affaires sociales par M.A. Bertrand. Acopted unanimously. 26 October 1954, AC AP PV ASOC-AC-0014.55-mai0050FR, HAEP.
26 27 June 1957, Annexe III Proposition de résolution relative aux conditions de vie et de travail dans la Communauté, AC AP PV ASOC-195706270010FR, HAEP.
27 Birkelbach, 9 July 1955, AC AP PV ASOC-195507090010FR, HAEP.
28 Georg Pelster, 27 February 1956, AC AP PV ASOC-195602270010FR, HAEP.
29 Nicolas Margue, 27 February 1956, AC AP PV ASOC-195602270010FR, HAEP.
30 René Leboutte, "Le rôle de la Communauté du Charbon et de l'Acier dans le développement des politiques de reconversion industrielle et d'essor économique régional," *Moving the Social. Journal of Social History and the History of Social Movements* 30 (2003): 33–41; Dirk Spierenburg and Raymond Poidevin, *The History of the High Authority of the European Coal and Steel Community: Supranationality in Operation* (London: Weidenfeld and Nicolson, 1994), 322–338.
31 April 14 1953, AC AP PV ASOC-195304140010FR, HAEP.
32 2 May 1956, AC AP PV ASOC-19560502-PM0010FR, HAEP.
33 28 October 1955, AC AP PV ASOC-19551028001FR, HAEP.
34 Sinot, 3 May 1956, AC AP PV ASOC-19560503-AM0010FR, HAEP.
35 11 January 1956, AC AP PV ASOC-195601110010FR, HAEP.
36 3 May 1956, AC AP PV ASOC-19560503-PM0010FR, HAEP.
37 11 May 1955, AC AP PV ASOC-195505110010FR, HAEP.
38 Note faite au nom de la Commission en réponse à la lettre de M.R. Motz, Président du Groupe de travail, en date du 20 juin 1955 sur l'extension des compétences de la Communauté dans le domaine social par M.G.M. Nederhorst, rapporteur, Septembre 1955, AC AP PV ASOC-AC-0001.56-novembre0080FR, HAEP.
39 Ibid.
40 27 June 1957, AC AP PV ASOC-195706270010FR, HAEP.
41 15 July 1957, AC AP PV SANI-195707150010FR; 5 September 1957, AC AP SANI-195709050010FR; 30 November 1957, AC AP SANI-195711300010FR, HAEP.
42 28 June 1957, AC AP PV SANI-195706280010FR, HAEP.
43 14 June 1957, AC AP PV SANI-195706140010FR, HAEP.
44 11 January 1956, AC AP PV ASOC-195601110010FR, HAEP.
45 18 October 1957, AC AP PV ASOC-195710180010FR, HAEP.
46 "Economic oases" was a comment made by Aloys-Michael Lenz. 11 January 1956, AC AP PV ASOC-195601110010FR, HAEP.
47 29 November 1957, AC AP PV ASOC-195711290010FR, HAEP.
48 10 December 1956, AC AP PV ASOC-195612100010FR, HAEP; 29 November 1957, AC AP PV ASOC-195711290010FR, HAEP.
49 Bericht im Namen des Ausschusses für Fragen der Sozialpolitik über die sozialen Aspekte des Berichts der Delegationsleiter des durch die Konferenz von Messina geschaffenen Zwischenstaatlichen Ausschusses an die Aussenminister, AC AP PV ASOC-AC-0002.56-novembre0010DE, HAEP.
50 Letter attached to Communication, 4 January 1957, letter dated 21 December 1956. AC AP PV ASOC-195701050030FR, HAEP.
51 8 October 1957, AC AP PV ASOC-195710080010FR, HAEP.
52 10 December 1956, AC AP PV ASOC-195612100010FR, HAEP.
53 Ann-Christina L. Knudsen, *Farmers on Welfare: The Making of Europe's Common Agricultural Policy* (Ithaca: Cornell University Press, 2009).
54 Nederhorst, 23 March 1959, AC AP PV ASOC-195903230010FR, HAEP; Bertrand, 24 April 1959, AC AP PV ASOC-195904240020FR; Gailly, 16 January 1958, AC AP PV ASOC-195801160010FR, HAEP.
55 Hazenbosch and Fohrmann, 10 October 1958, AC AP PV ASOC-195810100010FR, HAEP.
56 25 January 1960, AC AP PV ASOC-0196001250010FR, HAEP.

57 22/23 May 1959, AC AP PV ASOC-195905220020FR, HAEP.
58 Giacchero, 24 April 1959, AC AP PV ASOC-195904240020FR, HAEP.
59 Angioy, 24 April 1959, AC AP ASOC-195904240020FR, HAEP.
60 Nicolas Verschueren, *Fermer les mines en construisant l'Europe: une histoire sociale de l'intégration européenne* (New York: Peter Lang, 2012), 117–167.
61 10 October 1958, AC AP PV ASOC-195810100010FR; 13 February 1959, AC AP PV ASOC-195902130010FR.
62 René Pêtre, 25 September 1962, AC AP PV ASOC-196209250020FR, HAEP.
63 13 February 1959, AC AP PV ASOC-195902130010FR, HAEP.
64 9 September 1958, AC AP PV ASOC-195809090010FR, HAEP.
65 10 October 1958, AC AP PV ASOC-195810100010FR, HAEP.
66 13 December 1958, AC AP PV ASOC-195812130010FR, HAEP.
67 23 April 1958, AC AP PV ASOC-195804230010FR, HAEP.
68 13 February 1959, AC AP PV ASOC-195902130010FR, HAEP.
69 Ibid.
70 Drout l'Hermine, 24 April 1959, AC AP PV ASOC-195904240020FR, HAEP; Petrilli, 6–7 November 1959, AC AP PV ASOC-195911060020FR, HAEP.
71 23 April 1958, AC AP PV ASOC-195804230010FR, HAEP.
72 12 January 1959, AC AP PV ASOC-195901120010FR, HAEP.
73 Frageboden über die soziale Lage in den bäuerlichen Familienbetrieben in den Ländern der Gemeinschaft, 14. Mai 1959, AC AP ASOC-A0-0106.600030DE, HAEP.
74 7 November 1958, AC AP PV ASOC-195811070020FR, HAEP.
75 12 January 1959, AC AP PV ASOC-195901120010FR, HAEP.
76 See Knudsen, *Farmers on Welfare*.
77 13 February 1959, AC AP PV ASOC-195902130010FR, HAEP.
78 09/10 October 1959, AC AP PV ASOC-195910090020FR, HAEP.
79 Probst, 7 July 1959, AC AP PV ASOC-195907070020FR, HAEP.
80 6/7 November 1959, AC AP PV ASOC-195911060020FR, HAEP.
81 2 June 1961, AC AP PV ASOC-196106020010FR, HAEP.
82 Giacchero, 23 April 1958, AC AP PV ASOC-195804230010FR, HAEP.
83 28 January 1959, AC AP PV ASOC-195901270010FR, HAEP.
84 Vredeling 1961, AC AP PV ASOC-A0-0137.620030FR, HAEP.
85 14 April 1958, AC AP PV ASOC-195804140010FR, HAEP.
86 8 September 1959, AC AP PV ASOC-195909080020FR, HAEP.
87 Sabatini, 28 January 1959, AC AP PV ASOC-195901270010FR, HAEP.
88 28 January 1959, AC AP PV ASOC-195901270010FR, HAEP.
89 23 April 1958, AC AP PV ASOC-195804230010FR; Petrilli, 10 October 1958, AC AP PV ASOC-195810100010FR, HAEP.
90 7 July 1959, AC AP PV ASOC-195907070020FR, HAEP.
91 Stefano Giubboni, *Social Rights and Market Freedom in the European Constitution: A Labour Law Perspective* (Cambridge: Cambridge University Press, 2006), 7–93.
92 Milward, *The European Rescue*.
93 Fritz W. Scharpf, "The Asymmetry of European Integration, or Why the EU Cannot Be a 'Social Market Economy'," *Socio-Economic Review* 8 (2010): 211–250.
94 Antonio Varsori, "The Emergence of a Social Europe," in *The European Commission 1958–72. History and Memories of an Institution*, ed. Michel Dumoulin (Luxembourg: Publications Office of the European Union, 2014), 427–441, here 432.
95 Antonio Varsori and Lorenzo Mechi, ed., *Lionello Levi Sandri e la politica sociale europea* (Milan: FrancoAngeli, 2008); www.socialsummit17.se/wp-content/uploads/2017/11/Concluding-report-Gothenburg-summit.pdf, accessed 9 February 2018.
96 Daniel Vaughan-Whitehead, ed., *The European Social Model in Times of Crisis: Is Europe Losing Its Soul?* (Geneva: ILO, 2015).

2 From territorialized rights to personalized international social rights?
The making of the European Convention on the Social Security of Migrant Workers (1957)

Karim Fertikh

Introduction

The coordination of national social insurance systems is certainly the most lasting and important social achievement of European integration. While the internationalization of social insurances began prior to that time, it gained momentum after World War II. In many regards, the post-war decades witnessed the transformation and formalization of the interconnection of national social insurance schemes. At the time, various European players, taking advantage of the creation of new international organizations like the Council of Europe, the European Coal and Steel Community (ECSC) or the European Economic Community (EEC) pushed the agenda of a transnational social policy. This transnational social policy was not primarily conceived as a supranational policy, but it did articulate the competences of the national state, of international organizations and the social rights of individuals in a new manner. This chapter focuses on the making of the European Convention of the Social Security of Migrant Workers, which was signed by the six member states of the ECSC on 10 December 1957 and entered into force as EEC regulations (regulations 3 and 4) on 1 January 1959. It sheds light on the transnational coordination of social security and on the constellation of actors who promoted a European integration of social policy. This European Convention provided better social security for migrant workers and their families, defining the conditions of insurance when workers left their country of residence to work in another convention state, and guaranteeing the maintenance of social rights in such cases.

This achievement continued a trend in the development of social policy as a transnational phenomenon, which started in the nineteenth century. In the literature, control over national boundaries and international migrations have long been seen as a central component of state sovereignty. In the domain of the social policy toward migrants, a part of state sovereignty should be considered as the product of international negotiations. Since the nineteenth century, migrants have made up around 2.7% of the global population, and the number of international migrants amounted to 74 million in 1960.[1] State and social bureaucracies whose social policies are subject to conditions of nationality have had to deal with this social reality. In the nineteenth century, deporting to other countries the poor foreigners who could not earn their living or rely on local or national solidarity required negotiation between national administrations – indeed, deportation involves two countries and (at least) one border crossing.[2] The case of migrant workers gives us a window into the transnational dynamics of the Welfare State and into the place of international negotiations in the building of such states.

Social scientists are aware of the importance of the international dimension of welfare states. Historians have noted the importance of transnational networks of social reformers.[3] Since the nineteenth century, these networks have contributed to forging national social policies and have been instrumental in the synchronicity and similarities of certain reforms in that realm.[4] The creation of the International Labour Organization (ILO) in 1919 was a result of these actions; it institutionalized this nebula of social reformers at the international level.[5] The ILO offered transnational resources and a transnational scene, with regular meetings, to formulate international social demands. It was surrounded by a whole system of private or semi-public international organizations, offering an arena to discuss, compare and propose international instruments. Setting new reform agendas, defining (and recognizing) occupational diseases as social policy problems, and developing international standards and policies after World War I, the ILO was a kind of hub, centralizing the efforts of international policymakers.[6] In the continuation of these historical works on the ILO and reformers networks, some historians have produced actor-centred studies on the post-war period that highlight the continued importance of the transnational dimension of the social state and the growing role of certain international organizations.[7] This chapter follows this approach.

This approach aims at overcoming two limitations in contemporary research on the transnational dimension of the social state. Social sciences often neglect the actors of this policy. The literature on the post-1945 period has shed light on the continued importance of the internationalization phenomenon. In the social sciences, narratives usually describe a "Europeanization" of social policies, or the growing role of international organizations, going hand in hand with the decreasing role of national states in a "post-national" era. These narratives often emphasize general trends (towards "post-national" policies, Europeanization, or internationalization) that do not sufficiently account for the continued role of transnational networks in developing international labour protection (although admittedly these networks experienced transformations in the twentieth century). In sociology and political science, the literature is often biased towards abstraction, resulting in a certain lack of attention to actors and their concrete endeavours. The landmark synthesis of Maurizio Ferrera exemplifies this shortcoming: a genuine source of inspiration on post-sovereign social rights as a general analysis of the erosion of the link between state and social rights, his work says little about the *making* of these post-sovereign social rights in practice.[8] Crucially, the development of de-territorialized or individualized social rights, meaning social rights that are recognized independently of the territory where they are acquired or where social benefits are paid, has been a controversial topic in many international negotiations, including the negotiation of the European Convention on the Social Security of Migrant Workers. The analysis of these debates in this chapter sheds light on the legal, political and scientific conceptions that were confronted to de-territorialize (or individualize) social rights and define the extent of the de-territorialization. As they focus on outcomes, sociologists and historians have too often ignored processes and conflicting points of view on the coordination of social security schemes.[9] As a result, socio-historical and historical explanations are incomplete.

A second limitation of the studies addressing the internationalization of social security is that they often reproduce institutional categories (state, international organization) in the form of a "historiographical mimicry," akin to that discussed by Brigitte Studer in her research on communism.[10] All too often, the literature focuses on a single international organization – most frequently the European Union (EU) – and its relations with national states (or local administrations). In doing so, these studies analyse how national actors "use," so to speak, these international organizations. When migrations are analysed, the focus is often placed on the reaction of a single national state to the phenomenon. For instance, the stimulating work of Carl Ulrich Schierup and Stephen Castles investigates the reaction of Western social states to new migrations, but fails to identify a genuine transnational dimension in the (re)construction of the social state.[11] In a nutshell, in some of the current literature on the social rights of migrants, the transnational making of social policy often seems to be a blind spot.

A significant step on the path toward European integration, the European Convention on Social Security can offer us insights into this transnational making of social policy. Although the internationalization of social security had begun before the unification of the European labour market in the 1950s, the free movement of labour promoted by both the ECSC and by the EEC since their inception was an opportunity for systematizing the numerous bilateral or sectorial agreements concluded in the field of social security. Movement of labour required removing the barriers created by the lack of connection between the national (and infra-national) social security schemes. The name of the Convention on the Social Security of Migrant Workers reflected the importance of the movement of labour. The treaty was designed for "migrant workers" – not for European citizens in general – even if the worker, implicitly a male breadwinner, was in the end considered to have a family (although this was a subject of discussion). The general framing of EEC/EU cooperation in this domain has largely remained unchanged since the convention's adoption.

Under the convention, the worker must receive social insurance in his – the documents speak solely of men – country of employment within a reasonable timeframe. Regarding pensions and unemployment benefits, employment periods in countries other than his country of residence should be taken into account. Allowances must be paid in the country of residence if it differs from the country of employment. Children who do not live in the same country as their father should receive the family allowances. The cases of cross-border workers and of workers becoming ill in a country of short-term employment had to be dealt with, along with the mixed rights acquired in different systems. What should be done when a worker migrates with a sick family member? What if that person was to become ill before they were entitled to anything in their country of employment, considering some countries terminated health insurance coverage as soon as people left the country? In the debates, questions were also raised about how to compensate for benefits paid under the convention between the national social security funds. All these elements – country of employment, country of residence, duration of the stay, acquired rights, nationality – were argumentative or linguistic blocks used to construct the different provisions of the text. While the experts agreed on the principle of free movement and accordingly on rethinking the territoriality of social insurance, they had very different means in mind to achieve that goal, which this chapter will examine.

To analyse the making of the European Convention for the Social Security of Migrant Workers, I have explored a wide array of archives (ILO, European Union, French Labour Ministry) and documents to reflect the plurality of the players involved. The focus is specifically placed on the negotiation of the convention. From 1954 to 1958, it was prepared by governmental experts – i.e. heads of the national social insurances – in close cooperation with ILO officials and the High Authority of the ECSC. The EEC officials played their part later, as the convention was carried out as an EEC regulation. Other institutions and states intervened, including the UN High Commissioner for refugees, the government of the United Kingdom and Swiss officials. The expert meetings, one of which lasted two weeks, often took place at the ILO headquarters in Geneva, in the presence of a team of interpreters.

This chapter is divided into three parts. First, I examine the post-war context in which numerous agreements on social security and social rights were concluded in Europe and beyond. Second, I analyse the transnational milieu of experts, lawyers and politicians who form the human substratum of the production of these international rights. Last, I show how the 1957 European Agreement was produced and how it activated national and transnational legal categories.

The international framing of social security

In the post-World War II era, many international agreements were concluded in the field of social policy, especially in Europe, where work began on the European Code for Social Security (1964) and the Council of Europe's European Social Charter (1961) in the 1940s. International activity in the field was intense and publicized in numerous booklets.[12] These achievements also drew academic attention, and were the subject of many articles and monographs.[13] Efforts to synthetize these realizations were reflected in the 1951 ILO International Code for Labour Law and in the first known handbook for international labour and social security law, published in 1952 by the Belgian legal expert and minister Léon-Éli Troclet.[14]

At the time, the international framing of social security constituted an important part of this activity in relation to the liberalization of the movement of workers necessary to the constitution of the Common Market. The internationalization of social security – i.e., the construction of (personal, legal, institutional) bridges between the national social insurance systems – began long before 1945. In the early twentieth century, international agreements stabilized the relations between social insurances. In April 1904, the first known agreement linked the French and Italian social insurance systems as part of a broader trade agreement.[15] That same year, Italy and Switzerland concluded an agreement on occupational accident insurance, opening the way for a long list of other agreements on social insurances.[16]

Although social insurances existed long before the post-World War II period, it was then that their international architecture was rethought and systematized. Between 1946 and 1953, 135 international agreements were concluded.[17] This policy internationalization was a mainly European phenomenon, although some agreements were made in other countries (USA, Chile, Argentina, New Zealand, Australia). Eighty per cent of the agreements concluded between 1945 and 1955 concerned West European countries. While Western countries made the majority of these agreements, they also connected East and West: 9% crossed over the Iron Curtain.[18] Ten years later, there would be more than 400 such bilateral agreements, most of them (94%) in Europe.[19]

To be sure, some of these agreements concerned very small numbers of people. In the years following the reunification of Saarland with the Federal Republic of Germany, the French administration tried to sort out how many individuals fell under the agreements made with Saarland: 1800 Saarland workers were to receive their pension in Saarland from the French social insurance fund.[20] Some of the clauses that had been negotiated concerned so few people that they were dropped after a few years, like Article 15 of EEC regulation No. 3 concerning the right of French engineers in Saarland to keep their French social insurance. The negotiations on extending this provisional clause were terminated as the German administration observed that no one was actually benefiting from it.[21]

In the two decades following WWII, promoters of the development of international social rights saw the European continent as a special place, a laboratory for the making of international social policies. This vanguard role attributed to the European continent explains the crucial role played by the ILO in supporting the efforts of European administrations to conclude such agreements. The ILO played an especially important part in the drafting of European multilateral agreements on Social Security, as well as in the preparation of overall agreements to establish international social insurance standards launched by the Council of Europe. As the European Social Charter was signed in 1961 Jef Rens, the associate director of the ILO, insisted that Europe is

> the cradle of the world's social policy. Its contribution to the ILO is invaluable. Numerous ILO conventions are based on social legislations from European countries. [...] The continent remains, to a large extent, the soul and driving force of the International Labour Organization.[22]

This was why the ILO actively supported the preparation of the European Code of Social Security (1964) and of various European conventions for the Social Security of Migrant Workers. Prominent European legal experts predicted that the European social law would soon be the most advanced international social legislation.[23]

This idea that Europe had to become a "laboratory" for international social policy explains the support (especially the ILO's) for the development of international conventions on social security. International organizations provided technical support and the framework for these agreements. Whereas bilateral agreements were a longstanding tool of international relations, the use of multilateral agreements was a new development in the domain of social security. In 1950, the first multilateral agreement on social security, concerning Rhine boatmen, was prepared by ILO civil servants and ratified by the member states of the Central Commission for the Navigation on the Rhine River (CCNR). In 1953, the same players prepared a similar agreement for the ECSC, which laid the basis for the 1958 EEC regulations dealing with the social rights of migrant workers. The European Convention for the Social Security of Migrant Workers applied to the six founding countries of both the ECSC and the EEC (Belgium, France, Federal Republic of Germany, Italy, Luxemburg and the Netherlands). The third and fourth EEC regulations gave it legal force in 1959, and it was adapted in the 1970s because of the enlargement of the EEC. These agreements were not the only achievements of the post-war period. In 1964, the Council of Europe took up the issue and proposed a European Code of Social Security to develop social security standards and harmonize social charges.

The international dimension of social security was not regarded as a marginal phenomenon by the national players involved in reframing domestic social insurance schemes; it went hand and hand with the development of the social insurances themselves.[24] Considered as the "founder" of French social security in 1945, Pierre Laroque stressed the importance of this international work in the early days of social security in his 1993 memoirs. He noted that increasingly large amounts of resources were mobilized to tackle international issues (the first Bureau of the Directorate General was specialized in the international dimension of French social security), and that he took part in such activities himself:

> In my arguments so far, I have reasoned as if the issues raised by the Social Security were restricted to the French territory. Of course, these kinds of problems were of paramount importance, especially when the Social Security scheme was developed and implemented. However, international concerns were never neglected and became increasingly important as the organization established itself and its routine.
>
> I always insisted on dealing personally with every international problem, and there were many, with which we were confronted. [...] The First Office of the Directorate General was in charge of international issues pertaining to social security, which came to be its main and ultimately exclusive activity. [25]

In his memoirs, Pierre Laroque also describes his time-consuming international activities, including trips to faraway countries for international conferences. In 1950, his participation in the Commission for the Social Security of the ILO in Wellington (New Zealand) cost this high-ranking official and general director of French social security a month of his time.[26] Likewise, professional journals in the field of social security or labour policy devoted more space to the international dimension of these social policies in the 1940s/1950s than subsequently.[27] Laroque is no exception in this generation of "founding fathers" of both social security and international social law. The specialist of international social law Léon-Éli Troclet, who was several times after 1945 Belgian minister in charge of social insurances and labour, is another example: Troclet had since the 1920s been involved in efforts to establish international social standards in various capacities, especially at the ILO, whose governing body he presided over in 1950.

In post-WWII international social policy, many international negotiations in the domain of social policy and social security took place, resulting in numerous bilateral agreements on social security and in international conventions hosted by international organizations such as the ILO, the Council of Europe, the ECSC and the EEC. That period saw the advent of the European Code of Social Security, European Social Charter of the Council of Europe, European Convention for the Social Security of Migrant Workers in 1958 (and, in 1950, for social security for Rhine boatmen), and of European social policies implemented by the EEC and the ECSC. In all these negotiations, the importance of a limited circle of experts and civil servants in national administrations and international organizations is quite striking. This constellation of promoters of social policies and labour law designed these agreements in various international arenas.

The entrepreneurs of the internationalized social security

This transnational making of social security, embodied in meetings, committees, international conventions and agreements, must be analysed as the outcome of efforts by a singular post-war constellation of reformers (professors, trade unionists, experts, national and international civil servants) promoting an international social law. For technical reasons, the international coordination of social security systems was considered as central to the functioning of the national social insurances – and especially as a necessary counterweight to the liberalization of goods and capital exchanges – and, for more idealistic reasons, some of the (socialist or left liberal) members of the constellation of reformers saw international social regulation as part of a politically progressive agenda to improve the situation of workers at a time when moderates saw communism as a threat to liberal West European democracies. All the achievements of European social law were conceived together, as a whole, in the experts' writings.[28] Even if there was no plan afoot – instead, rather vague watchwords such as "social Europe," "social progress," "harmonization" – these networks played a role in forging legal categories and institutions that embodied the connection between the national systems. The negotiations of the European Convention brought together governmental and international experts who were already collaborating. The governmental experts – Jacques Doublet (France), Armand Kayser (Luxembourg), Kurt Jantz (Germany), Carlo Carloni (Italy), Adrianus van de Ven (Netherlands) – as well as many other players in the negotiations (the Belgian Minister Troclet, the ILO officials and so on) were already acquainted, contributing to the existence of the "even minimalist interpersonal trust" necessary in international negotiations on migrations.[29]

Private and public international organizations played a major part in this endeavour. The ILO and its employees in the Social Security Division of the International Labour Office were at the centre of the international network. NGOs specialized in labour and social security law gravitated around the ILO. The International Social Security Association was founded in 1927 under the auspices of the ILO. It was designed to foster cooperation between social security agencies. The association played a significant role, as it dispatched the standard models of international bilateral agreements that laid the basis for the actual agreements. Working in partnership with the ILO, the International Society for Labour and Social Security law was founded in 1958 after a first congress held in 1957, and brought together leading labour jurists.

The ILO cooperated with regional European organizations such as the Western European Union, the Council of Europe, the ECSC and the EEC to make good on their proclamations on achieving "social progress." At the time, the European regional organizations and the ILO developed a close cooperation, because of the latter's technical competence. Exchanges of documents, joint studies and the creation of common institutes were signs of this closeness. The ILO received annual funding for technical support from the ECSC.

The cooperation between the ILO and the European institutions was not always peaceful. This milieu of reformers did not constitute a unified "epistemic community of labour [in this case, social security] experts," not the least because of their organizational interests.[30] One of the reasons for this, as ILO employees put it, was the competition for "social prestige,"[31] meaning international recognition in the field of social policy. The European Convention for the Social Security of Migrant Workers might provide an example for this. ILO civil servants were involved in the negotiations and in the preparation of the convention text. Most of the expert meetings were held at the ILO headquarters in Geneva. At one point, as the document was nearly ready, the ILO officials began to fear that the ECSC would

> try to squeeze the ILO out of the picture in connection with activities undertaken jointly [...] Moreover, one cannot exclude the possibility that the intergovernmental committee for the *relance européenne* [sic] (the so-called "Spaak" Committee), entrusted with the drafting of the Common Market and Euratom treaties, might take up the convention with the agreement or connivance of the High Authority, and wish to have it signed under its own auspices, as a European achievement.[32]

The ILO feared, as it put it, "a 'separatist' manoeuver" on the part of the ECSC, which would have deprived the ILO of the credit for its actions in the preparation of the agreement. Worse yet, the ILO officials feared that the organization would be deprived of any means to intervene in the concrete coordination of the social security should it be kept out of the Administrative Commission of the social security, which had to be set up to carry out the agreement.

All the same, this milieu was densely interconnected through the numerous international organizations listed earlier, and the arenas (European assemblies, expert committees, conferences, negotiations, seminars) these organizations contributed to shaping.[33] These professionals considered the newly created European institutions as venues to push their agendas, but their networks pre-existed. For instance, in July 1950, the European Movement organized a "Social Conference" in Rome, where social experts, professors, high civil servants, officials from the ILO and the Council of Europe, and social insurance employees, driven by a certain European idealism, discussed both the importance of social security for "the development of personality" and the importance of its international coordination.[34]

This network revolved around a few specialists of international social law. Georges Spyropoulos, a high civil servant at the ILO, was a former student of Paul Durand, who supervised his PhD dissertation on trade unionism. A professor at the Sorbonne University in Paris, Paul Durand had been one of the founders of the International Society for Labour and Social Security Law and was active in the preparation of reports for various international organizations. He helped the legal expert Jacques Doublet, the successor of Pierre Laroque as head of the Directorate General for social security at the French Labour Ministry, to develop the French position on "social harmonization." Jacques Doublet conducted the French expert team on the European convention. The Luxembourgian expert Armand Kayser was himself a member of the International Society for Social Security Law and of the EEC Administrative Commission for social security (where he sat, among others, with the German expert Jantz).[35] Many of the experts in the national teams were involved in the drafting of the European Social Charter at the time.[36] Many were also involved in the expert committees of the EEC in the late 1950s and the 1960s. Close examination of the expertise demanded by the EEC and the ECSC reveals the importance of the construction of transnational knowledge, relying on international comparisons and the development transnational concepts (for harmonization purposes, among other things). The EEC's General Directorate for Social Affairs mobilized (and financed) the ILO and the scientific bureaus of the trade unions, as well as many national experts – professionals or scientists. Kayser, Van de Ven, Troclet, Doublet, and Laroque were among those who worked as experts for the EEC, even though some of them left to pursue academic careers in the 1960s.[37]

The professionalization of international social policy was instrumental in the making of this international milieu, as the backgrounds of the individuals involved in negotiating the European Convention reflect. Jean Dedieu, a top-level civil servant at the General Directorate of social security in Paris, was one of the French negotiators for the International Agreement for the Social Security of Migrant Workers in the 1950s. In 1958, Dedieu became a top civil servant at the Directorate General for Social Affairs of the EEC Commission. A specialist in the mathematical aspects of insurance and an ILO official, Wilhelm Dobbernack worked on drafting the European Agreement on Social Security.[38] He had been a civil servant at the Federal Labour Ministry since the 1930s and transferred to the ILO in 1952. This transnational milieu forged transnational categories in the field of social law that I shall explore further in the final part of this chapter.

The European Convention and the connection of the national social security organizations: from "national interests" to personalized international social rights

The fabric of the debates on the 1957 European Convention reveals the existence of this social milieu. Many decisions were left to the experts, without intergovernmental discussions. At the end of the negotiation process in 1957, the ministers met to reach an agreement on only two points (family allowances and employment insurance).[39] Many different kinds of arguments were put forward in the debates: legal, "philosophical," social and even moral, as when the Luxembourgian expert Armand Kayser voiced his wariness of "speculators," meaning insured persons who would pick out the best place to receive certain social benefits. In these debates, the players framed a European discussion on international social rights that can be understood partly in light of national positions and socializations and partly as an attempt to forge genuinely transnational categories. I will first try to explain how "national interests" could be expressed in such a technical debate, and, second, to examine the making and use of the transnational categories of "individualized" or "personalized" and "territorialized" rights.

First, the convention would not have existed without national systems: the experts did not aim at constituting a supranational social security (i.e. purely individual social rights). It required, as Roland Burke convincingly demonstrated in his study of the Universal Declaration for Human Rights, "a world of states for its provisions to be realized, set within an international architecture that supported their promotion."[40] The experts spoke in the name of their administrations, and hence as *national* experts. They took into account and defended the interests of national insurances, but there were a few moments when national interests were defended without being discussed in the context of more complex arguments. The non-negotiable conditions presented by some experts were sometimes absent in the provisions of the final agreement. What one could name "national interests" could be seen in another light, namely as the expression of the peculiarities of national social schemes and as an attempt to preserve their functioning. In the post-war era, international social rights were not philosophically perceived to be above and beyond borders. Rather, an effort was made to combine individual rights and national insurances by coordinating social security systems, possibly under a supra- or intergovernmental agency.

Preserving national social security systems was arguably one of the reasons for coming to an international agreement on the subject. The sustainability of national insurances was an argument in the debates. Armand Kayser, the Luxembourgian expert, explained that his country's insurance system considered certain insurance periods irrelevant for calculating pensions.[41] Should these periods be taken into account for foreigners, the whole system would be in danger, he claimed. More broadly, the debate was largely shaped by the French officials' active support for social harmonization in an attempt to protect the country's social security achievements from what contemporary parlance calls "social dumping."[42] Jacques Doublet defended such a harmonization during the negotiations of the Treaty of Rome, with some success (provisions were included in the treaty on the harmonization of social legislations and gender equality). The social security debate was a means to push this idea into new areas. One of the key features of harmonization was to be the constitution of a European Social Security Fund, financed by the national social security organizations, the ECSC and by a special payroll tax paid by the coal and steel industries' employers to finance a reserve fund in case of unemployment in the steel and coal industries (and amounting to 0.1% of the annual ECSC payroll).[43] The minutes of the discussion suggest that the experts linked this European fund with the harmonization of social costs. The ECSC representative, Giuseppe Glisenti, remarked that in his institution's experience, such funds had helped to achieve the unification and the harmonization of national regimes (helping for instance to establish a common market for steel and coal).[44] The question of the financial sustainability of the national funds was not the only question raised: the political coherence of the national social security systems was at stake as well.

Some countries had to stop subjecting benefit eligibility to the nationality principle in order to connect their systems with the other European systems. This was the case in the Federal Republic of Germany. In that country, the "social reform" (meaning the post-war reform of social insurances) was spearheaded by academic law expert Kurt Jantz (1908–1984) who served from 1935 to 1938 in the administration for insurance (Reichsversicherungsamt) and from 1938 to 1945 as advisor to the Labour Ministry. After the war, he left the ministry – by choice or not, we do not know – and worked for various Protestant churches. In 1951, he resumed his former duties at the Labour Ministry.[45] In his writings on social rights, Jantz developed the view that social rights and insurances are at the crossroads between individual freedom and the needs of the community (*Gemeinschaft*). Social policy accordingly faced the responsibility of building an "organic" social order.[46] Jantz insisted on the necessity to treat nearly eight million German refugees[47] on an equal footing with the non-refugees. Hence, the rationality principle played a part in the attribution of pensions. Should a foreigner entitled to a pension move out of the Federal Republic, he would lose this right. With a German national, refugee or non-refugee, the territoriality principle did not apply. As Jantz explained in his book *Das neue Fremdenrenten- und Auslandsrentenrecht* (1961), the same idea was then used in the application of the international agreements on social security and the nationality condition was dropped for the EEC countries.

One of the main problems discussed by the experts was the problem of family allowances and maternity benefits. These social benefits were part of social security, and the agreement tended to widen their scope to cover migrant workers and their families as well. This extension came up against a demographic argument.

Under French logic, supported by the dominant "populationists" (linked with the "population sciences"), ensuring the growth and quality of the population was the main problem for French society. The French founders of social security partly saw the system as a "biopolitical" means to govern the population.[48] They used the creation of social security as an incentive to produce more and better people. Jacques Doublet, born in 1907, can be seen as a member of the populationist network. A doctor in law, he had been a high-ranking civil servant since the 1930s. A member of the State Council from 1932 onwards, Doublet specialized first in questions of immigration, social affairs and family. In 1939, he served as General Secretary of the High Council for Family.[49] During WWII, as a civil servant under the Vichy regime, and in the post-war era, he was a promoter of the French variant of eugenics supporting both a growth of the population in quantity and its "qualitative improvement" (under the terms of this modernized eugenics), through housing and health policies especially. Doublet argued that social security was a tool for lawmakers to influence "the size and the quality of population."[50] In this sense, social security was used to assimilate migrants into the French population: migrant workers were expected to live with their families in France, in decent accommodations; full support to migrant children born in France was denied, as they were eligible for French nationality.

This *populationist* body of knowledge and practice informed the distinction made by French experts in the negotiation between insurance benefits (in the convention) and "demographic" policy (which did not require equal treatment). Doublet's "demographic" argument was taken up by the French minister Albert Gazier in 1957.[51] To begin with, social rights were not the rights of the worker – the "family head," as Doublet wrote[52] – alone, but of the worker and his family. The French negotiators insisted on this familial dimension, even if it meant additional costs for the national institutions, as Doublet praised himself for. The generosity of the system was seen by Jacques Doublet as a necessity to meet the need for manpower in France and, according to him, many other nations.[53] Furthermore, the right to social benefits was restricted in three major ways. First, a time limit was applied to the provision of family allowances: three years were seen as enough time for the worker to find a *decent housing solution* – housing being one of the means to improve the population's quality. The restriction could be expected to provide an incentive for him to settle down with his family in his country of employment and live in a "normal" family setting. The initial idea was to introduce a two-year cap unless the worker could prove he had failed to secure "decent" housing (but the experts feared this would lead to litigation).[54] A second restriction concerned children who were born on the territory of the country of employment. French negotiators insisted on removing maternity benefits from the agreement, as foreign workers could claim French citizenship for their children. A third restriction to social benefits stemmed from the presence of colonial workers in the French metropolis. While this was left unsaid during the meetings, Algerian migrants in France did not receive full family allowances for their children who had stayed in the Algerian colony, and foreigners could not be treated better than "national citizens." Since the international system had to be embedded in the pre-existing imperial system, the French official insisted that the benefits paid in the country of employment could not exceed those paid in the country where the children lived.

While arguably the convention relied on a "world of states for its provisions to be realized,"[55] and even to be conceived, the expert meetings gave exposure to genuinely *transnational categories of an international social right* that led to the specific loosening of the territoriality principle of social insurances. The discourse on social security made these agreements a desirable achievement per se. International social security was considered as a civilizational goal (making "social security for the human race as a whole" or an interconnected European system, according to the conclusions of the 1951 European Movement conference). This idealism found expression when the International Social Security Association defended these international agreements as a way to "remove barriers between nations [and] providing opportunities for the cross fertilization of ideas and experience and by forcing the legislators and administrators to look afresh at many of the principles which they have hitherto accepted as fundamental."[56]

> It helps to create a more liberal conception of social security. The ultimate goal of social security for the human race as a whole may still seem a remote ideal, but no one can doubt that every new reciprocal agreement marks a further step towards the achievement of that ideal.[57]

The same text expressed "admiration" toward the administrators who prepared and implemented these agreements. At a time when various European organizations were being set up, the European Convention in particular was regarded as a means to "contribute to the European unification," and it relied "not only on a technical argument of rationalization, but on a European motive."[58]

During the negotiations, the debate's main focus was on how to organize the de-territorialization of social rights. The personalization of social rights – the idea that social rights had to be attached to individuals independently of the territory where they lived or worked – was defended as a moral issue by some experts. In a memorandum, Armand Kayser criticized one of the convention's draft provisions, which refused to guarantee the rights of an insured person to a disability pension in Luxembourg in the three months following their migration to another country. "No civilized law," he continued, "could accept to deny these rights acquired at the cost of considerable financial sacrifice."[59] Here, the logic is moral and individual. In a memorandum, the Italian expert Carloni considered it a basic principle of the convention, and so did the other experts (including the Dutch expert Van de Ven).[60]

While the idea of loosening the territoriality principle formed the basis of the agreement, how to proceed was another story. The experts' arguments revolved around the dichotomy between territorialization and individualization (or personalization) of social rights. Many solutions were proposed. The Luxembourgian Kayser considered the controversy hypocritical. He defended the point of view "that social security being a redistribution of wealth, it was only convenient to take the wealth where it is accumulated. The notion of personality and territoriality are only the ideological superstructure expressing the diverging national interests of immigration and emigration countries."[61] In this sense, the opposition between "territorialization" and "individualization" would have been the expression of a national-interest-driven controversy between the important immigration countries, France and Belgium, and Italy.[62] In a projection of the costs stemming from the convention, $6.5 million would be required to carry out the external payments; $2.9 million would be provided by France alone (60%) and $2.1 million by Belgium (32%).[63] Nevertheless, I argue that the question of territoriality was used to dramatize the debate, and to promote the creation of a supranational institution to standardize social security costs (which did not come to be). In these negotiations, the territoriality principle, hence, was used to lower the French contribution, but had the broader purpose of paving the way for another step of Europeanization – something akin to the Europeanization of social security.

Countries with a high immigration rate (chiefly France and Belgium) supported the creation of a European Social Security Fund, which would have reduced their burden. An analysis in sheer terms of national interest could not do justice to the situation. The suggested supranational arrangement would have led to a loss of sovereignty for all national administrations as the counterpart for a repartition of the financial costs between all stakeholders. France argued that such a fund would de-territorialize the payment of benefits, when it was legally impossible for the French social security to pay a social benefit outside French territory. This was non-negotiable for the French government, which intervened directly in the debate, as it stated in a note to the experts in 1955:

> The French government would under no conditions agree with a text that would force the country of affiliation to almost singlehandedly support the costs of the benefits paid outside its territory, which would happen if the compensation fund were just an empty shell.[64]

The French government and the experts tried to push forward the idea of a harmonization of social costs through an international payroll tax. Jacques Doublet insisted on this European fund, threatening that France would stick to the territoriality principle if it was not implemented. This payroll tax solution was a way to promote France's "harmonization" agenda, but was not only meant to lower France's financial contribution (which was eventually achieved through other administrative means). French officials used a hard-line defence of the territoriality principle to push the transnational agenda of harmonization indirectly. The memorandum stated that the compensation fund would finance a "European Center for Social Security" headquartered in Luxembourg. "The Center," continued the memo, "[…] may also be entrusted with other missions in the field of health and social action. The value of such a Center for the European integration has not escaped the attention of the French government."[65] The French experts used the promise of deepening European integration as a means to gain support from other delegations by outlining a European interest. In the negotiation, the

French views appeared to lack the necessary support. Widening the frame, and in the process defining a genuinely European interest, was a means to attract additional backers. Examination of the fund's proposed distribution key suggests that there was more at stake than just reducing the burden on immigration countries: the international payroll tax and the ECSC's contribution reflected a supranational vision. The Italian expert Carloni remarked that such a fund would contribute to "the standardization of social security costs."[66] As the experts did not reach an agreement on the compensation fund, social rights were personalized (individualized) through inter-administrative arrangements, which ensured the clearing of the funds. The costs were divided between country of residence and country of employment by distributive keys, but no mechanism ensured social harmonization.

Conclusion

The European Convention for the Social Security of Migrant Workers was a means to internationalize social rights, by attaching social rights to an individual rather than a territory or nation, in order to make social rights and migration compatible. The European experts were part of a broader international network revolving around the ILO and associations (International Social Security Agency [ISSA], International Society for Labour and Social Security Law) promoting social rights both in national and in international frameworks. They imported and reshaped transnational categories in the EEC, giving rise to enforceable individual social rights, and loosening the territoriality or nationality principles of the national insurances. In doing so they forged a genuinely international law that has shaped the destiny of the coordination of social policy in the EEC/EU up to the present day. They protected the acquired social security rights of a migrant, putting personal rights above nationality and place of residence. At the same time, they stabilized the architecture of the national social insurance systems and gave an international scope to the action of the ministries in charge of social affairs. This chapter underlines that they did so not mainly to promote an international social policy as a means to improve the workers' condition, but in order to protect national arrangements (so that economic competition did not impact social protection) and as a technical means to improve and control the migrant population (hence the importance of the debates about family allowances). In the dynamic of the negotiations, national interests were not absent, but they were not always sufficient to gain enough support. In addition to relying on technical transnational categories, the negotiators framed a discourse that went beyond the expression of national interests, and, in their effort to gain support for their views, they constituted a transnational (here: European) interest.

In their negotiations, these experts established a resilient institutional architecture that connects national insurance schemes, an international clearing system and individual rights. While no supranational institution was created to supervise and expand the European social security, this does not mean that there was no institutionalization whatsoever. The European social security scheme was, in a sense, institutionalized by foreign policies conceived in Labour and Social Affairs Ministries. Due to the technical nature of the conventions, foreign affairs ministers and professional diplomats were effectively kept out of the loop: indeed, this chapter evidences the existence of a social diplomacy carried out by specialists of social policies. Following the EEC regulation of 1959 (i.e. the application of the European Convention), the member states created administrative centres to implement this agreement alongside numerous other bilateral agreements (for example the French Centre de sécurité sociale des travailleurs migrants – Centre for the Social Security of Migrant Workers). These centres played a role in the expansion of an unofficial social diplomacy that has shaped the transnational dimension of "welfare." For a long time these highly technical agreements were kept out of the spotlight. Recently, however, debates on "benefit tourism" and on the impact of the impending Brexit on the social rights of British migrants in Europe and European migrants in Britain have shown the extent to which they affect the lives of European citizens. The technicality of the arrangements seemed to have protected them to a certain extent, at a time when the EEC countries had similarities and, hence, could show solidarity with one another. It could be argued that the enlargement has resulted in greater dissimilarities – not only inequality in wealth, but perhaps perceived cultural differences – and contributed to calling these lasting arrangements into question.

Notes

1 Randall Hansen, Jobst Koehler, and Jeannette Money, "Incentivizing Cooperation," in *Migration, Nation States and International Cooperation*, ed. Randall Hansen, Jobst Koehler, and Jeannette Money (London: Routledge, 2011), 1–13, there 1.
2 Paul-André Rosental, "Migrations, souveraineté, droits sociaux. Protéger et expulser les étrangers en Europe du XIXe siècle à nos jours," *Annales. Histoire, Sciences Sociales* 66, no. 2 (2011): 335–373; Lutz Raphael, "*Grenzen von Inklusion und Exklusion. Sozialräumliche Regulierung von Armut und Fremdheit im Europa der Neuzeit,*" *Journal of Modern European History* 11 (2013): 147–167.
3 Sandrine Kott, "From Transnational Reformist Network to International Organization. The International Association for Labour Legislation and the International Labour Organization, 1900-1930s," in *Shaping the Transnational Sphere: Experts, Networks and Issues from the 1840s to the 1930s*, ed. Davide Rodogno, Bernhard Struck, and Jakob Vogel (New York/Oxford: Berghahn, 2015), 240–258; Christian Topalov, ed., *Laboratoires du nouveau siècle. La nébuleuse réformatrice et ses réseaux en France (1880–1914)* (Paris, Editions de l'EHESS, 1999). See also Rainer Gregarek, "Le mirage de l'Europe sociale. Associations internationales de politique sociale au tournant du 20e siècle," *Vingtième siècle. Revue d'histoire* 48 (1995): 103–116; Glenda Sluga and Patricia Clavin, *Internationalisms: A Twentieth-Century History* (Cambridge: Cambridge University Press, 2017).
4 See, for instance, Stein Kuhnle, "International Modelling in the Making of the Nordic Social Security Models," in *Beyond the Welfare State: Transnational Historical Perspectives on Social Policy,* ed. Pauli Kettunen and Klaus Petersen (Cheltenham: Edward Elgar, 2011), 65–81; Dietrich Rueschemeyer and Theda Skocpol, eds., *States, Social Knowledge, and the Origins of Modern Social Policies* (New York: Princeton University Press, 1996). Also see Daniel Béland and Klaus Petersen, eds., Analysing

Social Policy Concepts and Language: Comparative and Transnational Perspectives (Bristol: Policy Press, 2015).
5 Sandrine Kott, "Les organisations internationales, terrains d'étude de la globalisation. Jalons pour une approche socio-historique," Critique internationale 3, no. 52 (2011): 9–16; Sandrine Kott, Bismarck (Paris: Presses de Sciences Po, 2003); Sandrine Kott and Joëlle Droux, eds., *Globalizing Social Rights: The International Labour Organization and Beyond* (New York: Palgrave MacMillan, 2013). See also Cédric Dunand, *Die internationale Arbeitsorganisation (ILO) und die soziale Sicherheit in Europa (1942–1969)*, thèse d'histoire, université de Genève, 2002; and Lorenzo Mechi, Guia Migani, and Francesco Petrini, eds., *Networks of Global Governance, International Organization and European Integration in an Historical Perspective* (Cambridge: Cambridge University Press, 2014), chapters 6 and 10. Cf. Martti Koskenniemi, *The Gentle Civilizer of Nations: The Rise and Fall of* International Law 1870–1960 *(Cambridge: Cambridge University Press, 2001)*.
6 Sandrine Kott, "Constructing a European Social Model. The Fight for Social Insurance in the Interwar Period," in *ILO Histories: Essays on the International Labour Organization and Its Impact on the World during the Twentieth century*, ed. J. van Dæle, M. Rodriguez Garcia, G. van Gœthem, and M. van der Linden (Bern: Peter Lang, 2010), 173–195; Paul-André Rosental, "Introduction to Health and Safety at Work: An Issue in Transnational History," *Journal of Modern European History* 7, no. 2 (2009): 169–173; Paul-André Rosental and Catherine Omnès, eds., "Maladies professionnelles. Genèse d'une question sociale," *Revue d'Histoire moderne et Contemporaine* 56, no. 1 (2009): 5–11.
7 For instance, Sandrine Kott, "Un modèle international de protection sociale est-il possible? L'OIT entre assurance et sécurité sociale (1919–1952)," *Revue d'histoire de la protection sociale* 1, no. 10 (2017): 62–83; Matthieu Leimgruber, *La doctrine des trois piliers: entre endiguement de la sécurité sociale et financiarisation des retraites (1972–2010)* (Yverdon-les-Bains, Artias, 2010); Paul-André Rosental, ed., *Silicosis: A World History* (Baltimore: John Hopkins University Press, 2017); Nicolas Vershueren, *Fermer les mines en construisant l'Europe. Une histoire sociale de l'intégration européenne* (Brussels: Peter Lang, 2013); Monika Eigmüller and Stefanie Börner, eds., *European Integration: Processes of Change and the National Experience* (Basingstoke: Palgrave Macmillan, 2015); Willem Maas, "The Genesis of European Rights," *Journal of Common Market Studies* 43, no. 5 (2005): 1009–1025.
8 Maurizio Ferrera, *The Boundaries of Welfare: European Integration and the New Spatial Politics of Social Protection* (Oxford: Oxford University Press, 2005).
9 Simon Roberts, "A Short History of Social Security Coordination," in *50 Years of Social Security Coordination: Past, Present, Future*, ed. Yves Jorens (Brussels: European Union, 2010), 8–28.
10 Brigitte Studer, "Verschleierungstaktik als Herrschaftspraxis. Über den Prozeβ historischer Erkenntnis am Beispiel des Kominternarchivs," *Jahrbuch für historische Kommunismusforschung* (1995): 306–321.
11 Carl-Ulrik Schierup and Stephen Castles, "Migrations, minorities and Welfare State," in *Migration in the Global Political Economy*, ed. N. Philipps (Boulder: Lynne Rienner Publishers, 2011), 15–40.
12 For instance, Council of Europe, *L'Europe des travailleurs*, Strasbourg, 1961; Council of Europe, *Un sang nouveau en Europe*, Strasbourg, 1962.
13 For instance, Jeanne Rentier, *L'activité du conseil de l'Europe dans le domaine social* (Paris: Pedone, 1954); or Albert Delpérée, *Politique sociale et intégration européenne* (Paris: Librairie du droit et de la jurisprudence, 1956).
14 *Le code international du travail 1951*, Geneva, BIT, 1954; *Législation sociale internationale*, Brussel, Librairie encyclopédique, 1952.
15 Rosental, "Migrations, souveraineté, droits sociaux," *Annales* 66.

46 *Karim Fertikh*

16 T.C. Stephens, *Les accords de réciprocité en matière de sécurité sociale* (Rome: Editions internationales, 1956), 7.
17 International Social Security Association, *Reciprocity in Social Insurance* (Geneva/Roma: Editions internationales, 1956).
18 Stephens, *Les accords de réciprocité*.
19 John Holloway, *Social Policy Harmonisation in the European Community* (Gower: Farnborough, 1981).
20 Paris, archive of the Labour Ministry, letter of the Head of the Centre de sécurité des travailleurs migrants (Center for Social Security of Migrant Workers) to the director of the Bundesverband der Ortskrankenkassen, 3 February 1966.
21 Paris, archive of the Labour Ministry, letter of the Minister for Industry to the Minister of Labour, 10 January 1961.
22 Council of Europe, *L'Europe des travailleurs*, Strasbourg, 1961, 10.
23 These legal experts saw the construction of a European social law as a necessity to gain the support of the working class for the European project, which, according to Troclet, would need to be pursued further due to "an inexorable sociological law," see Léon-Éli Troclet, *Eléments de droit social européen* (Brussels: Institut de sociologie de l'Université libre, 1963); XVI or Gérard Lyon Caen, *Cours de droit social européen 1965–1966* (Paris: Cours de droit, 196), 5. See also Karim Fertikh, "La construction d'un droit social européen. Socio-histoire d'une catégorie transnationale (années 1950-années 1970)," *Politix. Revue des sciences sociales du politique* 29, no. 115 (2016): 201–224.
24 Studies on the history of transport infrastructure have pointed out that national transport networks were not created prior to the time of their internationalization: Frank Schipper and Johan Schot, "Infrastructural Europeanism, or the Project of Building Europe on Infrastructures," *History and Technology: An International Journal* 27, no. 3 (2011): 245–264, there 254.
25 Pierre Laroque, "La Sécurité sociale," in *Au service de l'Homme et du droit. Souvenirs et réflexions* (1993), 211.
26 Laroque, "La Sécurité sociale," 238 and following.
27 Jean-Pierre Le Crom, "Les années 'fastes' de la Revue française du Travail (1946–1948)," *Revue française des affaires sociales* 4, no. 4 (2006): 23–43.
28 See Jacques Doublet, "Problèmes de sécurité sociale et Communauté européenne du charbon et de l'acier," *Annuaire français de droit international* 3, no. 1 (1957): 568–585.
29 Randall Hansen, "Making Cooperation Work," in *Migration, Nation States and International Cooperation*, ed. Randall Hansen (London: Routledge, 2011), 14–27, there 18–19.
30 Sandrine Kott, " Une "communauté épistémique" du social?," *Genèses* 2, no. 71 (2008): 26–46. At the same period, there were attempts to constitute European organizations for labour and social security that would be independent from the ILO, such as the European Labour Organization promoted by the European Movement or the Conférence internationale d'experts de la Sécurité sociale promoted by Pierre Laroque. On this last point, see Cédric Guinand, "A Pillar to the Economic Cooperation: The ILO and the Development of Social Security in Western Europe," in *Networks of Global Governance: International Organizations and European Integration in a Historical Perspective*, ed. Lorenzo Mechi, Guia Migani, and Francesco Petrini (Cambridge: Cambridge University Press, 2014), 121.
31 "Faced with the criticisms constantly levelled at it, aware that only practical results in the social field will silence the critics, and convinced that in these circumstances the sharing of *'social prestige'* with other organizations though joint venture is undesirable, the High Authority (of the ECSC) now tends to go it alone." Geneva, ILO, box 197239: Brief for the Director General in connection with the forthcoming meeting

with the president of the High Authority of the ECSC (End 1956, beginning 1957). Emphasis mine.
32 Geneva, ILO, box 197239.
33 Madeleine Herren Oesch and Sacha Zala, *Netzwerk Außenpolitik. Internationale Organisationen und Kongresse als Instrumente der schweizerischen Außenpolitik 1914–1950* (Zürich: Chronos, 2002).
34 Florence, AHUE, ME 816.
35 Armand Kayser contributed to the book written to honour the German expert Jantz with a text about the European Convention: Armand Kayser, "Die soziale Sicherung der Wanderarbeitnehmer in der Europäischen Wirtschaftsgemeinschaft," in *Sozialrecht und Sozialpolitik. Festschrift für Kurt Jantz zum 60. Geburtstag*, ed. Horst Peter (Stuttgart: Kohlhammer Verlag, 1968), 17–22.
36 Julien Louis, "Quelle autorité européenne pour les droits sociaux? Les négociations de la Charte sociale européenne du Conseil de l'Europe (1953–1961) et la création du Comité des experts indépendants," conference ' Politiques de l'indépendance," Paris-Sorbonne, 12 January 2017.
37 Florence, AHUE, BAC 237/1980 – 453.
38 Martin Münzel, "Neubeginn und Kontinuitäter. Das Spitzenpersonal der zentralen deutschen Arbeitsbehörden 1945–1960," in *Das Reichsarbeitsministerium im Nationalsozialismus. Verwaltung – Politik – Verbrechen*, ed. Alexander Nützenadel (Göttingen: Wallstein, 2017), 494–549, there 516.
39 Geneva, BIT 197310: decision of the Council of Ministers of the ECSC, January 1957.
40 Roland Burke, "The Internationalism of Human Rights," in *Internationalisms: A Twentieth Century History*, ed. Patricia Clavin and Glenda Sluga (Cambridge: Cambridge University Press, 2016), 287–314, there 311.
41 See Martin Lengwiller and Milena Guthörl, "Le 'crise' de l'Etat social vu par les réseaux internationaux," *Revue d'histoire de la protection sociale* 1, no. 10 (2017): 124–147.
42 Lyse Rye, *The Rise and Fall of the French Demand for Social Harmonization in the EEC 1955–1966* (Trondheim: Trondheim Studies in History, 2004).
43 Geneva, ILO, box 197309: note of the ILO (1955).
44 Geneva, ILO, box 197309: meeting of the expert committee, 13 April 1955.
45 See Horst Peter, ed., *Sozialrecht und Sozialpolitik. Festschrift für Kurt Jantz zum 60. Geburtstag*.
46 Kurt Jantz, *Grundsatzfragen sozialer Sicherheit* (Stuttgart: Verlag Kohlhammer, 1964).
47 See Cornelius Thorp, *Gerechtigkeit im Wohlfahrtsstaat. Alter und Altersversicherung in Deutschland und Grossbritanien von 1945 bis heute* (Göttingen: Vanderhoeck & Ruprecht, 2015), 68.
48 See Paul André Rosental, *Destins de l'eugénisme* (Paris: Seuil, 2016).
49 Paul André Rosental, *L'intelligence démographique* (Paris: Seuil, 2003).
50 Jacques Doublet, "Des lois dans leur rapport avec la population," *Population*, no. 1 (1949): 39–56, there 39.
51 Geneva, ILO, box 197310: decision of the Council of Ministers of the ECSC, January 1957.
52 Doublet, "Problèmes de sécurité sociale," *Annuaire français de droit international*, 574.
53 Doublet, "Des lois dans leur rapport avec la population."
54 Geneva, ILO, box 197310: experts meeting (22–25 May 1955).
55 Burke, "The Internationalism of Human Rights."
56 International Social Security Association, *Reciprocity in Social Insurance*, 57.
57 Ibid., 59.
58 Geneva, ILO, box 197309: Third Experts Meeting (October 1955).
59 Geneva, ILO, box 197309: memorandum by the Luxembourgian delegation (11 June 1955)

48 *Karim Fertikh*

60 Geneva, ILO, box 197309: memorandum by the Italian expert Carloni (1 August 1955), p. 1.
61 Geneva, ILO, box 197309: Third Experts Meeting (October 1955).
62 See Emmanuel Comte, *The History of the European Migration Regime: Germany's Strategic Hegemony* (New York: Routledge, 2018), 55–56.
63 Geneva, ILO, box 197307: Second Preparatory Experts Meeting (April 1955), Note of the ILO: "Les charges du fonds de compensation et leur répartition."
64 Geneva, ILO 197309: memorandum of the French Government to the experts concerning the first draft of the European Convention: "L'harmonisation des regimes de sécurité sociale" (the harmonization of social security systems).
66 Ibid.
66 Geneva, ILO, box 197309: Third Experts Meeting (October 1955).

3 The ILO and the shift towards economic liberalization in the international professional rehabilitation policies of people with disabilities after World War II

Gildas Brégain

Introduction

Created in 1919, the International Labour Organization (ILO; for which the International Labour Office acts as the secretariat) aims at promoting reformist solutions to social problems, using dialogue between social actors to avoid social and economic conflicts. A universal and lasting peace is possible only on the basis of social justice. ILO's tripartite composition (employers, employees, states) radically breaks with the model of state-controlled economy implemented in the USSR. We can thus consider the ILO the result of a first Cold War.[1] During the interwar period the ILO worked on a number of social reforms in order to control industrial and agricultural working conditions in the context of a capitalist economic system. These reforms were inspired by socialist-reformist and social-liberal traditions, with standards developed by experts. They have been legitimated as conventions or recommendations, and therefore have a universal reach.

The ILO had been interested in the vocational rehabilitation of the war-disabled since 1920, when it created an administrative service to deal with this question. ILO intervention was necessary to protect the placement of injured soldiers and the wages they receive. Directed by Adrien Tixier, a Frenchman, in 1922 and 1923 this service organized two international conferences of experts on assistance to injured veterans, which legitimated the standards used in the countries of continental Europe (right to free prostheses for injured veterans, legal obligation for the government and private companies to hire a high percentage of injured veterans, salary continuation for workers with war injuries).[2] In the middle of the 1920s, the ILO legitimized the rights of disabled workers to medical rehabilitation (free care, prostheses) adopting various international conventions on the subject, but it only hesitantly committed to their vocational rehabilitation.

If the subject of the vocational rehabilitation of the disabled had disappeared from the ILO agenda by the middle of the 1920s, it reappeared at the end of World War II, because many countries were forced to find vocational opportunities for millions left with disabilities by the war. In the 1950s, during the International

Labour Conferences, the government representatives of the two power blocs promoted in their speeches labour measures inspired by their respective ideologies. In a Cold War context, the main point was to demonstrate which ideological system was more effective in the employment of citizens. The capitalist governments' representatives in the ILO focused on a free economy, and they accused socialist countries of violating the freedom of workers, while socialist governments' representatives focused on social rights and equality, and emphasized the capitalist exploitation and the false freedom of the workers in a "non-regulated market."[3] The rehabilitation of disabled citizens became part of this ideological competition between the two power blocs within the ILO. Seeking qualified workers, the socialist governments strongly favoured the vocational rehabilitation of the disabled in order to quickly increase their available labour supply. The Asian and African countries were only marginally involved in these debates, however, they played a central role in the debates on self-determination within the UN Human Rights Commission during the same period.[4]

The International Labour Office promoted a new policy of vocational rehabilitation of the disabled which clearly differed from its earlier policy. This policy reorientation was facilitated both by the leadership role of the United States and the United Kingdom within the International Labour Organization (ILO), and by the replacement of all the civil servants working on the subject. Between 1948 and 1970 the ILO was led by David Morse, an American civil servant. Dr. H.A. de Boer was the first person in charge of the medical rehabilitation of the disabled within the industrial hygiene division beginning in 1946. In 1953, the vocational training section (within the manpower division) of the ILO pre-empted and managed the ILO vocational rehabilitation policy. Briton Arthur Bennett began working there in 1953, followed by Vera Marinova, from Bulgaria, hired as an assistant in 1958.[5] In 1961, these two civil servants were assigned to this newly created vocational rehabilitation section of the manpower division. Two other civil servants joined them in 1964 and 1965: Isamu Niwa, from Japan, and Norman Edward Cooper, from the UK.

In 1945, the committee on employment of the ILO management board prepared a report on the employment of the disabled, which promoted experiments inspired by economic liberalism carried out in English-speaking countries in the field of vocational rehabilitation. This report stated, in particular, that the legal obligation to employ disabled persons was not absolutely necessary and instead recommended selective placements as the main solution to employment problems.[6] However, the contents of the ILO vocational rehabilitation policy had been seriously discussed only from 1953, with the preparation of a new international standard on vocational rehabilitation by the International Labour Conference. In these debates, the government representatives of capitalist countries confronted the government representatives of socialist countries, while the employers' representatives faced off with the workers' representatives. They led to the adoption of the Vocational Rehabilitation (Disabled) Recommendation (No. 99) by the 38th International Labour Conference in 1955.

This chapter examines the actions of the ILO in the sector of vocational rehabilitation both internationally and nationally. Its hypothesis is that after World

War II the policies of vocational rehabilitation shifted in a liberal-economic direction. I will explore this issue in two steps. Firstly, I will look at the construction of the main normative text related to the vocational rehabilitation of the disabled (Recommendation No. 99). Secondly, I will study how this standard circulated on the international level and what impact it exerted on national debates.[7] To demonstrate this, I will discuss the contents of the technical assistance given by the ILO experts in vocational rehabilitation in several developing countries (Argentina, Brazil) during the 1950s and 1960s. While this chapter contributes to the debate on the role of the ILO in the expansion of the modern welfare state, it does not aim to analyse the complex influence of the actions of the ILO on the development of legal standards in the field of vocational rehabilitation in Argentina and in Brazil.[8]

I undertake a close reading of the relevant ILO documents and place them in an international context. In order to understand the repercussions of Recommendation No. 99, I analyse the debates that took place within the committees on vocational rehabilitation and during the plenary assemblies of the 37th and 38th International Labour Conferences. In order to examine the technical assistance given by the ILO experts in vocational rehabilitation in Latin American countries, I carried out research in the administrative files of the ILO, in particular in the personnel files and the files of the programme of technical assistance, as well as in a number of government and associations files in Argentina and in Brazil.

The institutionalization of a liberal legality in the field of vocational integration for the disabled

In 1952, the ILO management board decided to include the vocational rehabilitation of the disabled on the agenda of the 37th International Labour Conference. The international harmonization of the programme of vocational rehabilitation was necessary in order to rationalize the management of this workforce and to promote social justice. The civil servants of the ILO vocational rehabilitation service (Arthur Bennett and Vera Marinova) wrote a report and a draft recommendation starting from the answers sent by the government members of the ILO. On this basis, many debates took place within the committees on vocational rehabilitation and during the plenary assemblies of the 37th and 38th International Labour Conferences. In a Cold War context, the positions adopted by the representatives of the leading countries of the two blocs were strongly ideological. The measures they promoted in their speeches reflected only a part of the measures that existed in the countries of each bloc; a few countries may have had very different experiences.

The rejection of the proposals of socialist countries

Socialist countries were strongly represented during the debates. Whereas Poland and Czechoslovakia had been members of the ILO since 1919, the USSR had left the ILO in 1939, that is to say five years after its adhesion, and had then renewed its membership only in 1954.[9] The government representatives of socialist countries wanted the regulation on vocational rehabilitation to take the form of a *convention*, in order to guarantee access to this benefit for all the disabled. But this proposal was overwhelmingly dismissed (192 votes against 10).[10] The majority favoured the adoption of a *recommendation*, i.e. a sufficiently flexible regulation so that each country could act according to its economic conditions and its possibilities of development.

Socialist countries defended the idea that all the disabled should have the right to access to vocational rehabilitation and employment, including the severely disabled, regardless of the employment situation in the country. The government adviser of Poland, Aleksander Hulek, argued that "the difficulties arising out of the economic structure of some countries, such as unemployment, should not hamper the development of vocational rehabilitation."[11] But this idea was rejected by the majority. In accordance with the position defended by a number of capitalist countries (including the USA), Recommendation No. 99 limited the benefits of vocational rehabilitation to the disabled who had reasonable prospects of securing and retaining suitable employment.

Socialist countries' representatives also required that this vocational rehabilitation be the exclusive responsibility of public authorities and be entirely free for the disabled.[12] But many members of the committee on vocational rehabilitation were opposed to it and underlined the role of private organizations in their countries. The recommendation adopted in June 1955 just indicated the role of public authorities in the control and development of vocational rehabilitation policies, and their mission of coordination and support to the action of private institutions.

As has been mentioned before, the proposals of socialist countries as regards rehabilitation were in conformity with socialist ideology (free services, social security, right to employment, cooperatives, state control). They were articulated in public during the international conferences in order to build a symbolic opposition between the two blocs (socialist/capitalist) and to demonstrate the unity of the Soviet bloc.[13] The rejection of the socialist proposals was not a surprise, and the same situation repeated itself on other subjects because the socialist countries were marginalised within the ILO.

A largely moderated quota system resulted from the protest of employers and of a number of capitalist countries' governments

In the first draft recommendation, the civil servants of the vocational rehabilitation section of the ILO had suggested including an article (No. 29) with coercive measures to support the employment of the disabled. This article stipulated that:

> 29. Wherever appropriate in the national circumstances, and consistent with national policy, measures should be taken to promote the employment of disabled persons by
>
> (a) compelling employers to employ a quota of disabled persons;
> (b) reserving certain designated occupations for disabled persons;

(c) ensuring that seriously disabled persons are given preference for employment in certain occupations considered suitable for them.[14]

During the discussions of the Committee on Vocational Rehabilitation convened during the 37th Conference, the employer members recommended removing the whole Article 29. They argued that "such schemes were often against the best interests of the disabled since they caused employers to engage no more than their quota, that they singled out disabled persons and that experience in certain countries was against such schemes."[15] Other experts defended the utility and effectiveness of this type of measure in countries with a high rate of unemployment and pointed out that the text allowed each country the freedom to legislate on the matter. The committee finally rejected the amendment of the employers, and Article 29 was approved during the plenary assembly in June 1954.

During the 37th session, the representative of the government of Iran, Mr. Habib Naficy, suggested adding a new subparagraph aimed at encouraging the creation of cooperatives of disabled persons. This amendment was approved by the majority. The phenomenon of the cooperatives of disabled persons constituted then a central element of the employment policy carried out by two socialist republics (Poland and Czechoslovakia). Thereafter, the government of the United States declared itself opposed to the inclusion of this measure in the article on the employment of the disabled, considering that the creation of cooperatives was only justified "in areas where employment in the competitive labour market is not available or there is no such competitive labour market."[16] Hence, it should not be a general measure of common practice for all countries. Conscious that these criticisms were related to a minority of countries, the ILO did not modify this subparagraph.

Upon being consulted by the ILO, the Australian, American, Canadian, Norwegian and Finnish governments positioned themselves against measures for compulsory employment of the disabled.[17] In the United States, the compulsory employment of disabled workers was perceived as counterproductive, discriminatory and in contradiction to the method of selective placement. Taking into account these disagreements, the ILO civil servants chose to moderate the content of the article in the draft recommendation, which was to be presented during the next International Labour Conference. They replaced the phrase "compelling employers to employ a quota of disabled persons" with "requiring employers to employ a quota of disabled persons" in Article (a) of the paragraph.[18]

The committee on vocational rehabilitation convened during the 38th Conference again discussed this article. The rapporteur of the project, Mr. Gordon Charles Henry Slater, who was also the representative of the government of the United Kingdom, proposed a new text to replace that of the ILO, reconciling the different points of view. His text replaced the gerund "requiring" with the term "engagement," which offered more flexibility in the interpretation of the text. These proposals were approved. During the debates in plenary assembly, the technical adviser of the Polish government regretted the rewriting of this article "which, to some extent, opens the door to philanthropy in tackling the problem of employment of disabled persons."[19] Finally, the 38th International Labour Conference approved the following text unanimously:

> Wherever appropriate in the national circumstances, and consistent with national policy, the employment of disabled persons should be promoted by means such as
>
> (a) the engagement by employers of a percentage of disabled persons under such arrangements as will avoid the displacement of non-disabled workers;
> (b) reserving certain designated occupations for disabled persons;
> (c) arranging that seriously disabled persons are given opportunities for employment or preference in certain occupations considered suitable for them;
> (d) encouraging the creation and facilitating the operation of cooperatives or other similar enterprises managed by, or on behalf of, disabled persons.[20]

Resulting from negotiations between employers' representatives, workers' trade-unions and government representatives, the text of Recommendation No. 99 represented a compromise between antagonistic visions on the access to employment. Those in favour of compulsory employment managed to keep it mentioned in the declaration, and their opponents managed to clearly moderate this idea with the following sentence: "Wherever appropriate in the national circumstances, and consistent with national policy," and by the absence of the word "compelling." The coercive solution did not disappear from the recommendation, but its adoption in a country was from now on subjected to the existence of specific circumstances in this country (without specifying these circumstances). Although the text did not clarify it, the general idea defended from 1955 by the ILO was that the application of this type of compulsory measure should be limited to public administrations and social security authorities, but should not affect private companies in order not to hurt the good will of employers, who were supposed to train and to accommodate the rehabilitated workers. However, the implementation of compulsory employment in private and public companies was allowed (at least temporarily) in the countries affected by a war.

The solutions to support the employment of the disabled, the implementation of which had been recommended in all the member states of the ILO, were not very ambitious (promotion of the working capacities, improvement of the tools, exemption of the employers' responsibility in case of a new accident, sheltered workshops, promotion of freelance work). In addition, the recommendation prohibited any wage discrimination due to a disability, but did not guarantee to disabled workers equal wages for the same number of working hours as the other workers. Indeed, the employers' representatives refused categorically to be compelled to give disabled persons the same wage as able-bodied workers for a lower output.[21]

An individualized solution of placement for a collective problem

Recommendation No. 99 of the ILO promoted professional training, vocational guidance and selective placement for all disabled people who had a reasonable prospect of securing and retaining suitable employment, whatever the nature and the origin of their disability. This text dogmatized the practice of a remunerated professional activity in the context of a liberal market economy. It excluded less productive disabled workers from ordinary work placements and expected them to work in sheltered workshops, as freelance workers or condemned them to the absence of remunerated activity. The development of sheltered employment was considered necessary for the employment of severely disabled and underproductive persons, and even disabled persons fit for competitive work but excluded from employment because of a high unemployment rate.[22] Sheltered employment was a recent concept, included in public policies developed by the British and American authorities at the beginning of the 1940s, in the context of the market economy. The implicit idea was to help private companies and public administrations preserve their high standards of productivity by avoiding hiring severely disabled people, who were perceived as less productive. The principles and the running of sheltered workshops had to conform to the minimum working conditions existing in factories, in order to facilitate their future transfer to employment in a competitive market. Sheltered workshops had to be non-profit-making entities subsidized by public authorities, so that they could concentrate their efforts on the employment of the severely disabled.[23] The sheltered industries organized in the United Kingdom after the adoption of the Disabled Persons (Employment) Act of 1944 represented an international model. A decade later, the Disabled Persons Employment Corporation (Remploy) managed 90 factories and employed 6000 severely handicapped persons, "unable to compete in a normal industry," thanks to grants given by the Ministry of Labour.[24] The experiment of the Russian sheltered workshops, placed within industrial plants, was also highlighted, since it enabled severely handicapped people to be in touch with a normal industrial and social life.[25]

According to prevailing ideas in English-speaking countries, this international text conveyed the idea of equal professional opportunity and implied complete freedom of action for the employer. This document favoured thus the defence of equal professional opportunities over the defence of the right to employment (advocated by socialist countries' representatives). Instead of solving the problems of employment through a complete restructuring of the social organization of the labour force, the representatives of capitalist countries favoured the solution of the selective placement of the disabled in private companies and public administrations. The selective placement method had been developed in several Western countries (United States, United Kingdom, then in Canada, Finland, Denmark) for twenty years and consisted of a careful selection of a placement in conformity with the capacities of the worker and the needs of the workplace. Introduced in the 1920s, this method then earned its reputation thanks to the development of scientific instruments (statistics on the performances and the productivity of the disabled in the industry, use of psycho-technical tests). A disabled person had to be placed in an employment "in which its disability does not constitute a work handicap."[26] Only disabled persons who had reached the necessary standards of competence and productivity were allowed to enter the ordinary job market, in order not to impact the profits of the employers. According to the ILO, this method widened the scope of professional opportunities for the disabled, while improving their personal capacities, and contributed to overcoming the prejudices employers might harbour regarding the capacities of disabled workers.

The shift towards liberal legalities in the field of vocational integration of the disabled

This recommendation ratified the swing of the policies of vocational integration of the disabled towards liberal (in the economic meaning of the term) legalities.[27] It included all the legal standards on the vocational integration of the disabled that exempted large private companies from their legal responsibility for organizing work based on solidarity, in order to maintain high profits in the hands of a minority of individuals.[28] These liberal legalities could take different forms: the first one disputed any form of compulsory employment (orthodox vision of liberalism defended by the American representatives), while the second accepted the adoption of compulsory measures as regards social security organizations and public administrations. Last, by extension, it appears relevant to add to the list of liberal legalities a third form: the legal standards which, although they included measures of quotas, did not include any strict control measures for their implementation (such as dissuasive fines) and/or incorporated devices aimed at guaranteeing a high rate of profits for large private companies (very strong tax exemptions, exclusion of disabled workers considered to be the least productive from compulsory employment chances, etc.). Indeed, these softened measures in the introduction of quotas deconstructed its solidarity-based nature.

The first and second forms turned the legal duty of private companies to employ disabled workers into a mere moral duty. The ILO favoured the second form, which was considered an inspiring example for private companies and a way to offer job opportunities for the rehabilitated disabled. This form was the one to be internationally institutionalized, and the one that the ILO experts developed in Latin America.

Nevertheless, from the middle of the 1960s, the ILO admitted in its manual on selective placement that a slightly different policy of placement of the disabled could be considered in developing countries. Indeed, a strong unemployment rate in these countries made it difficult to secure access to employment for rehabilitated disabled workers without a limited compulsory measure. So even if it was reaffirmed "[t]hat compulsion is wrong in principle,"[29] developing countries could consider introducing a measure involving weak quotas, restricted to large companies of the capital city. Before adopting this type of measure, each country had to have an effective system to register the disabled, a service of selective placement and an inspection system to supervise the employers' compliance with their obligations.[30]

Recommendation No. 99 mainly favoured the liberalized methods of vocational integration of the disabled (selective placement in a competitive market, depreciation of the quotas measures, creation of sheltered workshop, etc.), but its content and its form were sufficiently flexible to be interpreted in a number of different ways by the actors (association representatives, employers' representatives, etc.) according to their strategic interests. Disabled persons were encouraged to apply for a job in a professional environment based on merit and success, which led to massive failure: At the end of the 1970s, disabled persons living in developed countries were still massively exposed to unemployment, and their situation became further exacerbated by the economic crisis of 1974.[31] Moreover, most of the disabled workers laboured in sheltered industries and in a restricted number of professions (crafts, secretariat, telephony, etc.).

Since its adoption, Recommendation No. 99 of the ILO has been widely spread throughout the world by ILO publications and technical assistance missions. The relatively non-binding nature of this regulation, and its liberal economic guidelines produced strong international criticism by several non-governmental organizations (International Society for the Rehabilitation of the Disabled, International Federation of the Blind, World Council for the Welfare of the Blind, etc.) from the beginning of the 1960s. Representatives of these NGOs required the adoption of more binding measures (a convention at the international level, some legislation at the national level) in order to compel the states and private companies to employ disabled people.

In 1963, the rehabilitation committee of the Fédération internationale des mutilés du Travail et des invalides civils required the ILO to adopt an international convention in order to secure better protection for injured workers.[32] Aleksander Hulek, an influential member of the International Society for the Rehabilitation of the Disabled, had advocated since 1960 for the creation of an expert commission that would take care "of the implementation of the ILO recommendation no. 99 on a larger scale."[33] Finally, a vocational rehabilitation expert commission was organized within the ISRD, and its conclusions remained very respectful of the ILO's action, because one of its members was an ILO civil servant. In 1968, this vocational rehabilitation expert commission concluded that "the enactment of appropriate legislation requiring employment of disabled workers could be one of the means open to governments to ensure that the disabled have a fair share of employment opportunities."[34]

The same year, the Chilean government representative to the International Labour Conference, Mr. Hernán Santa Cruz, submitted a draft resolution inviting the ILO director general to carry out research on the employment policy of disabled workers, in order to have an international instrument which can secure their right to work. The main objectives of this new international instrument should be to proclaim the rights of disabled workers to rehabilitation, to employment retention (with the same salary), and to "the establishment of an employment and job reservation policy designed especially to identify preferences, or percentages, or both, with a view to the filling, in undertakings, of certain vacant posts with a job content particularly suited to disabled workers."[35] The employers' representatives in the Resolutions Committee fought against this resolution, arguing that "there were limitations to the possibilities of organizing jobs in undertakings to suit such workers. The primary aim of the undertaking was, of course, economic and the organization of jobs to suit disabled workers was only one factor that had to be taken into account.[36] The Canadian government representative and the United States workers' representative were reluctant, too. The US workers' representative considered that "it is impossible to set percentages." All these criticisms led to the approval of a totally different resolution, which invited the director to carry out research on how to widen possibilities of employment for disabled workers, setting aside research on a quota system or on the reservation of vacant posts.

The International Labour Conference partially answered the associations' claims and adopted on several occasions (23 June 1965, 24 June 1968, 24 June 1975) a number of enabling resolutions that reinforced the right of the disabled to vocational rehabilitation, without, however, contesting liberal legality.

The exportation of a liberal economic legality in the field of vocational rehabilitation of the disabled in Latin America (1955–beginning of the 1970s)

At the end of the 1950s, the Argentinian and Brazilian governments requested the ILO to send an expert in vocational rehabilitation in order to promote the activities of vocational rehabilitation in the recently created national institutes of rehabilitation in São Paulo (Instituto Nacional de Reabilitação, INAR) and in Buenos Aires (Instituto nacional de rehabilitación del Lisiado, INR). The ILO accepted this request, and sent several experts to Argentina and Brazil for varying periods of time. We will examine the work carried out by these experts in order to analyse the way they interpreted and applied Recommendation No. 99 in these Latin American countries.

The choice of experts in vocational rehabilitation qualified in selective placement

The experts sent on mission were selected by the civil servants of the ILO Personnel Office (in particular, R. Lyman), with the advice of the leader of the vocational rehabilitation programme, Arthur Bennett. The ILO civil servants used a number of criteria to make their choice among a large number of candidates: their technical skills (in particular their knowledge of industrial activities) and their degree of practical experience (in particular in the selective placement of disabled people) represented the main selection criteria. These elements determined their capacity to plan and run a rehabilitation centre, to investigate and to build coherent recommendations for the governments of the developing countries. During the preliminary interview of the applicants, the ILO civil servants were also sensitive to the way each applicant viewed vocational rehabilitation and its practical methods of implementation in developing countries: the civil servants wanted the experts to have a "flexible" approach, and not an intellectual or theoretical approach.[37] Their personality (self-confidence, stable temperament, sociability, etc.) and their knowledge of the local language were also taken into account because these would determine their capacity "to become a government adviser at the highest level," and their capacity to remain unperturbed in the face of the multiple delays and generally observable frustrations in the missions of short duration.[38] Almost all the selected experts were men: being a woman was not a reason for being excluded, but it represented a discriminating element when the mission aimed at organizing the vocational rehabilitation of disabled men.

Once chosen, the applicant had to sign a declaration of discretion and honesty with respect to the ILO, and had to undergo a medical examination. In practice, these experts often kept close links with their country's government.[39] The candidature of the expert was then submitted to the host country's government for approval, which was generally granted.

In 1957, the ILO sought to select an applicant to carry out a one-year mission in Brazil to promote vocational rehabilitation services for disabled people within the INAR of São Paulo. For this matter, the ILO requested the advice of its Canadian office, which quickly favoured the candidature of John Alfred Humphreys. Born in the United Kingdom in 1905, Humphreys attended the Duke of York's Military School, and then held many different jobs in the commercial sector. From 1943, he had been in charge of rehabilitation in the Workmen's Compensation Board of British Columbia. In addition to his long professional experience in the field of vocational rehabilitation (as well as in the field of the vocational guidance and selective placement), he also gained experience in the management and organization of a rehabilitation centre. He enjoyed the support of the National Coordinator for Civilian Rehabilitation in Canada, Ian Campbell, and of the chief rehabilitation officer for the Workmen's Compensation Board of Ontario.[40] During his interview, Humphreys was considered "highly qualified" for the mission projected in Brazil.[41] This expert knew only English, but the language problem was overcome when he decided to learn Portuguese on his own initiative (in October 1957), and when it was agreed that he would work under the direction of a Portuguese-speaking United Nations' expert, Paul Albright. Humphreys was thus sent to São Paulo from 2 March 1958 to February 1959. Even though the Brazilian government, the UN and the ILO wished to extend the mission of Humphreys until June 30, 1959, the Workmen's Compensation Board of British Columbia refused to extend his leave of absence and required his return in February.[42] The mission of the expert ended thus on March 2.

In 1960, the civil servants of the ILO personnel office wanted to recruit a very experienced expert to carry out a two-year mission in Buenos Aires in order to organize a vocational rehabilitation programme. After considering several candidates, they chose Georges-Yves Rouault, a Frenchman who ran a rehabilitation centre for tuberculosis patients in Germany (American zone) for the International Refugee Organization (1947–1952).[43] He was selected to carry out the mission in Argentina (December 1960–December 1962), and this mission was extended until December 1964. Rouault asked in 1961 that an expert in selective placement be sent to assist him in order to organize a more intensive action in this field. The

ILO personnel office considered then several candidates among the experts recommended by the London office and chose Norman Phillips.

At the end of the war, from 1946 to 1953, Phillips was responsible for a number of vocational rehabilitation and placement units for the disabled in the Ministry of Labour in Manchester. He was then chief of the Employment Exchange Newton Heath of the Ministry of Labour (Manchester) until September 1962. In spite of his long experience and his recognized skills, his perception of rehabilitation in developing countries had seemed too theoretical and not very thorough to the ILO representatives. Although his candidature had been rejected for other missions, he was more positively considered for the Argentinian mission projected in 1962, because it had a more restrictive character (selective placement) and because he would be supervised on site by Rouault. Technically qualified in selective placement, Phillips was selected for this mission, after his writing and oral skills in Spanish had been checked.[44] He went to Buenos Aires from 14 September 1962 to 25 August 1963 to organize a vocational rehabilitation programme. After that, he carried out short missions in Chile, Costa Rica, Peru and Brazil.

To carry out missions in Latin America, the ILO civil servants generally selected experts in vocational rehabilitation, who came from English-speaking or Scandinavian countries, because these countries represented the most advanced policies in vocational rehabilitation and selective placement. In the same way, when the ILO awarded grants for specialization in vocational rehabilitation to Brazilian or Argentinian professionals, the scholars were primarily sent to the countries that applied selective placement methods (United States, United Kingdom, Canada, Norway, Sweden). Otto Marques da Silva, a Brazilian, obtained a grant from the ILO from 10 June to 4 November 1960 to visit vocational rehabilitation institutions in the United States and Canada.[45] In Argentina, Jose Cibeira, the chief officer of the rehabilitation centre, got a grant from the ILO from October to December 1967 to visit institutions in England, Norway and Denmark. However, the Argentinian Antonio Lacal Zuco carried out his training course in vocational rehabilitation in France, Switzerland and Belgium, from 27 September 1966 to 21 March 1967, because he had a very poor command of English and a good command of French.[46]

The slow and difficult promotion of vocational rehabilitation and selective placement activities in rehabilitation institutes

In the two countries, the ILO experts developed a vocational rehabilitation policy in the national rehabilitation centres: the INAR in São Paulo and the INR in Buenos Aires. Since his arrival in Brazil, John Humphreys had faced many obstacles. He managed to quickly train two Brazilians, Otto Marques da Silva (as placement officer) and Wilma Seabra Mayer (as vocational guidance adviser), but these two specialists did not work full time in the INAR and maintained difficult relations with it. Moreover, until the end of 1958, Humphreys failed to organize vocational rehabilitation services, because the majority of the people receiving care could not be professionally rehabilitated. So the two Brazilian specialists who had been trained did not have enough patients, i.e. disabled persons able to be professionally trained and to find a job.[47] The situation changed in November 1958, following the pressure exerted by representatives of the United Nations and the ILO on the director of the INAR, Dr. Godcy Moreira. The latter finally agreed to promote vocational rehabilitation within the INAR.[48] The following month, Humphreys managed to organize an independent pre-professional unit, but for a long time the INAR management team refused to finance the recruitment of a supervisor for this pre-professional section. This section started to work fully from December 1959, giving training in watch-making, and radio and shoe repair. From 1958 to July 1966, 663 patients were trained, and approximately 320 were provided with permanent employment.[49]

The ILO experts also took part in the organization of the vocational rehabilitation services of the social security offices. As early as 1959, Humphreys spoke with the Ministry of Labour and the director of the rehabilitation services of the Instituto de aposentadoria e pensões dos industriarios (IAPI) in order to promote the vocational rehabilitation of disabled workers insured by the National Insurance Scheme. In 1960 and 1961, the IAPI created three vocational rehabilitation centres for disabled workers (Porto Alegre, Recife, São Paulo) that included professional training workshops and placement agencies. In December 1963, these three centres were transferred to the vocational rehabilitation services directorate of the social security offices (Superintendência de Serviços de Reabilitação Profissional da Previdência Social, SUSERPS), recently created in order to organize vocational rehabilitation on a national level. In 1966, the arrival of an ILO expert was considered necessary to advise the SUSERPS vocational rehabilitation centres and to prepare for the creation of new centres. Norman Phillips carried out a six-month mission in Brazil (from 19 May to 27 November 1966), a period during which he trained social workers in charge of selective placement in the three centres. Phillips considered that the work on selective placement carried out by these three centres was very ineffective (lack of knowledge of industrial activities, absence of an up-to-date register of the employers, lack of follow-up of the persons placed, etc.).[50] The expert also took part in a working group on the future vocational rehabilitation programme of the SUSERPS. Following his visit, he suggested that the SUSERPS establish a pilot unit of professional evaluation in São Paulo to accommodate forty trainees for six to eight weeks.

In Argentina, the Comisión nacional de rehabilitación del lisiado (CNRL) projected from 1959 to create a Centro de rehabilitación profesional in collaboration with the ILO. In 1962, a few months after his arrival, Georges-Yves Rouault built a large vocational training school, which would have no connection with the INR, and which would be able to accommodate between 300 and 500 boarders and day students. But economic difficulties and a lack of interest on the part of the authorities caused the project to be abandoned. Conscious of the limited funds available, Rouault favoured the fast installation of a vocational rehabilitation centre integrated into the INR.[51] This idea was belatedly realized in a limited way, thanks to the financial support of a private association (ACIR). Opened at the end of 1963, the centre accommodated about twenty male apprentices at the beginning, and then fifty students in 1968. The Centro de rehabilitación profesional ACIR was composed of a professional training service, responsible for training in manual occupations and industrial trades (tailor, shoemaking, mechanics, woodwork, mathematics, optics, electromechanical winding, radio) "to solve the problem of the disabled belonging to the lowest social class."[52] It was also composed of a selective placement service, which placed applicants on a case-by-case basis in factories or in sheltered workshops, or helped them open small independent businesses.

Rouault complained to the CNRL about the lack of specialized personnel in the professional training centre and about the lack of money for the construction of additional buildings. His requests for additional human and material resources were generally rejected. In June 1964, in a letter sent to the president of the CNRL, the ILO expert declared that "a professional centre cannot obtain the desired results with a lack of personnel, and with a failing basic organization."[53] In 1964, Phillips advocated that the CNRL set up additional employment agencies in the main industrial areas, taking the pilot agency established within the INR as a model.[54] He also recommended an increase in the staff of the disabled workers' placement service of the employment section of the Ministry of Labour in order to offer a complete and effective service.[55] But his requests remained a dead letter.

In both countries, the ILO experts organized the selection and vocational guidance of the disabled, using professional aptitude tests. They created vocational training services, and forced or persuaded the disabled to accept the discipline of industrial work (concept of performance and merit at work). The majority of the disabled submitted themselves to these conditions in order to obtain professional training and employment. A minority of them preferred to stay with their disability pension. The ILO experts also took part in the installation of small services of selective placement and sheltered industries. Nevertheless, they faced difficulties in implementing the planned programmes, either due to a lack of economic and personnel resources, or because of disagreements with the local leaders over the policies to be pursued. The rehabilitation professionals who had obtained an ILO grant (Antonio Lacal Zuco and Otto Marques da Silva) followed the action carried out by the ILO experts, and managed the vocational rehabilitation and selective placement services for several years. During the courses they gave, they widely disseminated the rehabilitation principles developed in English-speaking countries (downplaying the compulsory solution, promotion of the selective placement method, creation of sheltered workshops).

The socialization of local actors to liberal standards on professional insertion

In both countries, ILO experts and civil servants supported the legislative changes on the employment of the disabled in order to facilitate the recruitment of the rehabilitated disabled without compelling employers to hire them. They supported the inclusion of the most liberal measures contained in the ILO Recommendation No. 99 in the national legislation: non-discrimination because of a deficiency, the creation of a second injury funds, the introduction of tax exemptions for employers hiring disabled people and the creation of sheltered workshops to accommodate the less productive disabled. They advised the governments against the adoption of legislation on the compulsory employment of rehabilitated disabled workers in private companies. They also encouraged local actors (associations of disabled people, rehabilitation professionals, political officials) to accept the liberal principles of professional integration of the disabled (selective placement, rejection of the quota system for the private companies, utility of sheltered workshops).

However, association leaders and rehabilitation professionals had been aware of the European principles on the vocational redeployment of the war-disabled (principle of a high quota of recruitment of disabled and injured workers within administrations and private companies, maintenance of high wages) and were convinced of their relevance. Thus, in Argentina, many association leaders (gathered around the leaders of the Marcelo J. Fitte Club) said in 1957 that the state "would have to adopt laws so that there would be plenty of possibilities of employment [for the disabled], by requiring that a percentage of employment be reserved to the disabled in any industrial or commercial plant."[56] They called upon the ILO Recommendation No. 99 to legitimate their claim for vocational rehabilitation and employment. So the ILO experts had to deconstruct the legitimacy of the quota measure and to convince disabled leaders to relinquish it. Georges-Yves Rouault organized several conferences, including one for the disabled members of the Marcelo J. Fitte Club on 31 August 1962, during which he defended the idea "that it is necessary to train the disabled and to convince the employers that they must use their services."[57] Rouault's speech seemed to have been effective since this association stopped demanding legislation for compulsory employment.

In Brazil, John Humphreys wanted new legislation to be adopted in order to support the professional integration of the disabled. Indeed, the staff regulations of the civil servants of the federal union prohibited the employment or the retention of a "paralytic" within the administration. A new law was supposed to forbid any discrimination due to a disability and to support the recruitment of disabled worker thanks to the creation of a *second injury funds*.[58] These measures were inspired by American legislation, and in particular by Public Law 565 – Vocational rehabilitation amendments (1954).

In Argentina, Dr. Héctor Ruiz Moreno, a local delegate of the ILO, restrictively interpreted the unclear ILO recommendations during the third Argentinian rehabilitation congress in 1959. He began his speech by pointing out that the international recommendations had to be adapted to the characteristics of each country. In fact, that

> the compulsory placement of the disabled, necessary in countries that had experienced war, could be substituted in certain cases, in countries that had not experienced any war, by an action to promote the social, economic and technical benefits of hiring rehabilitated disabled workers.[59]

Moreno argued that compulsory employment was not called for in Argentina, since the country had not experienced a recent war. He quoted a number of measures planned by the ILO, for example the right to receive vocational training and the necessity to reduce the insurance premiums covering the accidents of rehabilitated disabled workers at work.

A few years later, Norman Phillips advised the Argentinian government against the adoption of legislation compelling private companies to employ disabled workers, at least not before the administrative organization was ready to manage the application of such measures. He said that "it is better to develop the idea that the disabled, when they are carefully selected and professionally rehabilitated if necessary, are as productive economically speaking as the able-bodied, and they thus do not need any particular protection."[60] Nevertheless, he considered that administrative departments and local authorities should study the possibility of employing voluntarily a given percentage of disabled workers (2%) in order to provide a model for private companies. During his stay in Brazil (1966), Phillips gave a rather similar speech. He declared he was in favour of offering jobs to rehabilitated disabled workers in social security institutions, then in the whole of the federal public service. For him, the placement of rehabilitated disabled workers in the public service would exert a positive effect on private employers, "who may be persuaded, rather than compelled."[61] He advised against the reinforcement of the existing legislation (Article 55 of Law No. 3807 adopted in 1960) compelling the employers to reserve a certain percentage of their jobs (between 2% and 5% according to their size) for rehabilitated disabled workers. He advised, however, the modification of the existing legislation on employment, so as to create exceptions to the minimum wage for workers in sheltered workshops, and for trainees in vocational rehabilitation.

In Argentina and in Brazil, the ILO specialists worked hard to convince all their interlocutors (doctors, associations, politicians, etc.) that it would be better to abandon any compulsory measures concerning private companies. Norman Phillips, and another ILO expert coming from West Germany, Kurt Müller, spread the same ideas during their missions in ten other Latin American countries during the 1960s. Over the same period, thanks to their enthusiasm, they managed to promote a rather restrictive (or rather liberal) interpretation of the ILO recommendations among rehabilitation professionals in Latin America. The leaders of the national rehabilitation services in Argentina and Brazil aligned themselves with this liberal legality, especially since it satisfied the interests of the employers' representatives, true partners of the implemented vocational rehabilitation programme. In both countries, lawyers close to the employers' representatives challenged the legitimacy of the compulsory employment of rehabilitated disabled workers within private companies. The Argentinian lawyer Dr. Mario Deveali stood against compulsory employment, referring to the ILO international resolutions.[62] The Brazilian lawyer Ubiracy Torres Cuoco called upon a recent publication by the ILO on the employment of the disabled – without quoting it expressly – in which the ILO "wondered if the legal solution was the right solution" in order to delegitimize the compulsory employment of a certain percentage of disabled people in private companies.[63]

If the socialization process of rehabilitation professionals and political officials to liberal orientations proved to be relatively easy, on the other hand, it was more difficult with the disabled, who had noticed a persistently high unemployment rate among their comrades. The disabled Argentinan Gino Andrés Valeri, a member of the Marcelo J. Fitte Club, stated he was shocked by the fact that an ILO representative promoted liberal legalities in the field of vocational rehabilitation, and he called for the adoption of compulsory employment measures.[64]

Conclusion

This chapter helps us to understand part of the role that the ILO played during the Cold War period, in a context of high political and ideological conflicts. In the middle of the 1950s, during the development of standards on the vocational rehabilitation of the disabled, the United States, the representatives of other capitalist countries and the employers' representatives succeeded in shifting international policies on vocational rehabilitation towards a more liberal economic policy. ILO Recommendation No. 99 legitimated the exercise of a paid professional activity in the context of a liberal market economy. It institutionalized the selective placement of disabled workers in a competitive job market and symbolically depreciated the use of compulsory employment quotas (by submitting its adoption to "specific conditions" and by drowning it in a high number of different possible measures). This recommendation excluded less productive disabled workers from ordinary work placement and expected them to work in sheltered workshops, as freelance workers, or condemned them to the absence of a remunerated activity.

An analysis of ILO reports and ILO Recommendation No. 99 shows that a true shift in the international vocational rehabilitation policies took place after World War II, with the depreciation of the ideas defended by the ILO after World War I (use of a system of quotas in public administrations and private companies to place the war-disabled, maintenance of integral wages). Among the multitude of solutions registered in Recommendation No. 99, the civil servants of the vocational rehabilitation section and the ILO experts sent to Latin America favoured the solutions tested in English-speaking countries (selective placement, depreciation of the solution of compulsory employment for private companies, creation of sheltered workshops). The ILO representatives played a fundamental role in the dissemination of liberal thinking in the field of vocational rehabilitation of the disabled in Latin American countries during the Cold War. They advised the local actors against the adoption of legislation requiring the compulsory employment of rehabilitated disabled workers within private companies. They were not the only foreigners to do it. The representatives of Goodwill Industries from Indiana (USA) and of the American rehabilitation organizations also promoted the American way of considering the employment of disabled persons in these countries.[65] These American ideas, which considered compulsory employment as useless and discriminating, were widely spread in Brazil and, to a lesser extent, in Argentina.

In conclusion, it is advisable to moderate our comments on the shift towards economic liberalization of international rehabilitation policies, because these policies evolved during the 1970s due to pressures from African and Asian countries and NGOs. A new international regulation on vocational rehabilitation was adopted by the ILO in 1983 (Convention No. 159 and Recommendation No. 168 on vocational rehabilitation). These standards reinforced the right to vocational rehabilitation and developed a number of solutions tested in socialist countries (cooperatives) and in developing countries (simplified vocational rehabilitation in agriculture), but did not strongly argue against the liberal economic orientation pursued since the 1950s. Moreover, the ILO representatives generally complied with the will of the governments, and sometimes encouraged the development of vocational rehabilitation policies inspired by certain socialist experiments (creation of production cooperatives) when they intervened in a number of countries in Africa or the Middle East (Algeria, Tunisia, Iran, Zambia, Tanzania).

Notes

1 Sandrine Kott, "Par-delà la guerre froide. Les organisations internationales et les circulations Est-Ouest (1947–1973)," *Vingtième Siècle. Revue d'histoire* 109, no. 1 (2011): 144.
2 Gildas Brégain, "Un problème national, interallié ou international ? La difficile gestion transnationale du problème des mutilés de guerre (1917–1923)," *Revue d'histoire de la protection sociale*, no. 9 (2016): 108–130.
3 Sandrine Kott and Joel Golb, "The Forced Labor Issue between Human and Social Rights, 1947–1957," *Humanity: An International Journal of Human Rights, Humanitarianism, and Development* 3, no. 3 (winter 2012): 321–335.
4 Steven L.B. Jensen, *The Making of International Human Rights: The 1960s, Decolonization, and the Reconstruction of Global Values* (Cambridge: Cambridge University Press, 2017), 44.
5 We have very little information about him because his personnel file is no longer in the ILO archives.
6 ILO, *The Training and Employment of Disabled Persons: A Preliminary Report* (Montreal: ILO, 1945).
7 Christoph Conrad, "Social Policy after the Transnational Turn," in *Beyond Welfare State Models: Transnational Historical Perspectives on Social Policy*, ed. Pauli Kettunen and Klaus Petersen (Cheltenham: Edward Elgar, 2011), 226.
8 David Strang and Patricia Mei Yin Chang, "The International Labor Organization and the Welfare State: Institutional Effects on National Welfare Spending, 1960–1980," *International Organization* 47, no. 2 (spring 1993): 235–262.
9 Gerry Rodgers, Eddy Lee, Lee Swepston, and Jasmien Van Daele, eds., *The International Labour Organization and the Quest for Social Justice 1919–2009* (Geneva: ILO, 2009), 31–32.
10 Conférence Internationale du Travail, 37ᵉ session, 1954, *Compte rendu des travaux* (Genève: BIT, 1955), 560.
11 Conférence Internationale du Travail, 37ᵉ session, 1954, *Compte rendu des travaux*, 333.
12 Conférence internationale du Travail, 38ᵉ session, 1955, *Compte rendu des travaux* (Genève: BIT, 1956), 389.
13 Sandrine Kott, "Par-delà la guerre froide. Les organisations internationales et les circulations Est-Ouest (1947–1973)," *Vingtième Siècle. Revue d'histoire* 109, no. 1 (2011): 145.
14 ILO, *Report IV (2): International Labour Conference, 37th session, Geneva, 1954* (Geneva: ILO, 1954), 130.

Shift towards economic liberalization 67

15 Conférence Internationale du Travail, 37ᵉ session, 1954, *Compte rendu des travaux* (Genève: BIT, 1955), 565.
16 ILO, *Report IV (2): International Labour Conference, 38th session, Geneva, 1955* (Geneva: ILO, 1955), 45.
17 Ibid., 50–51.
18 Ibid., 53.
19 International Labour Conference, 38th session, 1955, *Records of Proceedings* (Geneva: ILO, 1956), 370.
20 ILO, Vocational Rehabilitation (Disabled) Recommendation, 1955 (No. 99).
21 BIT, *Rapport IV (2): Conférence internationale du Travail, 38ᵉ session, Genève, 1955* (Genève: BIT, 1955), 42.
22 ILO, *The Training and Employment of Disabled Persons: A Preliminary Report* (Montreal: ILO, 1945), 169.
23 Ibid., 183.
24 J.L. Edwards, "Remploy: An Experiment in Sheltered Employment for the Severely Disabled in Great Britain," *International Rehabilitation Review* 77(1958): 147–158.
25 ILO, *The Training and Employment of Disabled Persons: A preliminary Report* (Montreal: ILO, 1945), 184.
26 Ibid., 223.
27 "Libéralisme," in *Dictionnaire d'Histoire politique du Xxe siècle* (Paris: Ellipses, 2005), 573–574.
28 Produced by the author himself, this definition is inspired by the definition of cosmopolitan legalities by Boaventura de Sousa Santos and César A. Rodriguez-Garavito, ed., *Law and Globalization from below: Towards a Cosmopolitan Legality* (New York: Cambridge Studies Press, 2005), 1–27.
29 ILO, *Manual on Selective Placement of the Disabled* (Geneva: ILO, 1965), 42.
30 Ibid., 43.
31 Norman Cooper, ed., "Conclusions and Recommendations," in *ILO European Symposium on Work for the Disabled, Vocational Rehabilitation and Employment Creation, Poland-Sweden* (Stockholm and Warsaw: ILO, 1979), 36.
32 Riksarkivet, Stockholm. SE/RA, 730032/1/F/F14a/3. Document titled "Session of the Rehabilitation Committee," Munich, 2–3 May 1963.
33 ILO Archives, NGO 20, ISRD, jacket 4 (1959–1963). Letter, 15 September 1960, M. Blanchard, director of Branch Office in Washington, to Director General in Geneva.
34 ILO Archives, NGO 20, ISRD, jacket 6 (1968–1972). Ian Campbell, Norman Cooper, James Garrett, B. Trampczynski, P. Trevethan, and Peter Quinn, *Guidelines for the Future in the Field of Vocational Rehabilitation of the Disabled*, n.d., p. 10.
35 Conférence Internationale du Travail, 52e session, 1968, *Compte rendu des travaux* (Genève: BIT), 544.
36 Ibid., 559.
37 ILO Archives, P. 10196. Note, 9 December 1957, Joan T. C. Smalley for the Director General.
38 ILO Archives, P. 7493. Lettre, Genève, 6 Septembre 1960, George-Yves Rouault à Mr Fuss; ILO Archives, P. 10196. Note, 9 December 1957, Joan T. C. Smalley for the Director General.
39 Sandrine Kott and Joëlle Droux, "Introduction: A Global History Written from the ILO," in *Globalizing Social Rights: The International Labour Organization and Beyond*, ed. Sandrine Kott and Joëlle Droux (New York: Palgrave Macmillan, 2013), 5.
40 ILO Archives, P. 8465. Note, 4/11/1957, R. M. Lyman to Mr. Blanchard.
41 ILO Archives, P. 8465. Telegramma, 25 September 1957, Rossborovait to ILO.
42 ILO Archives, TAP 0-9-10(C)-1. Copy of a letter, 2 December 1958, São Paulo, F. E. Godoy Moreira to Jansson.
43 ILO Archives, P. 7493. Formule d'enregistrement. George-Yves Rouault, 13 juin 1952.

44 ILO Archives, P. 10196. Note, 11/4/1962, Arthur Bennett to M. Harder.
45 ILO Archives, TAP 0-9-1 (C) FS-3. Otto Marques da Silva, *Report of the Month, October 10 to November 4*.
46 ILO Archives, TAP 0-2-1 (H) FS 2. Antonio Lacal, *Rapport à destination de Norman Cooper*, Paris, 7 Novembre 1966.
47 ILO Archives, TAP 0-9-1 (C)-1. J. A Humphreys, *Progress Report no. 5*, 12 November 1958.
48 ILO Archives, TAP 0-9-1 (C)-1. *Report by Mr B. Ghoshon his mission to Brazil (23 October–7 November 1958)*.
49 ILO Archives, TAP 0-9-1 (C). Norman Phillips, *Progress Report no. 2, 1st July to 31st August 1966*.
50 *Report to the Government of Brazil on The Vocational Rehabilitation and Placement of the Disabled* (Geneva: ILO, 1967), 44.
51 ILO Archives, TAP 0-2-1 (H)-1. G. Y Rouault, *Progress Report no. 7. March 19th to May 10th 1962*.
52 Pedro Kusmin,"Primeros Intentos de Rehabilitación Vocacional en la Argentina: Proyectos y Realidades," in *Primer curso sobre orientacion vocacional para Lisiados del Aparato Locomotor,* ed. AOI (Buenos Aires, 1964), 64.
53 ILO Archives, TAP0-2-1 (H)-1. Copia de una carta, Buenos Aires, 30 junio de 1964, G. Y. Rouault al Dr Carlos Ottolenghi.
54 OIT, *Informe al Gobierno de la Republica Argentina sobre la colocación selectiva de los inválidos* (Ginebra: OIT, 1964), 14.
55 Ibid., 15.
56 "[Carta] a la Magna Asamblea constituyente de 1957, reunida en la ciudad de Santa Fé," *En Marcha, organo oficial* del *Club Marcelo J. Fitte*, Buenos Aires, no. 10 (August 1958), 32.
57 Archives of the Marcelo J. Fitte Club, Buenos Aires. Acta de la reunión de la comisión directiva del Club Marcelo J. Fitte, Buenos Aires, 7 de septiembre de 1962.
58 ILO Archives, TAP 0-9-1 (C)-1. Copy of a letter, 2 December 1958, São Paulo, Prof. F. E. Godoy Moreira, to Mr Jansson.
59 Hector Ruiz Moreno, "Principales aspectos de la legislación internacional de protección al trabajador lisiado," in *Anales del 3e Congreso argentino de rehabilitación del lisiado, Buenos Aires, 8-12 diciembre 1959* (Buenos Aires, 1960), 465.
60 OIT, *Informe al Gobierno de la Republica argentina sobre la colocación selectiva de los inválidos* (Ginebra: OIT, 1964), 15.
61 ILO, *Report to the Government of Brazil on the Vocational Rehabilitation and Placement of the Disabled* (Geneva: ILO, 1967), 41.
62 *Revista Derecho del Trabajo*, Buenos Aires (abril de 1958), 315.
63 Ubiracy Torres Cuoco, "O direito do trabalho e o excepcional," *Mensagem da APAE*, São Paulo, no. 10 (setembro-dezembro de 1977), 32.
64 Gino Andrés Valeri, "Acaso la Ley prohibe trabajar al lisiado? No, pero tampoco lo protege!," *Revista del Club Marcelo J. Fitte*, Buenos Aires, no. 1 (abril de 1967), 13–14.
65 "Americanos elogiam atendimento aos excepcionais em Rio Grande-RS," *Mensagem da APAE*, São Paulo, no. 6 (maio-agôsto de 1976), 42–45.

4 Farewell to social Europe?

An entangled perspective on European disability policies in the 1980s and 1990s

Paul van Trigt

Introduction[1]

In a historiographical reflection on Brexit, historian Sandrine Kott points to the paradox that "the same people who blame 'Europe' for threatening their national welfare state" often "would agree that a special 'European social model' exists and that it provides a level of protection and redistribution unmatched anywhere else in the world." According to Kott, the International Labour Organization (ILO) was "instrumental in first defining what could be called a 'European social model,'" developed during the interwar period against the competing models of communism and fascism. After the war, this model was not initially institutionalized at the European level, but at the national level: the European institutions usually were aimed at an open economic market and left social policies to national governments. During the Cold War the European model that fostered social dialogue, self-administered insurance schemes and social rights was seen as the "middle-way taken by Western Europe, between the US attitude of 'laissez-faire' and the Eastern European welfare dictatorships." From the 1980s onwards the "social pact which lay at the heart of the European social model" was undermined, according to Kott, by conservative European political leaders, a development which appeared to be further strengthened by the fall of communist regimes since 1989.[2]

In this chapter I will address the way in which the European social model has become contested since the 1980s from a new angle, from the perspective of disability self-advocacy. Although it is often assumed that welfare states have improved the lives of people with disabilities, this assumption has been increasingly criticized by disability self-advocates since the 1980s. In the literature this critique is often framed as part of a paradigm shift from disability as a social-welfare issue to disability as a human-rights issue.[3] However, in the European context this shift was less straightforward than sometimes suggested, as I will show in this chapter by approaching the European institutions and self-advocacy from an entangled perspective. Using this perspective requires that I approach developments at the European level in relation to what happened at national and other international levels. Europe will be approached in a non-internalist way: the European sphere with European institutions and self-advocates cannot be understood only from an internal European perspective, but has to be investigated as entangled with institutions and self-advocates elsewhere.[4]

Although the historiography about disability and the welfare state is still growing, it is often put in "national boxes."[5] The scarcer literature about the history of European disability policies is often embedded in European studies.[6] The approach followed in this chapter is inspired by both the application of an entangled perspective to disability history and the increasing attention in the historiography of the European institutions to the entanglement with other international organizations.[7] In approaching European disability policies in a non-internalist way, this chapter will show that the support of disability self-advocates for the European social model was less self-evident than one would expect from this group: despite their critical perspective, they kept this model on board when the general support for the model became less evident, as Kott pointed out, after 1989.

In the first part of my chapter, I will sketch the evolution of European disability policies in the 1970s and 1980s, a period in which disability came to be seen as a policy area in its own right in the European sphere. This development was stimulated by the International Year of Disabled Persons (IYDP, 1981), an event initiated by the United Nations (UN) that has had an impact on disability policies around the world. My analysis in the second part of my chapter addresses developments inside and outside of Europe without which we cannot understand significant changes in the European disability policies in the 1990s. Because the available sources were limited, especially for the 1990s, this chapter has an exploratory character.[8]

A "considerable burden"

Considering that what is now the European Union (EU) started out initially as the European Coal and Steel Community and European Atomic Energy Community, and that one of the fundamental aims of this community was to foster the free movement of labour, it is not surprising that the initial concerns of the community regarding disabled (or handicapped, as they were then still called) people was their integration into the labour market, which was not at all simple in the free-market economy and particularly in times of crisis.[9] In 1973 the document called "Proposal for a decision on action by the European Social Fund to assist the social and occupational integration of the handicapped" declared that "in the countries of the European Community responsible circles are becoming increasingly aware of the problems of handicapped persons." It established that the number of those persons whose working capacity was reduced because of handicap was increasing, and although no precise statistics existed, it was estimated that several millions of people were affected in this way. The document then went on to state that

> In economic terms the existence of such large number is a *considerable burden*. Non-rehabilitated handicapped persons do not contribute to the production process, they are below average consumers, they do not pay taxes and they account for a considerable share of the social budget. The integration

of handicapped persons into active life makes it possible to reduce these disadvantages and provides a considerable contribution to the labour force. [...] Vocational and social integration, by giving handicapped persons fresh motivation and new dynamism, helps to make them *more independent and responsible*. This is one of the major factors in a social policy to help these people.[10]

With the aim to relieve this "burden," a great deal of policymaking in the 1970s revolved around health and safety regulations with the intention to help avoid industrial accidents. The rehabilitation of injured people to enable them to re-enter the labour market was another important goal. In European institutions disability was thus primarily seen as an issue related to a labour-based welfare state which was mainly organized at the national level but embedded in Europe. The framing of disability at the European level did therefore reflect the way in which the concept and the group were often approached in European welfare states.[11] As I will show in the next paragraph, the International Year of Disabled Persons as it was given shape by the UN in 1981 did not really contest this framing, but did nevertheless add new layers and strengthened certain tendencies.

New awareness

The main aim of the International Year of Disabled Persons was to integrate disabled people into the mainstream of life. In addition to the UN and its member states, the International Year was also observed at the regional level.[12] The European Parliament passed a resolution on 11 March 1981 which affirmed a commitment to promote social and economic integration for disabled people, in addition to their vocational integration.[13] During the International Year the development of a European community action programme concerning disabled people was considered, but mainly because of the economic crisis at that time, this remained only an idea.[14] Nevertheless, the International Year marks a change in European policies: up to this time, integration was first and foremost understood in terms of vocational rehabilitation. The broad focus of the International Year stimulated the Commission of the European Communities to further expand its efforts in rehabilitation for work with attention to the social integration of the disabled. For the first time, European institutions were challenged to set up a coherent and overall policy on all matters concerning the disabled with the aim to promote social and economic integration and an independent life.[15] In this way, the IYDP stimulated an integrated approach to disability that would become more and more common in Europe and elsewhere.

It took until 1986 before the European Council approved a new disability recommendation. The recommendation itself was meant "to promote fair opportunities for disabled people in the field of employment and vocational training." It also called for realistic targets for the employment of disabled people in firms and the preparation of a code of good practice. It was expected that the commission would coordinate the exchange of information and experience on the rehabilitation and employment of disabled people between national authorities. Moreover, the recommendation called for "giving particular priority to the active involvement of disabled people, whether in a representative or personal capacity, in the taking and implementation of decisions concerning them."[16]

The recommendation shows in the first place that employment remained an important focal point of European disability policies. Second, it makes clear how the "European social model" functioned: nation states were responsible for welfare and Europe facilitated the exchange between nations. Third, the recommendation acknowledged in line with the International Year the need to grant more autonomy to disabled people and to foster their initiatives. Within the European institutions this acknowledgement was already marked by the foundation of the "Disability Intergroup" in 1980 in which parliamentarians and self-advocates could informally meet.[17] Partly due to the informal character of the intergroup, however, the voice of disabled persons was hardly heard in the European institutions, let alone their opinion about the European social model. That would slightly change in the 1990s.

The institutionalization of self-advocates

In the 1980s the possibilities to use the European institutions for improving the situation of disabled persons were limited, certainly when compared to those offered by the UN and several countries. The International Year, as the current literature indicates, had initially the greatest impact on the national level, bringing disability activists in several countries together and challenging governments to deal with disability as an umbrella concept for groups previously approached separately.[18] The transnational exchange between disability activists as invoked by the International Year, most notably Disabled People International (DPI), proved crucial. This cross-disability organization was founded during the International Year out of disabled self-advocates' dissatisfaction with the dominance of non-disabled experts in the international sphere. With the International Year, the UN became an important venue for disability activists to raise their concerns, but it took a while before their ideas such as a (human) rights-based approach to disability were really picked up. One of the reasons why their new perspectives on disability encountered entrance barriers was the fact that disability was already institutionalized in other ways – a phenomenon that could be seen as "path dependency." Rehabilitation, for instance, was for a long time a much more central concept in the UN disability policies than human rights.[19]

When disability activists intensified their attempts to influence the European institutions in the 1990s, they ran into this "path dependency" of disability. It will not be a surprise that the path of European disability policies in the 1990s was still focused on labour. One of the main aims of the Community Action Programmes for Disabled People HELIOS I (1988–1991) and II (1993–1996) was the improvement of employment opportunities by stimulating the vocational training and rehabilitation of people with disabilities.[20] Europe was not alone in following its path as before. At the end of the International Decade of Disabled Persons (1983–1992), which followed the International Year, it became clear that human

Farewell to social Europe? 73

rights were not seen as the paradigm for the international disability policies of the future. Although the UN Commission on Human Rights gave some attention to the violations of the human rights of disabled persons, the idea of an international human rights convention was set aside by the UN in favour of the Standard Rules on the Equalization of Opportunities for Disabled Persons (1993). Under the rules as a non-binding instrument, countries and international organizations had no real obligation to change their disability policies. In the Asia-Pacific region for instance, the United Nations Economic and Social Commission for Asia and the Pacific (UNESCAP) declared an Asian and Pacific Decade of Disabled Persons (1993–2002) that in line with the international decade focussed on "the expansion of opportunities for the full participation of people with disabilities in society and their equality in the development process."[21] In Europe the welfare state remained the dominant lens through which disability was viewed.

However, continuity in policies should not disguise the increasing role of disabled self-advocates. The already-mentioned development of self-advocacy in the international sphere in the 1980s was not directly visible in Europe. Within Disabled People International, besides national councils, five regional councils were formed, including one for Europe. Resources within DPI were mainly used for developing countries, which means that there was no money available for Europe. Regional work was thus for a long time dependent on resources of individual members. DPI Europe was concerned with European initiatives like the computerized database Handynet, but this self-advocacy organization was only one of the myriad NGOs, many run by non-disabled people.[22] The influence of disabled people was, according to disability self-advocate Rachel Hurst, also limited during the HELIOS programmes.[23]

A closer look at these programmes and in particular HELIOS II teaches us that Hurst's observation is only partly true. In practice, the HELIOS programmes facilitated mainly the exchange of information and in this exchange the voice of disability self-advocates was probably not always heard. The HELIOS II programme, however, was seen as a way to realize a more "comprehensive, consistent policy." Moreover, the "dialogue group" that was already part of HELIOS I was formalized under HELIOS II: "this group comprises only representatives of the representative European non-governmental organisations, the aim being to exchange views on HELIOS II activities."[24] In the programme, disabled self-advocates became officially acknowledged as advisers of the European Commission. In this way, the first European cross-disability self-advocacy organization, the European Disability Forum (EDF), was formed as a working group and explicitly integrated into the HELIOS II programme.[25] With HELIOS II the European Commission took a step beyond general statements about the importance of self-advocacy: how could this official recognition come about?

Meanwhile, the World Council of Disabled People International could offer money and "lobbying skills learnt at the international level" with which DPI Europe could strengthen its influence in Europe from the early 1990s. When the European Parliament decided not to renew Helios I in 1991, DPI Europe together with other self-advocacy organizations used this decision to ask for a "more democratic consultative mechanism." Moreover, DPI succeeded in the 1990s together with the European Network on Independent Living in obtaining funding from the European Commission for several independent living programmes.[26] An important symbolic moment was the first European celebration of the International Day of Disabled Persons, which took place on 3 December 1992. DPI wanted to use this day, as announced by the UN, to raise awareness with "its message of human rights (not rattling charity cans at street corners!)."[27] After several requests and a threat of action, they received permission to use the official parliament chamber of the EU in Brussels to have a so-called "parliament of disabled people": 440 disabled people from all over Europe came to the parliament to talk with the Commissioner for Social Affairs, members of the European Parliament and commission officials. The attendees were impressed by the stories told by disabled people, and the European Parliament decided to support the "Disabled People's Parliament Resolution to support the UN Standard Rules" and "to research the real situation of disabled people in Europe and to find out what was happening with the rise of violence and fascism." According to Rachel Hurst, this day was a watershed moment and since then the voice of disabled people at the European level was strengthened.[28] The result of these actions was that self-advocates got the opportunity to start in 1993 a working group with self-advocacy organizations that became in 1997 the European Disability Forum and that continues to play an important role on the European scene.

Beyond a welfare state perspective?

From the evaluation of HELIOS II, it becomes clear that the strengthening of the voice of disabled people went along with the introduction of a new perspective that challenged the welfare state. In an interim evaluation report from January 1996 the Commission mentioned the innovative results of the programme, most notably the "active participation by the disabled people" and an "approach recognising the equal rights of disabled people as opposed to being based on assistance." According to the commission, this approach was part of "an approach to policy on the disabled in terms of human rights as opposed to a 'social welfare' approach." At the same time the commission noted "differing and sometimes contradictory views" in the programme, "reflecting the contradictions inherent in all policies concerning the disabled as implemented in the Member States, and in particular the tensions between the 'medical' and 'social' concepts of disability."[29] In the final report published in 1998, the programme was seen as a laboratory from which lessons had to be drawn. The focus on exchange was seen as the main limitation because "with limited resources," it remained very dependent on participants at national and local levels for its capacity to bring about "real" change (in services and policy for disabled people). Moreover, it also remained "very dependent on local and national participants for its capacity to bring about real participation and consultation for disabled people." Therefore the programme had, according to the commission, to be followed up by "steps to promote a rights based approach in the field of disability."[30]

As became clear from the 1998 report, Helios II marked the slow integration of a new, rights-based perspective on disability. Before I discuss the further institutionalization of this perspective, I will first discuss the context in which European institutions could become a venue for disability rights. Important developments in the process of European integration such as the Maastricht Treaty (1992) probably stimulated disability self-advocates to take aim at Europe. Moreover, two developments outside the direct influence of European institutions played a role in the rise of a rights-based approach to disability at the European level.

In the first place, the reluctance of international organizations to make disability part of their human-rights work seems to have stimulated the development of human-rights (law) expertise within and related to self-advocacy organizations on the European continent.[31] In 1993, during the international conference for and by people with disabilities in Maastricht titled "Eur'able," the German lawyer and self-advocate Theresia Degener mentioned the United Nations report Human Rights and Disability (1991) as the "first official study of the causal connection between serious violations of human rights and fundamental freedoms and disability." Although this study did not result in a direct change at the UN level, we can observe during the 1990s the increasing attention of European self-advocates to anti-discrimination law and disability and exploratory investigations of human-rights violations. The Dutch council of disabled people initiated a book project about human rights and disability, which was published in 1995 and contained several chapters written by lawyers.[32] The knowledge that was developed from this (human) rights perspective had already gained influence during Helios II and continued to do so afterwards. Contrary to what was suggested in the programme evaluations, however, I will argue in the following that the adoption of a rights-based approach did not naturally come at the expense of the welfare perspective.[33]

Second, the emancipation of people with disabilities in the United States of America came to be seen as exemplary. The understanding of disability as a (civil) rights issue inspired activists in the US to aim for anti-discrimination laws in the 1980s, resulting in the Americans with Disabilities Act (ADA) in 1990. This law was in an interesting way related to the welfare state. As research about the realization of the ADA shows, the relationship between this anti-discrimination law and the welfare state was framed to be almost mutually exclusive. The law was promoted on the grounds that discrimination not only "denies people with disabilities the opportunity to compete on an equal basis," but also costs the US "billions of dollars." This framing was crucial for the passage of this law: it was, according to Katharina Heyer, "good economic policy to turn people with disabilities from welfare dependents into productive taxpayers." In the lobbying for the law this "welfare argument" was frequently used. The Republicans and the disability community were even called "strange bedfellows," united in the conviction that "only the truly needy should receive welfare and that others should be given the opportunity to work and to become self-reliant and responsible citizens."[34] During the 1990s the ADA would become an international example. In the next section I will discuss the way in which this law was followed up by European self-advocates and the consequences for the European social model.

A Europeans with Disabilities Act?

Without these developments we cannot really understand the institutionalization of disability self-advocacy and the change in policies in Europe during the 1990s, most noticeably the inclusion of disability in Article 13 of the Treaty of Amsterdam (1997). Legal experts were heavily involved in the lobbying of the European Disability Forum to include disability in this treaty, an addition to the Maastricht Treaty (1992), which was the founding treaty of the European Union. The inclusion of disability in the Treaty of Amsterdam was not intended by the European institutions.[35] However, the EDF had developed an argument on how disability could be part of the broadening and deepening of existing anti-discrimination measures and received support from the Intergovernmental Conference Reflection Group that prepared the negotiations – with only one dissenting voice ("widely presumed to be the U.K. Conservative Government of the time").[36] The wish of the European disability NGOs for a general non-discrimination provision was not granted, but the inclusion of disability in the Amsterdam Treaty was seen as a breakthrough because European governments acknowledged for the first time the reality of the discrimination experienced by people with disabilities.[37] According to Mark Priestley, the Amsterdam Treaty gave momentum to the "disability rights" agenda and made possible the introduction of a Framework Directive on Non-Discrimination in Occupation and Employment in 2000 as the "first legislative intervention on disabled people's rights."[38]

Because of this, the impression could be given that European disability policy-makers made a shift from a welfare state and "social Europe" to an equal-rights approach. This impression seems to be underlined by the role played by British self-advocates at the European level. British activists belonged to the driving forces behind the European disability self-advocacy in contrast to the UK government, which played an obstructing role during the negotiations about Article 13 and the following Framework Equal Treatment Directive (2000).[39] They not only brought the social model of disability, as coined by Mike Oliver, to Europe, but in their own country and in Europe they fought for anti-discrimination laws.[40] These British perspectives included critical evaluations of the welfare state, although less critical and less legalistic than in the American context.[41] Can we therefore say that Europe in the late 1990s followed the Anglo-American shift to equal rights that did "replace and not complement measures of social security"?[42]

A closer look at the European discussions reveals that the Americans with Disabilities Act and the British Disability Discrimination Act (1995) could not easily be translated to a "Europeans with Disabilities Act" (Waddington) because of the tension "between the solidarity-based social welfare model, traditionally associated with Europe, and the more individualistic civil rights approach, traditionally associated with countries such as the United States."[43] In the literature about disability policies and movements, this tension is often framed in a negative way, opposing the welfare approach to the equal-rights approach. That seems, however, not to be intended by the European institutions. In the post-Amsterdam disability policies we still find a lot of attention to employment, as for instance in the case of the 2000 directive. Moreover, equal rights were often not seen in opposition to a welfare approach. Mabbett has pointed to a Comité des Sages, established by the European Commission in 1994 to reflect on the future of the Community Chapter, which argued "that the crisis of the welfare state called for a new unified approach to rights" beyond the separation of civil and social rights. She also mentions the development of the concept "social exclusion" that "widened the traditional focus of poverty policy beyond concern with income adequacy and towards issues of access to employment, housing, health care and education." The "inclusion of disability, age and sexual orientation" in Article 13 has therefore, according to Mabbett, to be seen as part of the "modernizing and restructuring" of the way "European welfare states regulate the life courses and family arrangements of their citizens."[44]

Moreover, the scholars who worked together with the European self-advocates were explicitly aiming at a fusion of the Anglo-American civil-rights model and the European social-welfare approach. The wish for a "Europeans with Disabilities Act" did not prevent scholars such as Lisa Waddington, who has worked together with the European Disability Forum, from arguing for a new synthesis between the two approaches and "a system based on a broader notion of social justice that stressed the right of each individual to a basic income and the opportunity for economic success" and a "set of economic and social rights that are grounded on principles of respect for human dignity."[45]

We can thus observe in both the European policies and in the literature of activist scholars an attempt to combine the European social model with a civil-rights and anti-discrimination-oriented model. Therefore we have to be careful about claiming a paradigm shift, as is already captured in the formulation of Waldschmidt that European disability policies changed during the 1990s from "a formerly disregarded branch of traditional social policy into a modern formation which comprises *not only* social protection and labour market integration, *but also* equal rights and non-discrimination."[46] Interestingly, the Convention on the Rights of People with Disabilities that was drafted by the United Nations in the years 2002–2006 includes rights that could be related to both an anti-discrimination and a welfare perspective. The inclusion of social rights seems not so much an effort of the European Union, which was involved in the drafting, but could partly be attributed to European international lawyers and self-advocates.[47] In the historiography of disability self-advocacy this relatively recent, positive engagement with the welfare state and the European social model is often overlooked.

Conclusion

What does this history of European disability policies and self-advocacy add to the historiography of the European welfare state? In the first place, it reminds us that the welfare state was supported by the European institutions – a construction that was called the European social model. During the 1970s and 1980s, Europe stimulated the transnational exchange of expertise about disabled persons. But also during the 1990s and 2000s, when disability was no longer exclusively seen through the lens of welfare, the idea of "social Europe" and the welfare state did not disappear. This chapter makes clear that in particular disability self-advocates did not say farewell to social Europe, a position that can be understood if we not only look at the interaction of the European arena with national arenas, but also take into consideration the influence of actors like the UN and disability activists from the US or outside the European institutions. Second, the chapter illuminates the influence of the (human) rights model of disability in the European context, which has hardly been addressed in the general historical literature until now. The model is often associated with a shift from a welfare perspective on disability to a civil-rights and anti-discrimination approach. In Europe we see the influence of this model, mainly brought in by British activists inspired by developments in the US. During the 1990s the European Disability Forum was successful in bringing the anti-discrimination perspective into the spotlight. However, in contrast to the US context and from what sometimes is suggested in the literature, this did not mean that the welfare perspective was put aside. This becomes clear if we take into consideration that the entrance of disabled citizens into the European arena went along with increasing attention to legal expertise. In this knowledge production, scholars tried to combine the anti-discrimination approach with the tradition of "social Europe." The increasing attention to equal rights since the 1990s has therefore to be understood as an extra layer to the perspective of the welfare state and "social Europe" and not as a paradigm change.

Notes

1 The author wishes to thank Karin van Leeuwen and Monika Baár for comments on earlier versions of this chapter and Johan Wesemann for his stories about European self-advocacy, and acknowledges the support of the ERC Consolidator Grant Rethinking Disability under grant agreement number 648115.
2 Sandrine Kott, "Social Europe, Democracy and Brexit," *Contemporary European History* 28, no. 1 (2019): 46–49.
3 Paul van Trigt, "Inequality in Global Disability Policies since the 1970s," in *Histories of Global Inequality*, ed. Christian O. Christiansen and Steven L.B. Jensen (Houndsmills: Palgrave MacMillan, forthcoming).
4 Sebastian Conrad, *What Is Global History?* (Princeton and Oxford: Princeton University Press, 2016), in particular chapter 4; Mark Priestley, "In Search of European Disability Policy: Between National and Global," *ALTER: European Journal of Disability Research/Revue européenne de recherche sur le handicap* 1, no. 1 (2007): 61–74.
5 Monika Baár, "De-Pathologizing Disability: Politics, Culture and Identity," *Neue Politische Literatur* 62 (2017): 281–303.
6 Anne Waldschmidt, "Behindertenpolitik (in) der Europäischen Union," in *Aufbrüche und Barrieren. Behindertenpolitik und Behindertenrecht in Deutschland und Europa seit den 1970er-Jahren*, ed. Theresia Degener and Marc von Miquel (Beilefeld: Transcript Verlag, 2019), 79–105.
7 Gildas Bregain, "An Entangled Perspective on Disability History: The Disability Protests in Argentina, Brazil and Spain," in *The Imperfect Historian: Disability Histories in Europe*, ed. Sebastian Barsch, Anne Klein, and Pieter Verstraete (Frankfurt am Main: Peter Lang, 2013), 133–153; Wolfram Kaiser and Kiran Klaus Patel, "Multiple Connections in European Co-Operation: International Organizations, Policy Ideas, Practices and Transfers 1967–92," *European Review of History: Revue européenne d'histoire* 24, no. 3 (2017): 337–357.

8 The archives of the European Disability Forum are not (publicly) available yet. The analysis in the first part of this chapter is partly derived from Monika Baár's paper "From Social Welfare to Human Rights: Disability Policy," based on an analysis of the reports on the social situation of Europe and presented during the conference Experts and Expertise in European International Organizations in Maastricht in 2014.
9 Anne Waldschmidt, "Behindertenpolitik (in) de- Europäischen Union," *Aufbrüche und Barrieren* 86.
10 Commission of the European Communities (CEC), "Proposal for a decision of the council on action by the European Social Fund to assist the social and occupational integration of handicapped persons," 16 November 1973, accessed 4 June 2019, https://eur-lex.europa.eu/legal-content/EN/TXT/PDF/?uri=CELEX:51973PC1958&from=GA. My italics.
11 Cf. Mark Priestley, "We're All Europeans Now! The Social Model of Disability and European Social Policy," in *The Social Model of Disability: Europe and the Majority World*, ed. C. Barnes and G. Mercer (Leeds: The Disability Press, 2005).
12 Monika Baár and Anna Derksen, "Das Internationale Jahr der Behinderten 1981 in historischer Perspektive," in *Aufbrüche und Barrieren*, 161–184; Monika Baár, "The European 'Disability Revolts' of 1981: How Were They Related to the Youth Movement?" in *A European Youth Revolt: European Perspectives on Youth Protest and Social Movements in the 1980s*, ed. Knud Andersen and Bart van der Steen (Houndmills: Palgrave MacMillan, 2016), 159–171.
13 Priestley, "We're All," 17–31, 19.
14 Baár, "European 'Disability Revolts'"; D. Driedger, *The Last Civil Rights Movement. Disabled People's International* (London: Hurst, 1989).
15 Anne Waldschmidt, "Disability Policy of the European Union: The Supranational Level," *ALTER, European Journal of Disability 3* (2009): 8–23; Priestley, "We're All."
16 "Council Recommendation of 24 July 1986 on the employment of disabled people in the Community," accessed 4 June 2019, https://eur-lex.europa.eu/legal-content/EN/TXT/PDF/?uri=CELEX:31986H0379&from=EN; Priestley, "In Search of."
17 Waldschmidt, "Behindertenpolitik," 99.
18 Baár, "The European 'Disability Revolts'"; Baár and Derksen, "Das Internationale Jahr"; Monika Baár, Chapter 7, and Anaïs Van Ertvelde, Chapter 8, this volume.
19 Van Trigt, "Inequality."
20 Waldschmidt, "Disability."
21 Osamu Nagase, *Difference, Equality and Disabled People: Disability Rights and Disability Culture* (master's thesis, Institute of Social Studies, The Hague, 1995); Penny Price and Yutaka Takamine, "The Asian and Pacific Decade of Disabled Persons 1993–2002: What Have We Learned?" *Asia Pacific Disability Rehabilitation Journal* 14, no. 2 (2003): 115–127; cf. Antony Anghie, "Whose Utopia? Human Rights, Development, and the Third World," in *Qui Parle* 22, no. 1 (2013): 63–80.
22 Rachel Hurst, "Disabled Peoples' International: Europe and the Social Model of Disability," in *The Social Model of Disability: Europe and the Majority World*, ed. C. Barnes and G. Mercer (Leeds: The Disability Press, 2005), 65–79, in particular 67–68.
23 Hurst, "Disabled," 68.
24 CEC, "Proposal for a Council Decision establishing a third Community action programme to assist disabled people (HELIOS II (1992–96))," 23 October 1991, accessed 4 June 2019, https://eur-lex.europa.eu/legal-content/EN/TXT/PDF/?uri=CELEX:51991PC0350&rid=2.
25 Official Journal of the European Communities no C 25/1, "Amended proposal for a Council Decision establishing a third Community action programme to assist disabled people – Helios II (1993 to 1997)," 28 January 1993, accessed 4 June 2019, https://eur-lex.europa.eu/legal-content/EN/TXT/PDF/?uri=CELEX:51992PC0482&rid=39.
26 Hurst, "Disabled," 71.
27 Ibidem, 73.

28 Ibidem, 73–74. Cf. Monika Baár and Paul van Trigt, "British and European Citizenship: Entanglements through the Lens of Disability," *Contemporary European History* 28, no. 1 (2019): 50–52.
29 CEC, "Interim Evaluation Report on the HELIOS II Programme," 23 January 1996, accessed 4 June 2019, https://eur-lex.europa.eu/legal-content/EN/TXT/PDF/?uri=CELEX:51996DC0008&rid=97.
30 CEC, "On the Evaluation of the Third Community Action Programme to Assist Disabled People (Helios II) 1993–96", 20 January 1998, accessed 4 June 2019, https://eur-lex.europa.eu/legal-content/EN/TXT/PDF/?uri=CELEX:51998DC0015&rid=3.
31 Priestley, "We're All."
32 Paul van Trigt, "A Blind Spot of a Guiding Country? Human Rights and Dutch Disability Groups Since 1981," *Moving the Social* 53 (2015): 87–102, 95.
33 Theresia Degener, "A New Human Rights Model of Disability," in *The United Nations Convention on the Rights of Persons with Disabilities: A Commentary*, ed. V. Della Vina, R. Cera, and G. Palmisano (Cham: Springer, 2017), 41–59.
34 Quoted by Katharina Heyer, *Rights Enabled: The Disability Revolution, From the US, to Germany and Japan, to the United Nations* (Ann Arbor: University of Michigan Press, 2015), 33–34.
35 Aart Hendriks, "Promoting Disability Equality after the Treaty of Amsterdam: New Legal Directions and Practical Expansion Strategies," in *Disability Rights in Europe: From Theory to Practice*, ed. Anna Lawson and Caroline Gooding (London: Bloomsbury Publishing, 2005), 187–198, 190; European Disability Forum, *Guide to the Amsterdam Treaty* (Brussels, 1998), accessed 4 June 2019, www.independentliving.org/docs3/edf98.html.
36 Theresia Degener and Gerard Quinn, "A Survey of International, Comparative and Regional Disability Law Reform," in *Disability Rights Law and Policy: International and National Perspectives*, ed. Mary Lou Breslin and Silvia Yee (Ardsley, NY: Transnational Publishers, 2002), 3–125, 106.
37 Degener and Quinn, "A Survey," 106–107.
38 Priestley, "In Search of."
39 Baár and Van Trigt, "British and European Citizenship"; Deborah Mabbett, "The Development of Rights-Based Social Policy in the European Union: The Example of Disability Rights," in *Journal of Common Market Studies* 43, no. 1 (2005): 97–120, in particular page p. 110.
40 Priestley, "We're All."
41 Heyer, *Rights Enabled*, 47–48; Priestley, "In Search of."
42 Waldschmidt, "Disability Policy," 21.
43 Hendriks, "Promoting," 188; L.B. Waddington and M. Diller, "Tensions and Coherence in Disability Policy: The Uneasy Relationship between Social Welfare and Civil Rights Models of Disability in American, European and International Employment Law," in *Disability Rights Law and Policy: International and National Perspectives*, ed. Mary Lou Breslin and Silvia Yee (Ardsley, NY: Transnational Publishers, 2002), 241–280.
44 Mabbett, "Development," 103–104 and 106.
45 Degener and Quinn, *Human* Rights, 118–119; Waddington and Diller, "Tensions," 278–279.
46 Waldschmidt, "Disability Policy," 8. My italics.
47 Theresia Degener and Andrew Begg, "From Invisible Citizens to Agents of Change: A Short History of the Struggle for the Recognition of the Rights of Persons with Disabilities at the United Nations," in *The United Nations Convention on the Rights of Persons with Disabilities: A Commentary*, ed. V. Della Vina, R. Cera, and G. Palmisano (Cham: Springer, 2017), 1–39.

5 The history of a phantom welfare state
The United States

Rose Ernst

> Perhaps it is its relative newness which accounts for the misconceptions and confusion which surround the term "welfare state." Its use during the last twenty years implies that some human societies can be classified as "welfare states" while others cannot. What then distinguishes such a state and by what criteria is it judged?
>
> —Richard Titmuss, 1963

> The stratification of our welfare system that distributes benefits according to race and gender also differentiates between two classes of inhabitants – citizens and subjects.
>
> —Dorothy E. Roberts, 1996

> The United States has never had a welfare state.
>
> —Sandrine Kott, 2017

Introduction[1]

Welfare state scholars have defended a non-existent entity for the past thirty years.[2] I coined the term *phantom welfare state* to describe this phenomenon.[3] The word "phantom" is meant not as a supernatural force, but rather in the sense of *phantom limbs* and *phantom pregnancies*. The *Oxford English Dictionary* defines a phantom limb as "the sensation of the presence of a limb after it has been amputated."[4] This, however, implies the existence of a welfare state at some point in the past – and that we are collectively feeling pain where an arm of the state used to exist. A more precise metaphor is phantom pregnancy, or as the *Lancet* described one case in 1887, "one patient was admitted who presented many of the signs of advanced gestation, but on examining her closely it was found to be a case of phantom pregnancy." The phantom welfare state concept builds on the idea of a physical feeling which mimics a real entity or condition: the collective sensation of an entity – fictive in reality – conjoined to the governing apparatus of a nation-state. The sensation exists, in part, as an origin or purpose story to accompany it. This fictive state is akin to a phantom pain – we were told the entity existed and therefore believed it did.

I introduce the phantom welfare state to provoke political and scholarly dialogue, not cast aspersions on welfare state scholarship. To the contrary, as a welfare state scholar myself – who has also devoted much time to welfare rights organizing – I am aware of the risks. While increasing assaults on poor people encourages foreclosure of critique in fear of further cuts, an urgent and honest conversation is necessary – not only about the motives of the original welfare state in the 1930s, but whether it makes sense to revive an entity that has never really existed.[5]

The phantom welfare state emerges through origin and purpose stories, retold by policymakers, administrators, scholars and the public. I organize the chapter around these sets of stories. The first story is an origin narrative: the welfare state emerged through the New Deal. Using a content analysis of speeches, I argue that even President Roosevelt did not articulate the raft of federal programs as a welfare state in the 1930s. The second set of stories includes the following: (1) social citizenship, (2) economic stimulus, (3) social control and (4) the welfare state as a hidden state. While each stand-alone story may be compelling, the co-existence of contradictory purposes of a welfare state undermines the idea of any general agreement on its contours in practice. The third set of stories emerges from a programmatic perspective. Regardless of era, the basic conundrum is this: which programmes, institutions and systems are integral to a welfare state? Next, I examine the role of federalism – particularly degrees of uniformity – in illuminating the existence of a phantom welfare state, especially in light of the competing narratives described earlier. A bottom-up analysis of perceptions and experiences with welfare state programmes reveals the importance of whose story is told. Finally, I consider the colonial and racial purpose of a phantom welfare state for maintaining a racial contract or white democracy.

First story: naming the welfare state

The first story is a New Deal narrative. Though the United States had proto-welfare state provisions at the local and state levels prior to the 1930s, President Franklin Delano Roosevelt's New Deal ushered in a national set of gendered and racially exclusionary programmes, represented symbolically by the 1935 Social Security Act (old-age insurance and assistance, unemployment, aid to the blind and Aid to Families with Dependent Children [ADC]).[6] The New Deal was a response to the Great Depression global economic crisis. Social insurance programmes included later in 1935 were part of a broader programme, which consisted of a host of economic regulations and foreign policies: "the Roosevelt Administration used two main tools to achieve one overarching goal: insulation and domestic intervention to create security."[7]

No doubt the torrent of federal policies created and reinforced a federal administrative structure, but was this hodgepodge of programmes conceptualized as a "welfare state" – even at the time? Outside the United States, the UK Beveridge Report in 1945 marks the emergence of popular welfare state terminology.[8] Wincott notes, however, that the phrase has earlier German origins: "*Wohlfarhtsstaat*

The history of a phantom welfare state 83

had been in use since the 1920s, if not earlier. More significantly, the traditional accounts of its 'origins' tend to imply that both the term, and a certain idea of the welfare state, gained a general currency from the 1940s."[9] Even as the term spread, however, the person ostensibly most responsible for the popularisation of the term, William Beveridge, distanced himself from it. According to Beveridge's biographer José Harris, he preferred the term "social service state" to "welfare state," which he thought had "Santa Claus" connotations.[10]

How popular was this term in the United States at the time of the New Deal? I examined the words of the public official most closely associated with the term in the United States: President Franklin Delano Roosevelt. In a content analysis of 2989 speeches, statements and press conference remarks made by FDR from 1932 – just prior to the launch of his presidency – through 1945, the term "welfare state" *does not appear, even once*.[11] As Figure 5.1 indicates, FDR did employ the word "welfare" on occasion, though he invoked it most frequently during the election of 1932.

After 1932, however, the number of mentions of welfare is relatively infrequent. As Figure 5.2 indicates, even when FDR does use this term, he uses it to refer to "the general welfare" rather than a set of social insurance or relief programmes.

Even during 1935 – the year of the Social Security Act – FDR used the word "welfare" (not welfare state) sparingly. Indeed, his signing statement of this signature act of his presidency – on 14 August 1935, does not include "welfare." The closest he came to describing a welfare state happened in a fireside chat on April 28, 1935: "[T]he Congress has devoted itself to the arduous task of formulating legislation necessary to the country's *welfare* ... The job of creating a program for the Nation's *welfare* is, in some respects, like the building of a ship. At different points on the coast where I often visit they build great seagoing ships." While the absence of the umbrella term to describe a set of policies as they are enacted

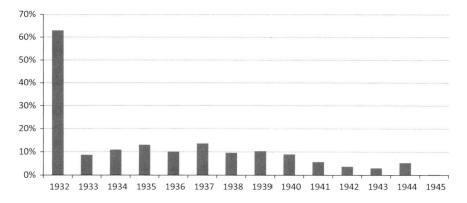

Figure 5.1 Percentage of FDR speeches including the word "welfare."

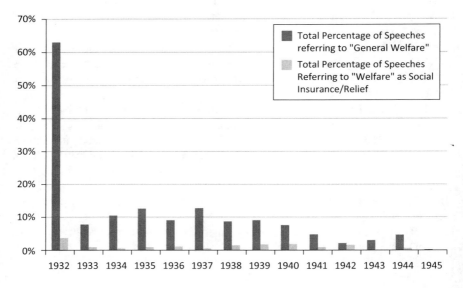

Figure 5.2 Comparison of "general welfare" versus social insurance/relief mentions in FDR speeches.

is explicable, the downward trend in the usage of the word "welfare" itself, over time, is puzzling. The most obvious explanation for FDR's sharp drop-off in usage of "welfare" after 1933 is the transition between a 1932 election campaign focus to an executive and legislative focus.

Second set of stories: conceptual meanings of a welfare state

Though FDR eschewed welfare state terminology, conceptual meanings in theory and in practice abound. Regardless of how compelling one story may be, the fact that these stories all co-exist undermines a coherent definition of the welfare state. I identify four general trends in scholarly definitions of the welfare state, particularly in reference to the United States.[12] The first trend includes conventional elements of social citizenship. Second, some scholars view the welfare state as a mechanism of social control rather than social citizenship, though they often make a chronological distinction between different welfare state regimes. Third, and closely related to the first, is a view of the welfare state as a Keynesian economic stimulus. Fourth is the view that the welfare state has a hidden purpose, even if scholars have different views on what that purpose might be.[13] That hidden purpose ranges from expansion of national state authority and governing structures to also providing social insurance, but in the form of "hidden" expenditures that actually make the US welfare state seem positively robust in terms of expenditures.

Social citizenship

Perhaps the most widely shared understanding of a welfare state is one that emphasizes expansion of social citizenship through social insurance and public assistance programmes. Consider the emphasis on well-being, offered by the *Oxford English Dictionary*: "A system whereby the state undertakes to protect the health and well-being of its citizens, especially those in financial or social need, by means of grants, pensions, and other benefits; a country practicing such a system."[14] Briggs offered one of the most influential, expanded definitions in 1961:

> A "welfare state" is a state in which organized power is deliberately used (through politics and administration) in an effort to modify the play of market forces in at least three directions – first, by guaranteeing individuals and families a minimum income irrespective of the market value of their work or their property; second, by narrowing the extent of insecurity by enabling individuals and families to meet certain "social contingencies" (for example, sickness, old age and unemployment) which lead other wise to individual and family crises; and third, by ensuring that all citizens without distinction of status or class are offered the best standards available in relation to a certain agreed range of social services.[15]

The first two directions, public assistance and social insurance, "serv[ing] both the poor and the middle classes" are fundamentally different than the third direction that ensures equitable treatment.[16] Indeed, the notion of public assistance and social insurance, as *guaranteed* by the state underscores the welfare state as part of a larger social contract between the governed and the nation-state. Briggs argues that the first two directions of the welfare state may be served by a "social service state," but not the third. The third direction, however, rests on providing the, "'optimum' rather than the older idea of the 'minimum.' It is concerned not merely with abatement of class differences or the needs of scheduled groups but with equality of treatment and the aspirations of citizens as voters with equal shares of electoral power."[17]

Briggs's 1961 formulation captured the tension between the welfare state as a "social concept" and an "ideology," at least in the United Kingdom: "As a social concept, it was used to describe a certain type of social and economic organization, coordinated and planned; as an ideology, it was interpreted within a total system of beliefs, values, assumptions, and goals shared by groups of people or individuals."[18] As Kott notes, however, this view of the welfare state as "striv[ing] to guarantee all citizens social security, social justice, social integration [and] individual freedom" is a view provided by "encyclopedias," not focused scholarship on the welfare state.[19] She notes conceptual differences in welfare regimes across time and geography. Even in the case of T.H. Marshall's expansive view of the British welfare state's role in promoting social citizenship, Wincott argues that Marshall "impl[ied] that social rights should exceed a certain minimum standard, he also viewed social citizenship as a product of (mass democratic) political action: social rights change mass democratic politics but also respond to political change. Thus the substance of social rights is not eternally fixed."[20] Thus, even among proponents of a social-citizenship narrative, rights derived from the welfare state are contingent – and subject to change at any time.

Social control

Moving away from lofty social-citizenship goals, I turn to ulterior-motive narratives. The first is social control.[21] A social control origin and purpose story is not separate from previous philosophical understandings of the welfare state. Neocleous argues that the genealogy of welfare- and police-state terminology reveals a close relationship:

> early discourse on policing was simultaneously a discourse on *Polizeistaat* or "police state," implying a state which engages in wide-ranging internal administration, welfare and surveillance. Given the negative connotations of the phrase "police state" in the 20th century, it might be argued that a far better means of understanding *Polizeistaat* is as an early welfare state.[22]

Hallsworth and Lea note though "social control was exercised less through overt coercion" in post-war Britain, the welfare state still rested on the notion of a "disciplinary society."[23] In moving from welfare state origins to contemporary analyses of the United States, Baskerville argues the transformation of the welfare state into a "miniature penal apparatus" makes it more overtly controlling than any paternalistic public benefits connection in the past.[24]

Economic development

Parallel to viewing public assistance and social control as two sides of the same coin, scholars have spun welfare state origin narratives of both economic upheaval and economic development. Proponents of a Keynesian welfare state offer perhaps the most well-known story in this area. Briggs also notes ties between economic development, state building, welfare and warfare in the UK: "the knowledge that large sums of money, raised through taxation at a level without precedent, were being used to wage war led without difficulty to the conclusion that smaller sums of money could produce a 'welfare state' in times of peace."[25] Piven and Cloward argue that the welfare state propped up capitalist waves of unemployment – much in the vein of a Keynesian argument – but one that looks at the welfare state as a social-control mechanism rather than as economic development: "The key to an understanding of relief-giving is in the functions it serves for the larger economic and political order, for relief is a secondary and supportive institution ... expansive relief policies are designed to mute civil disorder, and restrictive ones to reinforce work norms."[26] Like previous narratives, these stories emphasize limited, competing and/or fragmented views of overarching welfare state meaning. While moving us toward understanding origin and purpose, they do little to articulate a vision of what the welfare state is, exactly.

The hidden welfare state

Discrepancies between public views of government spending and what goes on behind the proverbial curtain are the métier of hidden welfare state narratives. Howard argues that the US welfare state is expansive if we include indirect federal government expenditures: "The hidden welfare state is roughly one-third to one-half the size of the visible welfare state of direct spending."[27] Howard also asserts that views of welfare state purpose are shaped by visible or direct expenditures: "Every commonly accepted definition of the welfare state makes room for both direct and indirect social spending ... *Scholarly convention, not reality, dictates that we equate the welfare state with direct spending.*"[28] This also reveals the real targets of spending: "middle and upper-income classes are the main beneficiaries of the hidden welfare state."[29]

Third set of stories: programmatic parameters

Imagine you write a list of every person dear to you, past and present. If someone's name does not appear, are they not important to you? Did they not exist because they are not on your list? This third set of stories highlights the list-creation challenge of welfare state programmes. Might the list include education, social insurance, tax breaks, health care, public assistance, work programmes, unemployment, disability, social security, veterans' assistance? Which programmes do not make the cut?[30] What is the difference between public park expenditures and those for public education? Both include outcomes of inclusion/exclusion, public spending, and affect the labour and property markets respectively.

In the wake of the post-1996 elimination of the federal guarantee of welfare (AFDC), Martin Gilens offers an inclusive list of federal welfare state programmes:

> [E]ducation, housing assistance, social insurance (such as pensions, unemployment insurance, and workers' compensation), health care, public assistance (means-tested cash aid for the poor), and programs for veterans. Together, federal, state, and local governments in the United States spent about $1.4 trillion on social programs in 1993, constituting 65 percent of all government spending.[31]

Gilens argues that "[o]utside of education, the remaining government social programs can [16] be divided into social insurance programs, which provide benefits to those who have made previous contributions through earmarked taxes, and means-tested programs, which offer benefits only to the poor."[32] If we consider the "hidden" welfare state or the "submerged" state, then we would need to include the Department of the Treasury, for example.[33] If we do this, however, and add on these programmes/tax loopholes to the already whopping 65% of the federal budget, the question becomes not so much what to include in a laundry list of the welfare state, but to ask, rather, which programmes are excluded? Agricultural subsidies? They certainly should be included in a hidden or corporate welfare state. This tension highlights the illusive quality of a potential behemoth state, on the one hand, or a ghostly apparition, on the other.

Perspectival perception and phantom pains

Phantom pains depend on perspective and perception. Scholars and policymakers are typical storytellers of the phantom welfare state narratives. They see and feel a welfare state through these stories – even though the stories often compete with one another. Scholars concur on the tension between federalism and a welfare state. Obinger et al. identify the paradox:

> At first glance, the institutional arrangements of contemporary federalism and welfare states seem to fulfill antithetical functions. Federalism is an institutional device designed to secure unity by allowing a certain degree of diversity, whereas the primary goal of the welfare state is normally to enhance equal social rights for all citizens. Federalism and the welfare state thus seem to be at the opposite ends of the diversity-uniformity continuum.[34]

Is a subnational welfare state a welfare state at all?[35] Do countries have welfare *states*, rather than a welfare state? Strong support of social citizenship by a central government is undermined if contingent on location within a nation-state; social citizenship is also undermined if administrators and policymakers systematically subject groups to surveillance, domination and exclusion.

I argue, however, the question of whether federalism undermines a welfare state definition is the wrong question to ask. Rather, federalism provides a useful lens, highlighting two difficulties of welfare state delineation: (1) bottom-up welfare state experiences (governors versus governed) and (2) distinctions specified in Dorothy Roberts's epigraph about welfare state "citizens and subjects."[36]

Subnational welfare states?

Federalism has played an ongoing role in maintaining white supremacy and settler colonialism in the United States. Any discussion of "devolution" of federal programs, such as AFDC/TANF (Temporary Assistance for Needy Families), requires recognition of this reality.[37] In this section, however, I argue the only plausible way to conceptualize a welfare state in the United States is to name it welfare states.[38] Even then, however, the definition fails because federal, state and local governments[39] are rooted in white supremacy and settler colonialism.[40] Even without this reality, significant variation between types of state (sub-national) and county policies as well as implementation would render them multiple entities as opposed to a uniform national welfare state.

From the perspective of "the people," or the governed, I examine the importance of a state-level analysis in three ways. First, I undertake a snapshot comparison of state welfare department programmes of the New Deal with those of contemporary Washington State.[41] While not easily comparable on a one-to-one basis, I note the contrast between types and numbers of state-administered social-service programmes.

Second, note the sheer number of department "clients" in Washington State. In 1938, using the same comparative programme data (outlined in Table 5.1), 25% of the state population were State Department of Social Security "clients."[42] In 2015, however, the Department of Social and Health Services (DSHS) reported that *over 40% of state residents were clients of the department.*[43] Regardless of quibbles about date or programme comparability, 40% of the state's population is significant. On the other hand, I argue it is difficult to envision that a majority of Washington State residents might identify themselves as clients, beneficiaries or subjects of a "welfare state" if asked directly.

This leads to the third point about a bottom-up approach: whether an individual experiences a programme as controlling and/or beneficial, will they (a) either know if this is a state-administered or state-funded programme – as opposed to one funded by the federal government – or (b) really care one way or another, even if they know the source?[44] And really, why should they care? This is not a flippant question – the existence of a phantom welfare state depends on it. From this perspective, the importance of a centralised welfare state as a precondition for a welfare state is null and void.[45] This matters for public officials, administrators and social movements, but matters little on an everyday level.

Racial contracts and white democracy

Racial citizenship is another sign of a phantom welfare state. If scholars agree that some degree of uniformity or coherence defines a welfare state – regardless of its origin or purpose – then the US is indeed a phantom welfare state. The US has always been a settler colonial state, as well as a state based on Charles Mills's racial contract: "But the peculiar contract to which I am referring, though based on the social contract tradition that has been central to Western political theory, is not a contract between everybody ('we the people') but between just the people who count, the people who really are people ('we the white people')."[46] The only alternative would be to call the US welfare state a white settler welfare state, modifying slightly the title of Deborah E. Ward's book, *The White Welfare State.*[47] This still implies, however, there might be some other welfare state in the future – if we just made it less discriminatory.[48] Even here, however, the problem is that the hidden welfare state then becomes the social-control state – because people of colour may experience as surveillance and control the same programmes that white people may experience as beneficial in some way.

This point holds true regardless of the origin or purpose story. In other words, if the purpose of a welfare state is to promote full citizenship, then it fails by definition if groups of people are excluded from this very definition of

Table 5.1 Comparison of state-administered "social service" programmes, Washington State

SDSS Programmes, 1938, Washington State	Department of Social and Health Services, 2015
Children's Programmes Blind Assistance Old Age Assistance Aid to Unemployables: General Public Assistance Care in County Farms, Hospitals & Sanatoria Aid to Employables: General Public Assistance	**Ageing and Long-Term Support** Adult Family Homes Adult Residential Care Assisted Living Comprehensive Assessments & Case Mgt In-Home Services Nursing Facilities Additional Services
Joint or Other Authority Programmes County Soldier's and Sailor's Indigent Fund Care in State Institutions Persons Dependent on FWP Security Wages Persons Dependent on Farm Security Administration Emergency Grants Civilian Conservation Corps Enrollees	**Substance Use Disorder Services** Assessments – General Detoxification Opiate Substitution Treatment Outpatient Treatment Residential Treatment Additional Services
	Children's Services Adoption Services Case Mgt Adoption Support Services Behavioural Rehabilitation Services Child & Family Welfare Services Case Mgt Child Care Services Child Protective Services (CPS) Case Mgt DLR Child Protective Services Case Mgt Family-Focused Services Family Reconciliation Services Family Voluntary Services Case Mgt Foster Care Placement Services Foster Care Support Services Other Intensive Services Additional Services
	Developmental Disability Services Employment and Day Programmes Field Services Individual and Family Services Other Community Services Personal Care Services Professional Services Residential Habilitation Centers & Nursing Facilities Residential Programmes State Operated Living Alternatives

Economic Services
Aged, Blind, or Disabled Assistance
Basic Food Programme
Child Support Services
Consolidated Emergency Assistance
  Programme
Diversion Cash Assistance
Pregnant Women Assistance
Supplemental Security Income-State
TANF and State Family Assistance
Working Connections Child Care
Additional Services

Juvenile Rehabilitation
Community Placement
Dispositional Alternatives
Parole
Institutions, Youth Camps & Basic Training

Mental Health Services
Children's Long-Term Inpatient Programmes
Community Hospital
Crisis Services
Evaluation and Treatment
Other Outpatient
State Hospitals

Vocational Rehabilitation
Medical and Psychological Services
Placement Support
Support Services
Training, Education, and Supplies
Vocational Assessments (Job Skills)
Vocational Rehabilitation Case Mgt

---

citizenship, by design. If we consider Joel Olson's analysis of "white democracy" in the United States, then the problem of any welfare state-citizenship linkage becomes clear:

> [T]he foundation of the American racial order is a *cross-class alliance* between the dominant class and one section of the working class ... This alliance, DuBois argues, produces two "worlds" of race, the white and the dark worlds. It results in a peculiar kind of democracy, a *Herrenfolk* democracy, in which the white world enjoys democratic rights and political equality while the dark world is subjected to the tyranny of the white majority.[49]

Any welfare state definition also fails because of the history of the US "welfare state" actively *denigrating* forms of citizenship. Consider welfare state participation in the systematic kidnapping of Indigenous children from their homes. If Indigenous peoples were considered ostensible "citizens" from 1924 forwards, then the implementation of genocidal "child welfare" removal programmes through the welfare state further demeans the idea of Indigenous citizenship.[50] This is not only a matter of exclusion. It is actually *inclusion* for the purposes of surveillance and control, which communicate a further denigration of status by the state.

Neoliberal crises

Myths about neoliberal language and crises mark the final signs of a phantom welfare state. The phantom welfare state feeds on the idea that neoliberalism has fundamentally changed or undermined a welfare state. While I cannot dispute the realities of retrenchment, I ask how our view of the welfare state shifts if we recognize: (1) the welfare state had neoliberal principles since its inception and (2) it has always experienced (perceived) crisis and scandal. These are big claims. I limit my argument to Washington State as a case study. Historians disagree about the degree to which the state was a progressive leader in implementation of the federal welfare state.[51] Nevertheless, significant early adoption of New Deal policies make it a useful state for my focus, along with the fact that it is a mid-to-large state in terms of population.[52]

Neoliberal principles

One would expect the mission of a Department of Public Welfare/Social Security would vary over the course of almost eighty years. I find remarkable similarity across time, however, in Washington State. This does not mean that neoliberalism does not exist, but rather that our nostalgic idea about a time before neoliberalism is misguided.

In 1938, Director Charles F. Ernst submitted a department annual report. In the conclusion, he identified recommendations based on internal department feedback, titled "Looking Ahead":

1. Applicants must try to help themselves.
2. Ask Advisory Committees to Stimulate Jobs and Community Responsibility.
3. Relatives Must Help.
4. County Commissioners Will Support Their Workers.
5. Human Needs Present Individual Problems and Must Therefore Be Treated Individually.[53]

In 2017, the mission and vision of various subunits of the Department of Social and Health Services (DSHS; the current equivalent of the 1938 Department of Social Security) included the following:

Rehabilitation Administration

Mission: To transform lives by creating pathways to self-sufficiency through effective rehabilitation services and meaningful partnerships.
Vision: Youth and adults succeed in rehabilitation with the support of an engaged community.[54]

Developmental Disabilities Administration
Mission: Transforming lives by providing support and fostering partnerships that empower people to live the lives they want.
Vision:

- Support individuals
- Continually improving supports
- Individualizing supports
- Building support plans based on the needs and
- Engaging individuals, families[55]

The 1938 and 2017 similarities are striking. In the 1938 report, one element of the department's mission was to "substitute a modern concept of Social Security for an outmoded attitude of poor relief to paupers." Director Ernst argued that unlike Elizabethan or colonial poor law, Social Security legislation emphasized "two factors, rehabilitation and prevention." He elaborated later in the paragraph:

> With our new emphasis *on prevention and rehabilitation*, however, we have come to look upon an individual in such circumstances as someone who not only needs immediate assistance, but who needs more opportunities which, in themselves, would assist him to be self-supporting. Lack of education and training, inadequate medical care, inadequate home environment, etc. have all proved to be contributing factors in making a person dependent.[56]

In 2017, the DSHS mission to "transform lives" offers this vision: "(1) people are healthy; (2) people are safe; (3) people are supported; and (4) taxpayer resources are guarded."[57] The last goal may strike the reader as uniquely recent, and as a hallmark of the retrenchment of the welfare state. While I can hardly argue that it is *not* a hallmark of retrenchment, I can argue that a similar state of affairs already existed or emerged in 1938.[58] Moreover, lest the reader object that I glossed over other periods as non-neoliberal eras in Washington State, consider the corporate rhetoric of Washington State Department of Social Security Director Roderic Olzendam's speech to county welfare administrators in 1949:

> What is the corporation [the department] doing? We have 148,000 people on our rolls ... Now, what are the dividends? Well, it seems to me that the dividends can be measured in what we are doing to help the native people of Washington, the people who are unfortunate for various reasons and who need help. We have been told by the stockholders that our job is to pay dividends by the expenditure of $206,000,000 to bring about better social conditions in this state.[59]

While this is hardly definitive evidence to call into question the concept of neoliberalism – or at least a chronology of it – this excerpt, along with other archival files, demonstrate welfare administrators' sensitivity to market-based language in maintaining welfare state structures, as well as a sense of perpetual crisis.

New crises?

A conventional history of the welfare state – as a grand narrative rather than a detailed history – implies a "Golden Age" welfare state either in time or place.[60] This myth undergirds the entire concept of a phantom welfare state because it implies a time or place when the welfare state was not in crisis.[61] In the United States, we have collective images of scandal-ridden agencies, as well as attendant stereotypical baggage about welfare state "clients." I do not argue these stereotypes do not exist now, but rather question *when* they emerged.

In 1940, a Thurston County Grand Jury investigated the State Department of Social Security (SDSS). In a memo to SDSS, Director Ernst detailed the Grand Jury's substantive findings which included charges of: "unwarranted" "over-expenditure" of millions of dollars; inappropriate influence of professional relief workers; diversion of funds away from relief purposes; "negligence and discrimination in the administration of the state Social Security Acts"; and "financial irregularities."[62] The Grand Jury also offered their own welfare state "recipient" stereotypes: "Food vouchers disclosed that some recipients were granted turkeys, expensive canned goods, beer and other luxury items." In 1949, at an internal department conference involving all state and local officials, participants discussed "welfare chiselers," along with racial stereotypes about recipients of public assistance. Thus, the internal as well as external perception of the department itself was, from its inception, hardly rosy, from the perspective of either the left or the right.

The phantom lives

Why does a phantom welfare state persist? While beyond the scope of this chapter, I speculate about the political purpose of such a state. Before this, however, I acknowledge two realities about US welfare state purpose and history.

The first reality concerns the results of an ostensible welfare state. In *Red Tape: Bureaucracy, Structural Violence and Poverty in India*, Akhil Gupta asks, "Why has a state whose proclaimed motive is to foster development failed to help the large number of people who still live in dire poverty?"[63] Gupta argues that poverty-related "excess deaths" number two million annually in India, which "overshadows the loss of human life resulting from all natural disasters globally."[64] Using related measurements, public health researchers found 728,200 deaths linked to "social factors" in the United States (2000), compared to 192,898 deaths due to the leading official cause of death, "acute myocardial infarction."[65] The US federal welfare state turned sixty-five years old in 2000. Poverty was the leading cause of death in the richest country on the planet. Surely this indicates welfare state failure or non-existence, contingent on different phantom welfare narratives.[66]

Washington State offers a state-level historical perspective. Community-based solutions to deprivation and capitalism emerged outside of state apparatuses in the 1930s. State responses to the Depression in the form of poor "relief" co-opted or shut down emerging community-based cooperative programmes.[67]

Racial implications

The phantom welfare state persists, I argue, because the word "welfare" itself – perhaps the most racially/racist maligned social policy ever created in US history – is a stand-in for the entire welfare state. Indeed, explanations for a relatively weak US welfare state couched in terms of values of individualism and private property ("American exceptionalism") crumble in the face of a racial analysis of the development of these sets of programmes.[68] Not only does a racial/gendered[69] analysis challenge American exceptionalism theories, but it also explains why the programmes developed as they did. Neubeck and Cazenave (2001) argue that *welfare racism*[70] plays a key role in *maintaining* state structures of white supremacy over time:

> The *racial state* – operating within the context of a racialized social system – has more often than not historically functioned as the *political arm of white racial hegemony*. Its policies have helped to protect and reinforce systemic inequalities along the lines of skin colour, both during the United States' long-term history of outright white supremacy and on into the contemporary period, when there is much denial on the part of European Americans that racism is any longer a serious social problem.[71]

Beyond welfare racism's administrative implications, we are left with the fact that because the word "welfare" itself is so heavily racially coded, it is hard to even argue that it is coded anymore. It is a "dog whistle" appeal to white people to makes them feel part of a democratic citizenry that is morally and culturally superior to people of colour.[72] In a 2016 Kaiser Family Foundation/CNN poll, 62% of white working-class respondents believed the federal government should receive all or most of the blame for "economic problems facing the working class." In that same poll, 57% of white working-class respondents reported their household receiving at least one of the following benefits in the past year: "Food assistance, Medicaid, unemployment, government assistance with utility bills or housing, government disability, Social Security, or Medicare." The majority of these named programmes are federal government programmes, even if they are jointly administered by the states. In the case of white college graduates, 48% agreed that the federal government should receive all or most of the blame for the economic situation of the working class. Though this percentage is much lower than the white working class itself, it is still a significant percentage – especially as 43% of these white college graduates' households received government benefits in the past year.[73]

We can see how the psychological wages of whiteness are supported by a phantom welfare state.[74] As we live in a white democracy or a racial contract system, the welfare state plays a pivotal role – as an image, not a fact – not only in maintaining systems of social control against people of colour, but as an ideological construct that appeals to white citizenry in both broad and specific class-based senses.[75] Call it a diversion, smoke screen, racial project or racial spectacle.[76] It is an old story, one that is a mind-numbingly repetitive and painful. Stretching back to the aftermath of Bacon's Rebellion in 1676, we can see the formation of white-settler democracy and the creation of internal division and conflict over the genocide and exclusion of people of colour as the central diversionary thread that motivates this conflict.[77] The phantom welfare state is a lurking, unexplored part of this long racial and colonial history.

Conclusion

The role of the left and right critiques of the welfare state – with the left arguing that it is too weak while the right complains that it is too big – surely play a central role in perpetuating the fiction of a welfare state. This fictive state creates the collective sensation that it is part of the governing apparatus of a nation state and has origin and purpose stories that accompany it. For many left scholars, the welfare state is a laudable goal to defend because we think it exists, or should exist. We want to wish it into existence in order to defend it. I share the concern, especially in an era of explicit and open political absurdity and violence in the United States, about immediate survival needs. This course of defence of something that has never actually existed – or at least not as anything other than a white-settler welfare state – should not prevent us from asking different types of scholarly and political questions. Indeed, it is more urgent than ever.

Notes

1 Thank you to Angelique M. Davis for her feedback and support in writing this chapter. Morgan Kimball provided tremendous research support throughout this project, including the content analysis of speeches. Thanks also to participants in the "Whose Welfare?" Workshop, most especially Monika Baár, Christine Bylund, Sandrine Kott and Paul van Trigt.
2 To be clear, I count myself among these scholars.
3 Daniel D. Huff and David A. Johnson, "Phantom Welfare: Public Relief for Corporate America," *Social Work* 38, no. 3 (1993): 311–316, uses "phantom welfare" to mean corporate welfare.
4 OED Online, s.v. "phantom," June 2017, Oxford University Press, accessed 22 June 2017, www.oed.com/view/Entry/142204?redirectedFrom=phantom+limb.
5 I argue the absence of the suffix "state" for groups of policies – other than the shadow state or security state – makes it more vulnerable to attack.
6 Suzanne Mettler, *Dividing Citizens: Gender and Federalism in New Deal Public Policy* (Ithaca: Cornell University, 1998); Kenneth J. Neubeck and Noel A. Cazenave, *Welfare Racism: Playing the Race Card against America's Poor* (New York: Routledge, 2001); Kiran Klaus Patel, *The New Deal: A Global History* (Princeton: Princeton University

Press, 2016); Jill Quadagno, *The Color of Welfare: How Racism Undermined the War on Poverty* (New York: Oxford University Press 1995); Social Security Act, Public law 74-271 49 STAT 620 (1935), accessed 9 December 2017, www.ssa.gov/history/35act.html#TITLE X.
7 Patel, *The New Deal*, 50.
8 Andreas M. Kazamias, "Spencer and the Welfare State," *History of Education Quarterly* 6, no. 2 (1966): 73–95; T.H. Marshall, "The Welfare State: A Sociological Interpretation," *European Journal of Sociology* 2, no. 2 (1961): 284–300; Daniel Wincott, "Social Policy and Social Citizenship: Britain's Welfare States," *Publius* 36, no. 1 (2006): 169–188; Daniel Wincott, "Images of Welfare in Law and Society: The British Welfare State in Comparative Perspective," *Journal of Law and Society* 38, no. 3 (2011): 343–375.
9 Wincott, "Images of Welfare in Law and Society, " 348.
10 José Harris, *William Beveridge: A Biography* (Oxford: Clarendon, 1997), 452.
11 Thank you to the American Presidency Project at the University of California, Santa Barbara.
12 The reason for this focus is that there is little indication in scholarly literature that policymakers favour the term themselves, even if they support the idea of the welfare state or its subsidiary programmes. Indeed, scholars themselves seem to be the ones most interested in the terminology, even if community organizers, NGOs and policymakers are concerned with the substantive effects.
13 Gøsta Esping-Anderson's conservative, liberal and social democratic welfare state regimes is helpful, but only to re-emphasize the primary point of phantom welfare states – an elusive encompassing welfare state definition. See Gøsta Esping-Anderson, *Three Worlds of Welfare Capitalism* (Princeton: Princeton University Press, 1990), 3.
14 OED Online, s.v. "welfare state," June 2017, Oxford University Press, accessed 22 June 2017, www.oed.com/view/Entry/226969?redirectedFrom=welfare+state+.
15 Asa Briggs, "The Welfare State in Historical Perspective," *European Journal of Sociology* 2, no. 2 (1961): 228. Emphasis added.
16 Christopher Howard, "The Hidden Side of the American Welfare State," *Political Science Quarterly* 108, no. 3 (1993): 411.
17 Briggs, "The Welfare State in Historical Perspective," 228.
18 Kazamias, "Spencer and the Welfare State," 73–74.
19 Sandrine Kott, "Der Sozialstaat," in *Deutsche Erinnerungsorte II*, ed. Etienne François and Hagen Schulze (Munchen: C.H. Beck, 2009), 486.
20 Wincott, "Social Policy and Social Citizenship," 83.
21 Mark Neocleous, "Social Police and the Mechanisms of Prevention: Patrick Colquhoun and the Condition of Poverty," *The British Journal of Criminology* 40, no. 4 (2000): 710–726; Simon Hallsworth and John Lea, "Reconstructing Leviathan: Emerging Contours of the Security State," *Theoretical Criminology* 15, no. 2 (2011): 141–157.
22 Neocleous, "Social Police and the Mechanisms of Prevention," 721.
23 Hallsworth and Lea, "Reconstructing Leviathan," 144.
24 Stephen Baskerville, "From Welfare State to Police State," *The Independent Review* 12, no. 3 (2008): 402.
25 Briggs, "The Welfare State in Historical Perspective," 227.
26 Frances Fox Piven and Richard A. Cloward, *Regulating the Poor: The Functions of Public Welfare* (New York: Vintage Books, 1971), xv.
27 Howard, "The Hidden Side of the American Welfare State," 405.
28 Ibid., 404. Emphasis added.
29 Ibid., 416.
30 State programmes can expand social rights/citizenship while also being a method of social control. Consider the example of a driver's license.
31 Martin Gilens, *Why Americans Hate Welfare: Race, Media, and the Politics of Antipoverty Policy* (Chicago: University of Chicago Press, 2000), 15.

32 Ibid., 15–16.
33 The submerged state is "existing policies that lay beneath the surface of US market institutions within the federal tax system." Suzanne Mettler, *The Submerged State: How Invisible Government Policies Undermine American Democracy* (Chicago: University of Chicago Press, 2011), 4.
34 Herbert Obinger, Stephan Leibfried, and Francis G. Castles, *Federalism and the Welfare State: New World and European Experiences* (Cambridge: Cambridge University Press, 2005), 2.
35 "'[O]ne of the very few areas of unanimity in the literature' with which 'writers from all the main competing explanatory paradigms' agree, notes Frank Castles, is 'that federal institutions are inimical to high levels of social spending.'" Wincott, "Social Policy and Social Citizenship," 169.
36 Dorothy E. Roberts, "Welfare and the Problem of Black Citizenship," *Yale Law Journal* 105 (1996): 1567.
37 Brown notes pervasive racial discrimination in AFDC in the 1930s. Michael K. Brown, "Ghettos, Fiscal Federalism and Welfare Reform," in *Race and the Politics of Welfare Reform*, ed. Sanford F. Schram, Joe Soss and Richard C. Fording (Ann Arbor: The University of Michigan Press, 2004), 48.
38 Lest the reader believe this means there are only 50 welfare states, the number may run well into the hundreds once we consider states that have county-based programmes, tribal governments, as well as other non-state colonial entities such as Puerto Rico. A central function of state government is to promulgate a system of public education, so by any definitional criteria, states already have greater responsibilities for welfare state provision than the federal government.
39 I focus here on the United States. My argument does not preclude other racism-based welfare states elsewhere in the world. Quite the contrary. Consider Kitschelt and McGann's identification of "welfare chauvinism" where "political entrepreneurs emphasise racist and authoritarian slogans but studiously stay away from an admiration of market-liberal capitalism." Herbert Kitschelt and Anthony J. McGann, *The Radical Right in Western Europe: A Comparative Analysis* (Ann Arbor: The University of Michigan Press, 1997), 22.
40 White supremacy is a "historically based, institutionally perpetuated system of exploitation and oppression of continents, nations and peoples of color by white peoples and nations of the European continent; for the purpose of establishing, maintaining and defending a system of wealth, power and privilege." Mickey Ellinger and Sharon Martinas, "The Culture of White Supremacy," Challenging White Supremacy Workshop (1994), accessed 16 December 2016, http://whgbetc.com/mind/culture-white-sup.html; Evelyn Nakano Glenn. "Settler Colonialism as Structure: A Framework for Comparative Studies of US Race and Gender Formation," *Sociology of Race and Ethnicity* 1, no. 1 (2015): 52–72; Andrea Smith, "Indegeneity, Settler Colonialism, White Supremacy," in *Racial Formation in the Twenty-First Century,* ed. Daniel Martinez HoSang, Oneka LaBennett, and Laura Pulido (Berkeley: University of California Press, 2012).
41 Though I focus on one state, there are no indications that this state – Washington State – is unique for the purposes of the following discussion.
42 State Department of Social Security, "Annual Report: Persons Dependent on Some Form of Public Assistance in the State of Washington, 1938," box A1, folder 21, Director's Files, 1933–1953, Washington State Department of Public Welfare, Washington State Archives, Olympia, Washington. This included the jointly administered federal WPA and CCC.
43 State Department of Social Security, Annual Report 1938.
44 Mettler cites a quote popularized in the media at the time of President Obama's health care plan debate: "At a gathering in Simpsonville, South Carolina, in August 2009, one man told Republican Representative Robert Inglis, 'Keep your government hands off my Medicare.'" Mettler, *The Submerged State*, 2.

45 I do not argue that there are welfare states either, for the same reasons it does not exist at the federal level – racial discrimination runs rampant with local discretion as well. Brown, "Ghettos, Fiscal Federalism and Welfare Reform." The point is individuals have a higher probability of direct contact at the state rather than federal level.
46 Charles W. Mills, *The Racial Contract* (Ithaca: Cornell University Press, 1997), 3. It is important to note that Mills's description of a racial contract is global in character.
47 Deborah E. Ward, *The White Welfare State: The Racialization of U.S. Welfare Policy* (Ann Arbor: The University of Michigan Press, 2005).
48 Even overarching changes to federal policy signal increasing benefits to white middle-class voters: "Changes in the racial composition of poor women remaining on the rolls expose the political trap at the heart of new welfare policy. In many states whites have left the rolls faster than blacks. The proportion of white families in TANF sharply dropped to 31 percent of all cases; racial minorities now account for over two-thirds. Meanwhile, states have amassed financial windfalls due to the rapid decline in caseloads and fixed federal financing. Most states are either hoarding this money or passing it on to white middle-class voters in the form of tax cuts and other subsidies." Brown, "Ghettos, Fiscal Federalism, and Welfare Reform," 48.
49 Joel Olson, *The Abolition of White Democracy* (Minneapolis: University of Minnesota Press, 2004), xxiv.
50 Indian Citizenship Act, Public Law 68-175, 43 STAT 253 (1924); Roxanne Dunbar-Ortiz, *An Indigenous People's History of the United States* (Boston: Beacon Press, 2014).
51 Bruce Blumell, *The Development of Public Assistance in the State of Washington during the Great Depression* (New York: Garland Publishing, 1984).
52 According to the US Census, Washington State's population was 1.5 million people in 1930 and 6.7 million in 2010.
53 Charles F. Ernst, "Report of the Department of Social Security," June 1938, box A1, folder 21, Director's Files, 1933–1953, Washington State Department of Public Welfare, Washington State Archives, Olympia, Washington.
54 Rehabilitation Administration, Washington State Department of Social and Health Services, "Strategic Plan: 2015–2017," accessed 2 June 2017, www.dshs.wa.gov/sites/default/files/SESA/spmrw/documents/current/Strategic%20Plans/RA.pdf.
55 Developmental Disabilities Administration, Washington State Department of Social and Health Services, "Strategic Plan: 2015–2017," accessed 2 June 2017, www.dshs.wa.gov/sites/default/files/SESA/spmrw/documents/current/Strategic%20Plans/DDA.pdf.
56 Ernst, "Report of the Department of Social Security."
57 Washington State Department of Social and Health Services, "Mission, Vision and Values," accessed 2 June 2017, www.dshs.wa.gov/strategic-planning/mission-vision-and-values.
58 Blumell reports Director Ernst's efforts to cut state department expenditures, even in 1936. Blumell, *The Development of Public Assistance*, 309.
59 County Administrator's Conference, Spirit Lake, June 23, 1949, box A5, folder 10, Director's Files, 1933–1953, Washington State Department of Public Welfare, Washington State Archives, Olympia, Washington, p. 14.
60 Wincott, "Images of Welfare in Law and Society."
61 Slavoj Žižek argues that the European welfare state has entered permanent crisis mode: "after decades of the welfare state, when cutbacks were relatively limited and came with the promise that things would soon return to normal, we are now entering a period in which a kind of economic state of emergency is becoming permanent: turning into a constant, a way of life." Slavoj Žižek, "A Permanent Economic Emergency," *New Left Review* 64, no. 1 (2010): 86, accessed 26 December 2016, https://newleftreview.org/II/64/slavoj-zizek-a-permanent-economic-emergency.

62 Charles F. Ernst, "Memo," January 23, 1940, box A1, folder 27, Director's Files, 1933–1953, Washington State Department of Public Welfare, Washington State Archives, Olympia, Washington.
63 Akhil Gupta, *Red Tape: Bureaucracy, Structural Violence and Poverty in India* (Durham, NC, and London: Duke University Press, 2012), 3.
64 Ibid., 5.
65 Sandro Galea, Melissa Tracy, Katherine J. Hoggatt, Charles DiMaggio and Adam Karpati, "Estimated Deaths Attributable to Social Factors in the United States," *American Journal of Public Health* 101, no. 8 (2011): 1462.
66 I do not argue for cuts to what passes as "benefits," because what little the poor can use to survive should not be denied them.
67 Blumell, *The Development of Public Assistance*.
68 Neubeck and Cazenave, *Welfare Racism*; Jill Quadagno, *The Color of Welfare: How Racism Undermined the War on Poverty* (New York: Oxford University Press, 1995).
69 Neubeck and Cazenave are careful to include an intersectional analysis of racist/sexist constructs of welfare state policies.
70 "[T]he organization of racialized public assistance attitudes, policy making, and administrative practices." Neubeck and Cazenave, *Welfare Racism*, 36.
71 Ibid., 23.
72 Ian Haney-López, *Dog Whistle Politics: How Coded Racial Appeals Have Reinvented Racism and the Wrecked Middle Class* (New York: Oxford University Press, 2014).
73 Kaiser Family Foundation/CNN. "Kaiser Family Foundation/CNN Working-Class Whites Poll," 20 September 2016, prepared by Liz Hamel, Elise Sugarman, and Mollyann Brodie, accessed 2 June 2017, http://files.kff.org/attachment/Report-Kaiser-Family-Foundation-CNN-Working-Class-Whites-Poll .
74 W.E.B. Du Bois, *Black Reconstruction in America: Toward a History of the Part Which Black Folk Played in the Attempt to Reconstruct Democracy in America, 1860–1880* (New Brunswick: Transaction Publishers, [1935] 2014).
75 Olson, *The Abolition of White Democracy*; Mills, *The Racial Contract*.
76 Michael Omi and Howard Winant, *Racial Formation in the United States*, 3rd ed. (New York: Routledge, [1986] 2014); Angelique M. Davis and Rose Ernst, "Racial Spectacles: Promoting a Colorblind Agenda through Direct Democracy," *Studies in Law, Politics and Society* 55 (2011): 133–171.
77 The Virginia white-planter class offered poor whites a "racial bribe" in the aftermath of this rebellion: "[they] extended special privileges to poor whites in an effort to drive a wedge between them and black slaves. White servants were allowed to police slaves through slave patrols and militias, and barriers were created so that free labor would not be placed in competition with slave labor." Michelle Alexander, *The New Jim Crow: Mass Incarceration in the Age of Colorblindness* (New York: New Press, 2010), 25.

6 Managing the transition from war to peace

Post-war citizenship-based welfare in Italy and France, 1944–1947

Giacomo Canepa

Introduction

The most relevant comparative studies on the impact of war on the patterns and pathways of Welfare State development have emphasized the importance of demobilization, welfare benefits and educational programmes for veterans and refugees among the long-term policy repercussions of the World Wars.[1] The relations between post-war policies, party politics and groups of victims, such as widows, orphans, disabled veterans and the unemployed, have been examined in depth especially for the post-WWI era. By contrast, the historiography on the aftermath of WWII has identified the role of Communist parties, the European-wide process of constitution-making, the integration of the labour movement into the active life of the state and a powerful commitment to welfare as the most important aspects of the post-war political transitions of 1945.[2] The post-war period, notably the aftermath of the war, is a key moment in the construction of European welfare states: on the one hand, military occupations, the circulation and propaganda of foreign models, and the presence on the ground of international organizations allowed for the entanglement of national and international actors and policies; on the other hand, the widespread awareness of the inadequacies of the collapsed existing systems and the social crisis created by the war called for reforms.

The aim of this chapter is to investigate the impact of the measures directed at categories of recipients other than wage earners, such as marginalized war-torn groups, on the systems of social protection. How did post-war needs impact existing welfare states? I will therefore seek to connect the reintegration of veterans and refugees into society and the labour market with the transformations of the Welfare State, by comparing post-war assistance in two European countries, France and Italy. I will examine Italian and French governmental structures devised to manage the transition from war to peace during the "post-war moment": the Commissariat, and later the Ministère des Prisonniers, déportés et réfugiés (Ministry for prisoners, deportees and refugees, MPDR, November 1943–November 1945), and its Italian counterpart, the Ministero per l'assistenza post-bellica (Ministry for Postwar Assistance, June 1945–February 1947).

Both these administrations, so far ignored by the historiography of the Welfare State, dealt with post-war assistance to all sorts of veterans, ex-deportees and "national" refugees resulting from wartime exoduses, massive civil destruction, and, in the Italian context, from the loss of its colonial empire and the redefinition of its borders. The social assistance measures directed at these groups – encompassing around 2.1 million prisoners, deportees and forced labourers, and 2.5 million civilians, above all refugees, in France (approximately 12% of the population); 4.7 million veterans and 3.3 million refugees and victims of the war in Italy (approximately 17% of the population) – marked the transition to a citizenship-based right and state-provided treatment. Poverty, destitution and displacement affected all social strata; the distinctions between the deserving and undeserving poor, and between workers and the economically marginalized, were increasingly blurred. The needs of these groups of war victims fell outside the existing welfare systems based on contributions and previous work activities. My analysis shows how social welfare was used to pacify citizens and how post-war emergencies acted to stimulate the development of the Welfare State and the framing of welfare provisions in terms of the entitlement of each citizen. I argue that the impact of war emergencies, far from being only a temporary economic burden for welfare systems, affected the process of construction of social rights and notably altered the meaning, the targets and the aims of social assistance.

Recent studies on the nexus warfare–welfare after WWI have shown how the fear of post-war social unrest as well as new pressures coming notably from veterans and war victims, forced the state to undertake extensive social reforms, in particular the adoption of unemployment insurance. The national "debt" of gratitude of the nation was to be paid not only through pensions, in accordance with the principle of compensation, but also through a public programme of economic protection and job reservation for disabled veterans.[3] Although this experimental legislation was cut down due to the deterioration of economic conditions during the 1920s, post-WWI disabled veterans' measures marked an important step in the development of the compensatory role of the state.[4]

After WWII, the unprecedented involvement of civilians in the conflict, the widespread violence, the challenge of assisting all the victims of war and the flows of internal refugees, as well as the disruption of governmental structures and the disintegration of social relations, stimulated state intervention and reforms of the existing systems of social protection. France and Italy offer interesting grounds for comparison because the two countries differed in international status, economic conditions and transition time frames. On the other hand, they shared some important aspects: Nazi occupation, the existence of collaborator and Allied-supported governments and a huge resistance movement, administrative traditions and customary state–society relationship. Both Italy and France were challenged by the reconstruction of democracy and the enlargement of citizenship capacities, which resulted in new post-war constitutions. Furthermore, in the 1940s both countries debated whether to reform their occupational insurance systems or introduce structural reforms based on universalist models.[5] The relationships between insurance and assistance systems, as well as the means of their financing, the categories of recipients and the levels of benefits, were at stake. How did policies towards veterans and war victims influence the broader development of the social protection systems? How did the resistances' vague commitments to change translate into a specific blueprint for social policy?

Through the analysis of the transformations of assistance systems and of post-war turning points in the development of welfare, this article deals in a critical way with Marshall's theorization of social rights: "the whole range from the right to a modicum economic welfare and security to the right to share to the full in the social heritage and to live the life of a civilized being according to the standards prevailing in the society."[6] According to Marshall, post-war European society added to traditional political and civic rights this third level of citizenship, following the Atlantic Charter motto of "freedom from want." The promise of the state to provide social protection represented a reward for wartime sacrifice and service, as well as an important cultural factor in stabilizing post-war societies. Marshall's definition was embedded within the British experience marked by the Beveridge Plan and in part by the Labour Reforms of 1945–1948. In continental Europe, the concepts of the Beveridge Plan were adapted to national discourses. Similar distortions affected the notion of social security, which appeared in 1935 in the USA and aimed to include different forms of contributory insurance, social assistance and other social services in a universal, comprehensive and egalitarian system.[7]

Marshall's heuristic definition did not comfortably fit the situation in France and Italy, where the social security systems, after some debate, finally rejected the principles of unity, homogeneity and universalism, which were at the core of the Beveridge Plan, because of corporatist reactions, pre-war policy legacies and different theoretical perspectives.[8] In France, policymakers Pierre Laroque and Alexandre Parodi planned to totally reform the social protection system by unifying the insurance schemes, by making the services uniform, by providing for the participation of recipients in the management of its services and, lastly, by extending them to the entire population. In Italy, two committees were set up in 1946 and 1947 to discuss the social safety net, the experiments underway in other European countries and possible reforms. But, in the end, the ambitious social security plan developed by Pierre Laroque in France failed, and in Italy the D'Aragona Commission, despite the great expectations for change, finally converted social security into the protection of professional revenues against specific social risks rather than an intervention providing a minimum income to the population.[9]

The analysis of the post-war turning point, characterized by the circulations of projects that promoted a shift from occupational towards universal systems and by the tensions between theoretical reflections, political decisions and grassroots dynamics of social groups, that ultimately nipped in the bud such a development, allows us to nuance the best-known Welfare State models. In post-war French and Italian insurance systems, the social rights of the occupants of work-based categories were recognized but not those of citizens as such. However, the transformations of public assistance systems – which promoted, by contrast, universalism – have rarely been put into this picture by the historiography. Assistance does not derive from contributions paid, as does insurance, but is an entitlement financed by taxation and based on human or social rights. It is precisely in this field that some elements of social rights based on citizenship were introduced.

In the view of French and Italian planners and leaders, assistance was supposed to disappear with the emergence of insurances.[10] The literature has often considered it as a remnant of the past, but, in fact, despite all expectations, assistance continued to represent an important item of public expenditures between the 1940s and the 1960s.[11] In association with the lack of coverage of the insurance systems, one of the causes of this permanence lay in the transformations that public assistance experienced mostly because of the post-war humanitarian crisis of prisoners of war (POWs), deportees and refugees. Existing systems of public relief were swamped by post-war needs, which overlapped with rising claims to social protection based on moral rights, caused by the unprecedented nature of the conflict that hit civilians as well as soldiers. The literature has underlined that these new claims for state protection from wartime violence and provisions were often politicized with the language of entitlements that preceded the attainment of any juridical standing.[12]

Given the wide scope of the issue, after providing some factual data on the two ministries, I will focus more specifically on the narrative of renewal and redressing that drove these non-permanent *administrations de mission* rather than on all the specific welfare measures adopted.[13] This formulation describes a public administrative body which is charged with a defined, circumscribed mission and provided with the specific competencies to manage the task and able to act in coordination with the classical ministries. This coordination is facilitated by establishing a link between the emergency post-war situations, broader welfare reforms, social rights and political participation. Treating the actors that framed this narrative and articulated the social contract of 1945 of rewarding popular patriotism with democracy and social justice, the chapter goes beyond a comparative model-based approach and looks at "border-crossing, international and global processes which interact with nationally construed social problems."[14] The striking similarities between the French and Italian administrations stemmed from bilateral French–Italian policy transfers. Yet, it is important to also take into account international actors and notably the United Nations Relief and Rehabilitation Administration (UNRRA), the first international organization created during the war to provide liberated countries with essential relief. UNRRA did not operate in support of veterans, deportees or national refugees within the French or the Italian boundaries. As part of the "global New Deal," however, UNRRA spread an idea of welfare that went well beyond mere relief and encompassed any action "for the personal rehabilitation of individuals requiring special help."[15] The focus on national administrations allows us to consider the articulation of rights in play between local, national and transnational spheres.

Repatriation in the context of recovery's ideology

The refusal of the French provisional governments to accept UNRRA intervention within its national boundaries is closely intertwined with the establishment, in November 1943, of the Commissariat des prisonniers, déportés, réfugiés (CPDR), that later, in the aftermath of the Liberation of Paris (after amalgamation with nine different Vichy administrative services). This body was to become a ministry under the same name (MPDR).[16] At that time the Comité Français de Libération nationale headed by De Gaulle was striving for international recognition. The Commissariat should be seen in the context of the preparation for the return and of the establishment of new state bodies aimed at reconstruction and of the reestablishment of French full national sovereignty.[17] In September 1943, Michel "Charette" Cailliau, De Gaulle's nephew, proposed to the Landing Commission, in charge of developing the measures to be taken upon the Liberation of France, the creation of a secretariat for prisoners and deportees, underlining their "political and military, current and future" importance.[18] Since the Vichy regime had turned prisoners into a cornerstone of its ideology of national redemption through sacrifice and closely intertwined their return with the development of its policy of collaboration, De Gaulle and the Commissioner of the Interior, the socialist André Philip, glimpsed the possibility of benefiting from studies already undertaken by Vichy government bodies and of winning the support of 1.5 million repatriates.[19] De Gaulle established a new office and raised it to the rank of commissioner for prisoners, deportees and refugees under the leadership of Henri Frenay, a former prisoner who founded the anti-communist resistance movement Combat.

Initially this administration was not involved in the development of social policies: humanitarian relief was delivered through private initiatives and the state had only the power to control, orient and coordinate them. However, the increasing role of the state was stimulated by a number of factors: first, the need to oppose Vichy's propaganda among POWs; and then, the presence of "international or foreign bodies interested in this action," that is the risk that UNRRA would take the repatriation of prisoners and refugees away from national governments.[20] De Gaulle wanted to demonstrate to the Allies the ability of the French to manage liberated areas and to eradicate the shame of Vichy collaboration. The French government, exhibiting a proud attitude of self-sufficiency, succeeded in avoiding foreign interference in the internal distribution of goods, while UNRRA kept the tasks of preventing epidemics, coordinating the activity of voluntary societies and organizing the repatriation of prisoners and deportees but only up to the national boundaries. Administering relief became a way to restore national prestige following the years of collaboration with Nazi occupation, and the CPDR engaged in the organization of an orderly, rapid and attentive return of POWs, political deportees and labour conscripts, as well as national refugees resulting from the evacuations of 1939–1940 and 1944, from air bombardments and from the German expulsions of Alsatians. Assistance for the victims of the war showcased the redistributive role of the state. It also spoke to the ideological dimension of the conflict and put into practice the programme of the Conseil National de la Resistance, which had included assistance to the victims of the war in a rather vague reform of the insurance system when imagining the social contract for peacetime.[21]

The CPDR did not want to limit its activities to the repatriation, but engaged in organizing a social policy for repatriates. Some proposals designed to mute, in the name of the commissioner, the words "prisoners, deportees, refugees" in "repatriation," that was considered as an activity "no longer only material, affectionate and charitable, but spiritual, political and economic," were rejected. In fact, Frenay looked at repatriation not merely as an organized transfer of populations, but as a national and political duty, which should have an effect on both the recipients of care and French society:

> Repatriation is not the sum of individual cases, but a nationwide exercise to allow as fast and as well as possible recovery of national economy, by bringing back to their places and to the course of business the citizens of both sexes displaced by the war, by ensuring or preparing their rehabilitation to national life.[22]

The fighting and suffering experienced both in camps and in occupied France had to be resolved and put to use in the name of national unity. This implied some administrative transformations: if Vichy had carefully differentiated the administrations for each category of recipients, after the Liberation of Paris the nine services already established by the Vichy regime were merged and managed as a whole. The staff of former Vichy services was partially purged, mainly in the higher echelons, and the appointments in the MPDR's local offices showed the circulation between the prisoners' political movement, resistance groups like Combat, and the public administration. Among the 8445 public servants working in MPDR, only 15% had formed part of the pre-existing wartime administrations, often belonging to the Movement of Prisoners, while former prisoners represented 35% of the male staff. In particular, the new leadership shared a common cultural background in resistance activity that was deemed to be necessary for the complex tasks required by the difficult repatriation operations. The composition of the staff caused some problems. This was especially the case when public servants claimed the right to demonstrate against the government alongside the other prisoners – but also made French officials reject the UNRRA approach based on psychological casework since, because of the divergent wartime experiences of French returnees and displaced persons, UNRRA's relief workers could not appreciate their sufferings.[23]

Only MPDR's public servants, coming from the camps or from the resistance, could use relief to reconcile the two sides of France, which had fought Nazism in the camps and in the woods. The aim of promoting social solidarity, through an interventionist state that encouraged public participation by developing decentralized services, was shared with the contemporaneous projects of reform of the insurance systems like that carried out by Laroque, as well as the will to address the non-economic dimensions of alienation and insecurity. Through the MPDR, this new generation of young public servants entered into public administration, where they brought to bear their previous experiences in the private sector and in resistance movements. They shared a certain impatience with formalistic legal logics and new concepts of governance, underlining the importance of the active participation of recipients, of building networks and of the search for a consensus in civil society. The sources and first-hand accounts unanimously reported administrative and financial disorganization. The MPDR, however, engaged in the elaboration of conceptual frameworks and bureaucratic labels that reflected the modernizing technocratic approach to relief, as well as pre-war ideas about large-scale state planning.[24]

The repatriation fostered the gradual expansion of social policies, even though Frenay thwarted the grander plans of socialists, aimed at including the whole population, and underlined that for state assistance to be effective it would have to deal only with repatriates and refugees. The new generation of public servants promoted a broader definition of poverty, which no longer took into account the principle of subsidiarity, namely the existence of other incomes within the family unit. Among the policies organized at the national level, the establishment of a "sanitary cordon" certainly responded to the necessity of avoiding epidemics and to the obsession with espionage. However, MPDR's mix of welfare and national pedagogy served to reconstruct the returnees' sentiment of belonging to a wider community, the nation. The project was closely linked with the political ambitions of Frenay himself, who in 1945 founded his own party, the Union socialiste et démocratique de la Résistance. The party's political programme aimed to give politics that moral dimension lost in the 1930s and to ensure the continuation of the social mixing that had characterized the Resistance movement, by combining the ideals of the French Revolution, of social Catholicism and of socialism. The MPDR had to foster the perpetuation of the atmosphere of rediscovered community that had characterized the Liberation, against the fragmentation of the social body caused by political clashes, and to stress the importance of a "moral economy of repatriation" culpably neglected in 1918.[25] For these reasons, each recipient had to be considered as a citizen. The definition of MPDR's recipients encompassed all the displaced victims of Nazi persecution, including forced labourers (identified as "labour deportees") and non-military foreigners denaturalized in previous years.

Facing the legacies of Mussolini's war

In Italy, the same process of standardization and unification of the categories of recipients represented one of the most important post-war structural changes in the social protection system. The economic difficulties of the end of the 1930s and the outbreak of WWII had irrevocably undermined the Italian system, which was disorganized, discretionary, based on the local level and characterized by the differentiation of benefits imposed by the fascist regime to distinguish each social group of recipients. As the end of the war approached, the return and reintegration of 4.5 million veterans, including 1.2 million POWs both under German and Allied control, became one of the most important concerns of the political class. Furthermore, in the long term, there were the problems of the demobilization of 200,000 partisans, and the Allied Control Commission repeatedly invited the Italian government to "establish a well-coordinated organization for the rehabilitation and welfare of the patriots," by underlining the political menace represented by unemployment. Finally, post-war social problems also encompassed several hundred thousand "national" refugees, considered ineligible for assistance by UNRRA, which took care only of nationals of countries which had joined the United Nations and victims of Nazism. National refugees were thus divided from foreign refugees who in their turn were excluded from Italian social protection.[26] In this respect, the state administrations reinforced the nationalism of the post-war period, and citizenship increasingly represented a dividing line in terms of access to social benefits.

In May 1944 an Italian high commissioner for refugees was first set up, followed by the creation of an office aimed at the reintegration of partisans and, in March 1945, of a high commissioner for veterans. Soon undermined by financial shortfalls and by the disruption of the public administration, at the end of the war they were replaced by a new social administration, the Ministry of Post-War Assistance (MAPB), which responded to the political priority of assisting resistance fighters and secondarily veterans and of reintegrating them into the economic system. For this reason, Emilio Lussu, a prominent member of the Partito d'Azione, a small liberal-socialist political party very active in resistance movements, was appointed as minister. The organizational structure of the MAPB, as in France, extended existing structures and ended up replicating the French approach. Italian planners appreciated French attention to the psychological aspects of the different categories of recipients and took from other national experiences the idea of improving through veterans' assistance the social infrastructure of the country. As in France, the Italian ministry had the obligation to recruit staff among the categories of recipients, considered as the vanguard of the nation. The department heads were former leaders of resistance groups and often members of the Partito d'Azione. This new generation of public administrators headed a large and enthusiastic but completely inexperienced staff of 6420 temporary officials, some of whom had gone directly from the Liberation days' fighting to the MAPB. The presence of the recipients inside the administration was designed to stimulate, in a logic of self-help, the cooperation of veterans' associations and their collaboration in the stability of the new democratic systems, by recreating the "union sacrée" of the Resistance movements: the associations must relieve MAPB's local officers of a significant part of the administrative burden. It followed that policies often emerged from the bargaining between the MAPB and the associations: for instance, MAPB was at the forefront of the efforts to give official and juridical recognition to resistance fighters. Public assistance was, however, given also to the 1940–1943 veterans, who had fought Mussolini's wars, because the aim of these policies was to respond to the problem of unemployment through income support and education and the vocational rehabilitation of veterans.

The officers of MAPB emphasized the political aspects, especially the management of the transition and the need to spread an updated concept of citizenship. This was based on social rights and duties and was expected to become able to bridge the gaps between individuals, civil society and the state created by the disintegration of state structures after the Armistice of 1943. The collapse of insurance systems made social assistance, financed by general taxation and by a special "fund of national solidarity," the markers of the direct commitment of the state to the well-being of its citizens. The MAPB, in that sense, represented the first national assistance institutional structure and replaced the traditional "public charity." The latter was managed by private, mostly Catholic, foundations and municipalities, controlled by the Ministry of Interior through prefects, which considered social protection as a matter of public order and not of welfare. A second innovation was that the MAPB established a language of social rights dependent on need and citizenship that replaced the arbitrary and the discretionary categories that had previously prevailed in the concept of "assistance to the poor." A list of provisions and subsidies was made mandatory on the national level in order to reduce local political constraints. A means-test continued to be a condition for entitlements, but it did not refer to the poverty standards: it was linked to supporting the basic needs of the family, even if the male breadwinners worked or had other assets in their place of origins. Provisions were continued after their return home in order to stimulate the rehabilitation of internal refugees.[27] Since the ideas of institutional renewal that shaped the MAPB's project could not rely on traditional administrative practice, the new generation of civil servants coming from the Resistance took into account the French, English and American experiences in managing the transition from war to peace. Despite the differences between France and Italy, and notably the high rates of unemployment, the experience of the MPDR taught Italian officers the need to not restrict post-war interventions to measures of private law and to place them at the core of a broader policy review aimed to culminate in the establishment of a social security system.[28] Furthermore, the reading of the French official records inspired MAPB officers to attach a brief statement of the reasons behind each measure adopted. Keeping citizens informed was deemed necessary to break an administrative culture marked by twenty years of fascism and to adapt the administrative language to the aim of the "construction, *toujours recommencée*, of a real democratic country."[29] Social assistance must have a pedagogical aim regarding the whole country, and in that sense the MAPB explicitly adopted the UNRRA concept of "rehabilitation," usually summed up in the motto of the organization "to help people to help themselves."[30]

From the experience of UNRRA, the MAPB drew attention to the problems of eligibility and to the definition of the categories of recipients, but also the idea that moral discomfort, and psychological and psycho-social problems were more urgent than material conditions.[31] Finally, the circulation of the US G.I. Bill, the most important package of post-war benefits for veterans in US history, showed the MAPB's administrative culture's admiration for New Deal policies, underlining the importance of demobilization politics in the planning of a state–society relationship:[32]

> [These provisions] require biological and psychiatric as well as political thinking, for to be effective they must enhance life first of all, rather than prestige and power. Perhaps the need is summed up in the words "social statesmanship" [...] What we do for the veteran [...] will set the pace for services and considerations for our whole population.[33]

The provisions of the G.I. Bill – subsidies, mortgage assistance, college education grants, housing and especially vocational training – represented also a public-sector model programme for more general and long-term ambitions, and outlined a "national policy of respect for the importance of the individual." These policies firstly dealt with the concerns that veterans, or ex-partisans, could represent seditious forces, like fascism after the WWI. MAPB's administrators stressed the importance of a cultural demobilization able to address the bellicose wartime representations of society, enemies and violence that had been part of total war. To disarm the fascist regime's rhetoric, it was necessary to grant assistance to all veterans and ex-partisans as citizens, even if they were able to work and needed only social reintegration. Citizenship, and not patriotic virtues or sufferings endured during the war, formed the basis for the entitlement.[34] The proposals of veterans' associations, which aimed to provide assistance to the soldiers who stood up during the conflict, were rejected. This was because it was impossible to make distinctions between combatants and non-combatants and any privileged condition was "unacceptable in a real democracy."[35] The problem of veterans boiled down to "the political education of Italians."[36] Through such assistance, the MAPB wanted to "remake Italians," providing them a moral re-education and contributing to promoting awareness of the rights and duties connected with democratic citizenship of which partisans were models. The MAPB thus played down any claims to a "moral economy of recognition," advocated by each veterans' association for their own, in favour of an approach not limited to the restoration of pre-war conditions but one that stressed social and individual development.

From "rehabilitation" to social services

In France, the abolition of the distinctions that at first differentiated provisions for each category of recipients paved the way to the elaboration of a set of social policies focusing on social and work reintegration for veterans, ex-partisans, internees, those incarcerated for political reasons, labour conscripts, refugees and victims.[37] Discriminating, in-kind distributions of goods gave way to subsidies, free health care, paid leaves, vocational training, student loans and student special programmes, discounts on taxes, facilities in family law, and assistance complements to the insurance system.

The right to some forms of social assistance was associated with citizenship, and this meant that any other parameter apart from need was removed, starting from Vichy's requirements regarding the (above all sexual) morality of recipients.[38] The role of private actors was reserved, with the claim that they could best respond to the diversity of individual distress and guarantee real reintegration into the national community. In both countries, the state refused to bear all the costs of social reintegration and encouraged the development of relief activities by veterans' associations or civil society.[39] The return was strictly linked to the patriotic rhetoric of recovery. Political deportees, for instance, embodied both resistance engagement and patriotic suffering that could ensure the redemption of "France's soul": their reception had to recreate the national community around new values. The traditional trust in private and mutual assistance acquired a discourse regarding political participation that re-adapted Leon Bourgeois's concept of solidarism.

This recurring topic in French history of welfare was linked to the new political contest and the necessity of freeing French people from the state of passiveness in which Vichy had confined them. According to Frenay, the task of social policy was to promote social solidarity and to bridge the gaps created not only by social conflicts but also by the war in French society. As in Laroque's broader projects, post-war social policies had therefore to stimulate an active citizenry and to provide citizens with a new sense of independence and self-worth, and to address the cultural and psychological causes of social unrest.[40]

Both the MAPB in Italy and the MPDR in France promoted through social policies for veterans a process of cultural demobilization and remobilization around new democratic values and specific patterns of national recovery. The main objectives of state intervention included prolonging the moral effort of resistance movements and promoting consensus with regard to the rising political systems. But this discourse about the development of civil society could have unintended implications. Financial shortfalls and the emphasis on moral aspects led governments to confer a large role on veterans' associations, thus integrating them into governmental action. The Italian Minister Emilio Lussu attempted to federate (rather than unify) the different associations of "patriots," including veterans of WWI in order to control and affect the politics of the associations, which in turn benefited from earmarks and political patronage.[41] In France, the same emphasis on participation was intended to guarantee to some associations close to Minister Frenay the political advantages deriving from the management of reception facilities and the care of former POWs and deportees.[42] Notable among these groups was the movement of prisoners, founded during the Vichy period. Following the street protests of June 1945 against the shortcomings of assistance, organized by the Communist component of the movement, the MPDR decided to hamper the creation of a big association of all war victims: the only link between these different categories would have been the claims against the state.[43]

For MAPB's high-ranking officials, post-war social policies represented a first-step measure towards making every citizen enter into the labour market and thereby be protected by a general social security system, which they aimed to correct on the basis of the English Labour Party reforms. This approach preferred considering the problem of unemployment as a whole, without granting veterans a privileged position. However, it conflicted with the legacies of past legislation, and with the economic conditions and the political needs of the national unity government, which emphasized not only the emergency situation, but, in continuity with traditional patriotism, the necessity of a job quota for veterans and refugees compensating them for the sufferings endured for the national honour.[44] The traditional patriotic semantic frameworks were not consistent with the political-institutional acceleration. In particular, the myth of the "military nation," bequeathed by the Risorgimento and by the First World War prevented the passage from assistance to the combatants (linked to the concept of the moral debt of the nation) to a modern social welfare system, aimed at all citizens, notwithstanding the forms of their participation in the war effort. The patriotic revival was supported, from December 1945, by the new Minister Luigi Gasparotto, an old member of the small Demo-Labour Party and a prominent representative of the WWI veterans.[45] Gasparotto ascribed a moral character to the MAPB, by presenting assistance as the caring attention of the state towards veterans and national refugees. The reintegration of veterans into the labour market was therefore promoted not only through making it compulsory for companies to rehire their former employees who had served in the war but also through enforced placement of veterans in companies. This measure, which had been conceived twenty years before for disabled and injured veterans, was now expanded to all veterans, enlarging compensation rights over and above physical injuries.

The assistance provided by the MAPB remained insufficient to meet the needs of all recipients or to compensate for the shortages in the health and insurance systems. Despite all the projects launched based on the MPDR and G.I. Bill models, in Italy most veterans and refugees benefited exclusively from modest subsidies, named "allowances" to emphasize citizens' entitlements.[46] The predominance of these forms of assistance, which were deemed a hindrance to the development of a spirit of initiative and collaboration, was increasingly criticized within the MAPB. But it was only during the last period of the MAPB, under the communist Emilio Sereni, that a plan was developed to replace welfare payments with public services. These were aimed at the entire population and included nurseries, care homes, foster homes and vocational training.[47]

Again, programmes of France and the USA served explicitly as models for Italian efforts. The MPDR had developed interventions aimed at social reintegration, which were considered as the final element of the emergency relief system.[48] The uncontrolled distribution of allowances had contributed to an inflationary escalation. By contrast, the development of public services, on the one hand, and the intervention into the labour market, on the other, allowed the channelling of all the resources available for modernization and emphasized professional reorientation or, at least, work reintegration as the best rehabilitation intervention. More significant were some measures undertaken for repatriates and refugees, but with the aim of extending them to the entire French population. The return of prisoners and deportees exposed the shortages of the French public health system. The MPDR, in an attempt to integrate existing structures and private initiative, already in February 1945 established that the state would take over medical treatment for all returnees as well as the sanitary control which took place at French boundaries. But the initial extension of free care provided for the injured WWI veterans proved to be insufficient, since those who had been persecuted for racial reasons and prisoners who had been kept as workers were not entitled to any rights. The MPDR decided therefore to rely on the health insurance system that returnees were enrolled in before the war, by providing refunds for treatment expenses. In addition, the creation of the Aide médicale temporaire provided complete, state-paid, high-level assistance for all returnees not enrolled in health insurance funds. The graft of an assistance addition onto the insurance system represented the germ of a project inspired by British reforms aimed at establishing a national health system and social services to assist repatriates and their families.[49] The plan, which was to be extended to the whole population on a citizenship basis, envisaged the creation of "a national medical and social assistance service" and the unification in a single "Ministry of population" of all responsibilities concerning social security and health:[50]

> Beyond the desire to give the country back healthy men, we would have liked to provide, in connection with the comeback of 2 million French citizens, the medical and medico-social framework that France did not already possess: public hospitals, nursing homes, health records, assistance law reform, social work and health service. The circumstances and especially the budgetary difficulties did not permit this.[51]

Malthusian anxieties and the hygienist logic that drove this project, elaborated before and during the war, made "human capital" a field of state action.[52] This was not a uniquely French situation: also in Italy, post-war agencies were linked to the broader projects of a comprehensive social welfare plan encompassing insurance and social assistance that must represent a safety net and not a guaranteed income. The Tremezzo conference, held in September–October 1946, brought together the UNRRA Mission and MAPB officials to discuss an "Italian New Deal." The project adapted to the Italian context the wartime developments of social welfare in the USA, by moving beyond a critique of the Italian organization for the low educational qualifications of its social workers; the discretionary margins in distributing aid; the fragmentation of efforts; and the political, clientelist and religious conditions imposed.[53] The conference noted the pressing problems of rationalization, coordination and unification of different systems, as well as the importance of rehabilitation and prevention policies. Post-war policies must foster an expansion and a transformation of social protection that targeted the root causes of misery, addressed psychological and material unrest, and fostered the growth of "collective morality."[54] The MAPB had to develop a plan of social interventions and to transform itself into a ministry of social assistance designed to take care of the entire population. At the same time, in parallel, the insurance system was to be replaced by a social security coverage based on needs, with provisions accorded to all workers and their families, notwithstanding the contributions paid.[55]

The end of an age of reforms and their legacies

The development of post-war policies in such broader projects was soon undermined by financial shortfalls, by the ending of emergency situations and by the changing political landscape. The MAPB and MPDR were explicitly temporary administrations that were expected to dissolve at the return to normality. The unprecedentedly rapid rise of social welfare expenditures in 1944–1945 strengthened the idea of the total disappearance of the social assistance public-sector intervention and of the triumph of a modern social security system, once the post-war emergences were over. In France, at the request of the Minister Frenay, unwilling to leave his ministry in the hands of another party, the dissolution came abruptly in November 1945. The MPDR was first transformed into the Ministère de la population, which also absorbed family and health policies and aimed at improving the standards of living of all citizens.[56] Nevertheless, soon after this project was downsized, and responsibilities for public health and demography were detached from social assistance, paving the way for the restoration of the pre-war Ministère pour les anciens combattants et les victimes de guerre. Its activity did not focus on the expansion of social policies, but ended up repeating pre-war policies of reserved enrolments for veterans and assimilated civilians, defined as "favourite creditors of the Nation."[57] The minister, the communist Laurent Casanova, criticized all solutions which aimed at including veterans and victims of the war in the public assistance system. This was considered as the stigmatizing bequest of a period during which the rights of the working class were not recognized. As the phase of emergency relief came to an end, the ministry preferred to underline the importance of re-evaluating pensions. A system of meticulous graduation of pensions differentiated each group of victims, by rewarding especially combatants and members of the Resistance. Assistance remained a pariah in the field of social policy, with the notable exception of rehabilitation policies.

In Italy social problems caused by the war proved difficult to be brought back to normalcy, and the MAPB lasted almost up to the collapse of the antifascist national unity governments. In February 1947, the MAPB's ambitious project was stopped, part of the staff fired and competencies simply redistributed among existing permanent structures, mostly to the Ministry of the Interior, which thus recuperated its traditional role of social control. The predominance of sector-specific measures brought forth an extremely selective intervention in the field of social reintegration, which was unable to trigger a real expansion of the social functions of the state.

The wait for structural reform dragged on for over two decades. By broadening the definition of poverty and by establishing social services, the MAPB and MPDR flanked transnational modes as a reference for the demands of rationalization and standardization of the assistance provisions that circulated all throughout the 1950s and concretized in various – and long unsuccessful – legislative proposals. Despite these shortcomings, the deep legacies of the post-war moment cannot be overlooked: post-war social policies succeeded in amalgamating the different war experiences of civilians, partisans and veterans and in promoting a reform of public assistance systems, which advanced a new pact between citizens and the state in order to create a democracy founded on the principle of social citizenship as "full membership of the community."

The specific management needs of the post-war transition impacted significantly on the social protection systems and made an important contribution to the move towards universalism. This impact has been downplayed because it concerned essentially public welfare, which has long been regarded as marginal and irrelevant in modern social policy. In both France and Italy, however, post-war assistance in favour of marginal populations was linked to citizenship, and social rights were no longer based only on work, occupational groups and subscriptions paid. Post-war assistance established the grounds for the progressive shift from a groups-based tool for ensuring public order to a system of individual rights aimed at prevention, personal development and participation in democratic life as part of citizenship. In both post-war France and Italy, citizenship-based provisions were largely extended, over and above the mere right to life. These developments call into question the importance of the failure of the attempts to shift from an occupational to a universal welfare state system, usually ascribed by the historiography to policy legacies; the centrality of labour; the effects of the Cold War and internal tensions; and the social divisions between employed workers, small-business owners, self-employed workers and marginal groups. These findings invite us to rethink welfare state typologies in historical research, to highlight the openness of the post-war period, and to take into account the intertwining between insurance and assistance. The building of a national assistance system represented a first essential step in the process of construction of individual rights to an adequate standard of living, to work and equal pay, to education and to cultural well-being. While demobilization after WWI fostered the introduction of specific programs for disabled veterans, twenty-five years later the linkage between social reintegration and population policies expanded these same provisions to non-disabled veterans as a matter of social rights.[58] Public assistance was no longer provided only to those unfit for work but to all the victims of the war, including able-bodied refugees and active men, who simply needed to be reintegrated into society and labour markets. The combination of social exclusion and poor health was no longer necessary for a citizen to be entitled to public assistance: a major innovation for Italy and France, where no unemployment assurance existed at that time. In that sense, the rationalization and the centralization of the assistance provisions were consistent with their inclusion in a wider, universal and reformed social policy including the elimination of unemployment, medical coverage, and the prevention of illness and disability, through hygiene and workplace safety. If social security was part of an attempt to transform the environment of the workplace, social assistance was tailored to the psycho-social demands of the integration of recipients, with the objective of making them more independent and responsible. Despite the failure of the project of a universal system of benefits that would cover the entire population, the impact of the war's emergencies on the welfare system spread new methods of social intervention of the state. Post-war state action provided a new rehabilitative meaning to social assistance, which became later its centrepiece during the post-war economic boom. In the post-war Italian and French contexts, social policy was centred on normalization and integration into the social and political reconstruction processes. The approach based on "rehabilitation," borrowed from UNRRA, increased self-help among the recipients, took care of their psychological needs, and boosted them to participate in society and the economy more effectively. The two ministries shared therefore a common model of normalization based on citizenship; contributed to reshaping the relationships between public social policies, local administrations and charitable private organizations; and participated in the building of the new social order of the Liberation.

Notes

1 Herbert Obinger and Klaus Petersen, "Mass Warfare and the Welfare State – Causal Mechanisms and Effects," *British Journal of Political Science* 47, no. 1 (2017).
2 Geoff Eley, "Legacies of Antifascism: Constructing Democracy in Postwar Europe," *New German Critique* 67, no. 1 (1996).

3. Deborah Cohen, *The War Come Home: Disabled Veterans in Britain and Germany, 1914–1939* (Berkeley: University of California Press, 2001).
4. Antoine Prost and Jay Winter, *René Cassin and Human Rights: From the Great War to the Universal Declaration* (Cambridge: Cambridge University Press, 2013), 25–33.
5. Paolo Mattera, "Changes and Turning Points in Welfare History. A Case Study: A Comparison of France and Italy in the 1940s," *Journal of Modern Italian Studies* 22, no. 2 (2017).
6. Thomas H. Marshall, *Citizenship and Social Class* (Cambridge: Cambridge University Press, 1950), 11.
7. Ilaria Pavan, "'These New Rights': Social Security in the Postwar Italian Debate," *Journal of Modern Italian Studies* 22, no. 2 (2017).
8. Ido De Haan, "The Western European Welfare State beyond Christian and Social Democratic Ideology," in *The Oxford Handbook of Postwar European History*, ed. Dan Stone (Oxford: Oxford University Press, 2012), 301.
9. Bruno Palier, *Gouverner la sécurité sociale, Les reformes du système français de protection sociale depuis 1945* (Paris: PUF, 2005), 101–106; Maurizio Ferrera, Valeria Fargion, and Matteo Jessoula, *Alle radici del welfare all'italiana. Origini e futuro di un modello sociale squilibrato* (Roma: Marsilio, 2012), 86–112.
10. Colette Bec, *L'assistance en démocratie* (Paris: Belin, 1994), 92–93.
11. Cf. Maurizio Ferrera, "Italy: Wars, Political Extremism, and the Constraints to Welfare Reform," in *Warfare and Welfare: Military Conflict and Welfare State Development in Western Countries*, ed. Herbert Obinger, Klaus Petersen, and Peter Starke (Oxford and New York: Oxford University Press, 2018), 117–123.
12. Nicole Dombrowski Risser, *France under Fire: German Invasion, Civilian Flight, and Family Survival during World War II* (Cambridge: Cambridge University Press, 2012); Leonardo Paggi, *Il popolo dei morti. La Repubblica italiana nata dalla guerra (1940–46)* (Bologna: Il Mulino, 2009).
13. Julia Moses and Martin Daunton, "Border Crossings: Global Dynamics of Social Policies and Problems," *Journal of Global History* 9, no. 2 (2014).
14. Christoph Conrad, "Social Policy after the Transnational Turn," in *Beyond Welfare State Models: Transnational Historical Perspectives on Social Policy*, ed. Pauli Kettunen and Klaus Petersen (Cheltenham: Edward Elgar, 2011), 218–240.
15. Silvia Salvatici, "Not Enough Food to Feed the People," *Contemporanea* 14, no. 1 (2011); Jessica Reinisch, "Auntie UNRRA at the Crossroads," *Past and Present*, suppl. 8 (2013).
16. Laure Humbert, "French Politics of Relief and International Aid: France, UNRRA and the Rescue of European Displaced Persons in Postwar Germany, 1945–47," *Journal of Contemporary History* 51, no. 3 (2016).
17. Andrew Shennan, *Rethinking France: Plans for Renewal, 1940–46* (Oxford: Oxford University Press, 1989), 60–61.
18. "Projet de constitution d'un Secrétariat Général aux prisonniers et aux déportés," 8 September 1943, Archives Nationales (AN), 3AG/1/270.
19. André Philip to Général De Gaulle, 5 October 1943, AN 3AG/1/270.
20. "Ordonnance du 2 October 1943," *Journal officiel de la République Française* (*JORF*) no. 25; Jean Monnet to Renè Mayer, 19 February 1944, AN F9/3116.
21. Philippe Hesse and Jean-Pierre Le Crom, *La protection sociale sous le régime de Vichy* (Rennes: PUR 2001), 341–347.
22. "Organisation du commissariat au rapatriement" [February 1944?], AN F9/3095.
23. "Note de la Direction des services internationaux," 15 May 1945, AN F9/3150.
24. Philip Nord, *France's New Deal: From the Thirties to the Postwar Era* (Princeton: Princeton University Press, 2012); Ben Shephard, "Becoming Planning Minded: The Theory and Practice of Relief 1940–1945," *Journal of Contemporary History* 43, no. 3 (2008).

25 Bruno Cabanes, *La victoire endeuillée. La sortie de guerre des soldats français (1918–1920)* (Paris: Seuil, 2004), 377–393.
26 "Memorandum Patriot Branch," 5 November 1944, NARA, Allied Control Commission, 10000/125/100; Pamela Ballinger, "Borders of Nations, Borders of Citizenship: Italian Repatriation and the Redefinition of National Identity after World War II," *Comparative Studies in Society and History,* 49, no. 3 (2007).
27 "Circolare 4257/ST," 22 August 1945, in *Assistenza post-bellica* (Lanciano: Carabba, 1946): 37.
28 "L'assistenza post-bellica negli altri paesi," *Bollettino dell'assistenza post-bellica* 1, no. 1 (1945): 22.
29 Antonio D'Andrea, *Filosofia e autobiografia* (Firenze: Cadmo, 1998), 90.
30 Enrico Berardinone, "Assistenza del primo intervento e avviamento all'assistenza sociale," in *Atti del convegno per studi di assistenza sociale* (Milano: Marzorati, 1947), 521.
31 Lucia Marsan Corti, "I problemi del dopoguerra," in *Atti del convegno per studi*, 518.
32 Glenn Altschuler and Stuart Blumin, *The GI Bill. The New Deal for Veterans* (Oxford: Oxford University Press, 2009).
33 G.S. Stevenson, "Foreword," in *Soldier to Civilian: Problems of Readjustment*, ed. G. Pratt (New York and London: Whittlesey House, 1944), xi.
34 *Al prigioniero che torna* (Poligrafico dello stato: Roma, 1946).
35 "Promemoria Frassineti," [Autumn 1945] Archivio centrale dello Stato, MAPB/1.
36 Roberto Battaglia, "Il problema dei reduci e dei partigiani," in *Atti del convegno per studi*, 544.
37 Pieter Lagrou, *The Legacy of Nazi Occupation: Patriotic Memory and National Recovery in Western Europe, 1945–1965* (Cambridge: Cambridge University Press, 2000), 118.
38 *Bilan d'un effort* (Paris: Imprimerie Nationale, 1945), 58–59.
39 "Réunion plénière," 7 February 1945, AN F9/3138.
40 Eric Jabbari, *Pierre Laroque and the Welfare State in Postwar France* (Oxford: Oxford University Press, 2012), 130–131.
41 "Affari generali," s.d., ACS, MAPB/1, 3.
42 Christopher Lewin, *Le retour des prisonniers de guerre français* (Paris: Publications de la Sorbonne, 1987).
43 François Cochet, *Les exclus de la victoire* (Paris: SPM, 1992), 198–199.
44 Aldo Giovanni Ricci (ed.), *Verbali del Consiglio dei ministri* (Roma: Presidenza del Consiglio dei Ministri, 1998), VI.1: 204–205.
45 Agostino Bistarelli, *La strada del ritorno* (Torino: Bollati Berlinghieri, 2007): 237.
46 "Circolare 8016/6-9," 13 May 1946, *Bollettino dell'assistenza post-bellica*, 1, 4–5 (1946): 22.
47 "Press conference," 31 July 1946, Fondazione Istituto Gramsci (FIG), Fondo Sereni/Attività governativa, 5/1946.
48 "Ordonnance 45-948. Exposé des motifs," 11 May 1945, Service Historique de la Défense (SHD), Caen-BAVCC/40R24.
49 Robert Debré, *Préface*, in *L'organisation de santé du rapatriement*, Pierre Valette (Paris: Imprimerie centrale des Grands Boulevards, 1945), 4.
50 Robert Debré, "Santé publique et sécurité sociale," *Population* 2, no. 2 (1947).
51 *Bilan d'un effort*, 146.
52 Paul-André Rosental, *L'intelligence démographique. Sciences et politiques des populations en France (1930-1960)* (Paris: Odile Jacob 2003), 112–113.
53 Jennifer Mittelstadt, *From Welfare to Workfare: The Unintended Consequences of Liberal Reform, 1945–1965* (Chapel Hill: University of North Carolina Press, 2006), 26–39.
54 "Intervention at the conference," 30 September 1946, FIG, Fondo Sereni/Discorsi, 5/1946.

55 Stefano Giua, "Nuovi orientamenti della previdenza sociale," in *Atti del convegno per studi*, 73–88.
56 Decree 45-013, 29 November 1945, *JORF Lois et décrets* 258, 7970; "Circulaire 744 DCC," 4 December 1945, SHD, Caen-BAVCC/40R29, 2.
57 *JORF*, Assemblée Nationale, 23 December 1945, 296.
58 Pierre Romien, "À l'origine de la réinsertion professionnelle des personnes handicapées: la prise en charge des invalides de guerre," *Revue française des affaires sociales* 59, no. 2 (2005): 238–239.

7 Disabled citizens and the neoliberal turn in Britain

Whose rights and whose responsibilities?

Monika Baár

Introduction[1]

The phenomenon commonly labelled as the neoliberal turn represented a key transitional moment in the history of the welfare states in Europe and beyond. It revealed both certain common characteristics and peculiarities confined to a number of individual states. This chapter reflects on the repercussions of this shift from the perspective of disabled people in Britain, where it coincided with the rise to power of Margaret Thatcher's conservative government in 1979. On the one hand, this period became associated with serious cuts in the welfare budget and the fundamental reshaping of the welfare landscape. These measures were justified ideologically as a means to "responsibilize" citizens, while in pragmatic terms they were justified by pointing to the circumstances dictated by the financial crisis. On the other hand, this era was characterized by an upsurge in disabled people's grassroots activities. This intensification of bottom-up activities owed not merely to domestic dynamics, but also resonated with international developments.

One such crucial event was the United Nations' International Year of Disabled Persons (in Britain usually referred to as International Year of Disabled People and in abbreviated form as IYDP), which was observed worldwide in 1981 with the aim to promote the rights of persons with disabilities and enable their integration into the mainstream of society. This chapter seeks to add new angles to recent insightful studies on the development of disability-related welfare policies in Britain in the post-war period and in particular on the neoliberal turn by placing the intensified discussions around the International Year and their repercussions at its centre. Using the International Year as its lens, it reveals that the late 1970s to early 1980s represented a compressed period during which epochal transformations took place: it was marked by the termination of the post-war welfare consensus, to which earlier British governments had committed themselves at the rhetorical level.

The Thatcher government expected that citizens, having benefited from the earlier welfare expansion, would now be ready to accept sacrifices. Yet, disabled people had been overlooked in the post-war British welfare settlement and this "benign neglect" made them reluctant to accept the rolling back of the state which had never rolled forward for them in the first place. They also found it ironic that a year which was dedicated to their cause brought about worsening living standards and restrictions on the already not too extensive service provision. This dissatisfaction catalysed the formation of new types of grassroots organizations which focused not only on services but also on rights, and adopted a more critical and confrontational approach that explicitly challenged the status quo. This transformation can also be traced in the change of the official title of the year, which was originally planned to be the International Year *for* Disabled People. The charitable connotations of this label, however, triggered a negative reaction from the target group and consequently, the initial designation was subsequently changed to the International Year *of* Disabled People. This shift indicated a move in the public discourses away from the mainstream charitable–medical approach towards a more socio-economic understanding of disability.

The chapter demonstrates that both the representatives of the disability rights movement and the representatives of the neoliberal state argued for a greater degree of autonomy and independence for citizens. For disabled people this crystallized, among other things, around two concepts: the right to work and independent living, both to be realized with appropriate supporting frameworks. These two desiderata did not merely provide the preconditions for self-sufficiency, but also constituted a key dimension of political autonomy. By contrast, in the neoliberal "version," the intention was reduced to individual employment and personal care, without the expectation to simultaneously support societal participation. In other words, the neoliberal state co-opted the disability movement's demands in a de-collectivized version and, as a consequence, it also removed any implications of social justice from those agendas.[2]

Conventional analyses of the welfare state have typically been based on government and policy documents, but recently academic debates have become invigorated by having recourse to the rich, albeit often uncategorized, holdings of the archives of voluntary associations. Another enriching factor has been the employment of the biographical approach, which utilizes the lived experience for exploring the intersections between the public sphere and private lives and interrogating the agency of disabled citizens.[3] Seeking to build on these new directions whenever possible, this study investigates and confronts the role of the state, the contribution of grassroots organizations, the media and selected individuals. In terms of source material, this chapter draws on the hitherto unexplored archival records of the Secretariat of the International Year of Disabled Persons held in the University of Liverpool Special Collections & Archives.[4] Following consultations between the government and leading voluntary organizations in late 1978, the Secretariat was organized by the National Council for Voluntary Organizations. In addition, the chapter utilizes a range of "grey materials" – leaflets, pamphlets, newsletters of voluntary organizations – many of which are available in the virtual Disability Archive UK maintained by the Centre for Disability Studies at Leeds University; and interviews with activists which have been published in lesser-known outlets.

Antecedents: the British welfare state and disability

As recently produced excellent studies, such as those undertaken by Jameel Hampton and Gareth Millward, have demonstrated, just as in several other European countries, in Britain the post-war welfare settlement had failed to accommodate disabled people within its cradle-to-the-grave provision. Governments consistently drew a sharp distinction between people whose disability had occurred from war – or industrial injuries – and the "rest." Those belonging to the latter category, implicitly perceived as "moral failures," were excluded from social citizenship and remained heavily reliant on non-statutory provision. Consequently, they were greatly exposed to poverty and exclusion. As one critique noted, the welfare state acted as "the ambulance waiting at the bottom of the cliff" for those in an acute financial status, rather than creating conditions which prevented impoverishment in the first place.[5]

It was this marginalized position which organizations such as the Spastics Society, the National Association for Mental Health (nowadays known as Mind) and the National Association of Parents of Backward Children (nowadays known as Mencap) sought to address with their activities and services. In the 1960s and 1970s, a number of new organizations came into being which operated with novel approaches and strategies. In 1965 two housewives, Megan du Boisson and Berit Moore, established the Disablement Income Group (DIG) whose goal was to tackle the problem of poverty. They fought for the introduction of a comprehensive statutory income for disabled people, which was to be based on the severity of their condition, irrespective of the cause of their disablement, marital status and age. As their memorandum of 1965 stated: "Disability should not be regarded as short term sickness indefinitely prolonged, but as a category of being for which special provision must be made."[6] DIG therefore contributed to the emergence of the notion of "civilian disability" as a category and as an object of policy. Britain's entry into the European Economic Community gave DIG members the opportunity to exert further pressure on the government by comparing British social policy unfavourably to those of other countries in the Community. For example, British disability policies needed to be revised in light of the European Council directive on equal treatment of men and women because they were found to be discriminating against disabled married women, whose position in the social security system was described by Barbara Castle as "second class citizens entitled to third-class benefits."[7]

Another organization that campaigned for the introduction of a comprehensive income scheme was Disability Alliance (DA), a federation comprising 70 institutions. It was founded in 1974 in reaction to the White Paper issued in 1974 titled "Social Security Provision for Chronically Sick and Disabled People." As one member later recalled, they were "united in fury" realizing that in the document the desired non-statutory allowance was relinquished altogether.[8] Unlike traditional charities, DIG and DA did not focus on one specific type of impairment (for example blindness or physical impairment); they were pan-disability organizations. They lobbied the government employing "insider tactics": this entailed forging close relations with influential officials and presenting them with a sound evidence base. Nevertheless, successive Labour governments throughout the 1970s rejected the target of a general allowance for disabled people with the excuse that it was incompatible with the contributory principle of National

Insurance. Although the morally justified nature of disability benefits was not called into question, they were considered legitimate only as long as they did not place an unreasonable financial burden on the state.[9]

Different attitudes towards priorities, membership and strategies could and did lead to frictions even among organizations fighting for the same fundamental goals. For example, the Union of the Physically Impaired Against Segregation (UPIAS) emerged on the scene in 1974 out of a frustration: its founders Vic Finkelstein and Paul Hunt protested in this way against what they believed was DIG's "colonization" by professional academics. UPIAS (of which more later) campaigned for independent living and direct payments which could allow disabled people to take control over their own finances and live according to their own life schedules rather than according to the rigid frameworks imposed on them by inflexible statutory services.

Welfare expenditure in Britain saw a reduction from the 1970s onwards, which can be attributed to a great extent to the worldwide financial crisis. Yet, with the election of Margaret Thatcher in 1979, this retrenchment also acquired a sound ideological basis. One of the fundamental tenets of the neoliberal turn was the emphasis on obligation over rights: "citizenship of entitlement" was to be replaced by "citizenship of contribution."[10] Along these lines, the Tory government relinquished the idea to develop comprehensive, state-led initiatives to address the problem of poverty. Its intention was not to abolish the welfare state, rather, to marginalize its relevance for the all but the poorest segments of society, for whom it was still expected to act a safety net. The government reduced service provision in the belief that it encouraged welfare dependency and impeded economic growth. Hence, the new policy supported profit-driven private providers, and instead of thinking in broader terms of societal protection, they focused on the individual rights of customers. The emphasis on the virtue of self-help and the push towards market-based provision thus became pivotal constituents of Thatcher's moralistic–individualist policies.[11]

The official response: charitable action and "we have to do something"

It was in this tensed climate that amid much fanfare the International Year was launched in Britain in January 1981. The official contribution entailed declarations, reactions and activities in multifarious spheres and by a host of actors: the royal family, the government, political leaders, the media and a number of established charities which enjoyed a certain degree of approval and/or sponsorship by the government. A Central Committee was established to coordinate the response of the central government, and, as in the majority of United Nations member states, an IYDP Secretariat was also created with branches in England, Wales and Northern Ireland. The government expected, however, that the main response to the International Year should come from the voluntary and private sectors.[12] The IYPD Committee therefore reached the decision that it would not engage in fundraising. Instead, the charities and voluntary organizations were expected to increase their fundraising capacities.[13] Of the members of the royal family, the Queen, Prince Charles and the spouse of Princess Margaret, the Earl of Snowdon, became involved in the International Year. Cherishing the legacy of the Commonwealth, the IYPD Committee of New Zeeland requested the Queen to dedicate her Christmas Speech of 1981 to the International Year. As a significant gesture on her part, the Queen accepted this request, as the following fragment from her speech demonstrates:

> Last July we had the joy of seeing our eldest son married amid scenes of great happiness, which made 1981 a very special year for us. The wonderful response the wedding evoked was very moving. Just before that there had been a very different scene here in the garden at Buckingham Palace when three and a half thousand disabled people, with their families, came to tea with us. […] The International Year of Disabled People has performed a very real service by focusing our attention on their problems. We have all become more aware of them and I'm sure that many of you, like myself, have been impressed by the courage they show. […] Their courage in handling their difficulties and in many cases living an almost normal life, or making abnormal life normal, shows our own problems to be insignificant in comparison. […] We have seen in 1981 how many individuals have devoted themselves to trying to make life more tolerable for handicapped people, by giving loving care and by providing money and effort to improve facilities and to hasten research.[14]

This speech was a quintessential manifestation of the conventional charitable approach to disabled people: it implied that "us" (the able-bodied) and "them" (the disabled) represented two entirely different worlds, and it expressed some pity towards those "unfortunate people" belonging to the latter category. Moreover, in a typical fashion, it showered praise on those who displayed courage and succeeded in overcoming their difficulties. The event itself mentioned in the speech – afternoon tea – likewise fit into the conventional charitable templates. The patron of the International Year was the Queen's son, Prince Charles, whose wedding happened to take place in 1981, and so the wedding also became a site of charitable activities. For example, the sale of souvenirs at the royal wedding was offered for charity purposes and some of the wedding presents were in fact donations to charities involved in the International Year. A further connection to the royal family was forged through the appointment of Antony Armstrong-Jones, the Earl of Snowdon, as the International Year's president for England and making him the chair of a special committee bearing his name. Snowdon had contracted polio at the age of 16, which motivated him to engage in disability campaigning. Nevertheless, the remit of the Snowdon Committee did not entail the addressing of concrete problems. Rather, it operated as a kind of "popular tribunal" that received an extraordinarily large number of letters. This indicated that many disabled people did not know where to turn with their problems.[15] Virtually all the letters received a standard reply, including, for example, the one written by the Ladies' Committee of the Help Action Research for the Crippled Child. This letter extended an invitation to Lord Snowdon to undertake a portrait sitting. The Ladies' Committee's plan was that the completed portrait would be offered to the highest bidder and the income would be used for charitable purposes. However, the plan did not materialize: "I am afraid Lord Snowdon is not able to accept this kind invitation. Normally, Lord Snowdon would answer your kind letter personally but due to the quite overwhelming amount of correspondence he has receiving concerning the International Year he is unable to do so. If there is a concrete problem they pass it onto the authorities."[16]

Discussions in Parliament revolving around the International Year were undertaken by the political parties, the All-Party Disablement Group, and a number of MPs also expressed special interest. The All-Party Group reminded both parties of the promises that they had made in their run-up for the elections in 1979 in their respective manifestos. Conservatives declared: "Our aim is to provide a coherent system of cash benefits to meet the costs of disability, so that more people can support themselves and live normal lives," whereas Labour promised to "introduce a new disablement allowance to include the blind, varying according the severity of disablement."[17] The All-Party Group called attention to the confusing and inequitable nature of the existing system of benefits, which were based on the cause of the disability rather than need. The All-Party Group reminded its peers and the public that improving the system was not a party-political issue. The All-Party Group proposed a campaign for a comprehensive disability income scheme, but not with short-term effect, rather to be implemented "*when the economic situation improves.*"[18]

While fundamental improvements with immediate effect were ruled out in this way, there existed consensus among politicians that it would be an embarrassment for a prosperous country not to do *something*. In 1981 the liberal MP Lord Winstanley delivered a speech during the parliamentary debates which commenced with the following words:

> My Lords, in my view Britain leads the world at talking about the disabled, though I am bound to say that the Americans come fairly close. Perhaps we lead the world in understanding the social, economic and political needs of the disabled. But do we lead the world in what we actually do? I very much hope that the international year will prove to be a year, not in which we talk a lot more about the disabled but in which we do something.[19]

The government's intention "to do something" became manifest in its rushing through the Disabled Persons Act 1981, which focused on the problem of access in a particularly narrow way. As Alf Morris, a disability campaigner and Britain's first Minister for Disabled People (from 1974 to 1979), noted in the *Sunday Times*: "the act not only had its teeth removed, but its gums as well."[20] Another manifestation of the "we have to do something on the cheap" mentality was the redefinition – in fact narrowing – of the focus of the International Year from full participation and equality to two issues: improving access and changing attitudes. Regarding the former objective, the minute book of the IYDP Committee stated, "Far more could be done, particularly to improve access. At Leeds Castle, for example, the Trustees have succeeded in opening up many more parts of the Castle and its grounds for disable people, without having to spend too much money."[21] Regarding the latter objective, educational campaigns aimed at improving attitudes were launched. For example, a national poster campaign was mounted with the motto: "Do disabled people make you feel uncomfortable? If so, their greatest handicap could be you and your attitude. So, think of the person. Not the disability."

During the International Year, disability as a theme received generous exposure in the media, and for the first time, some of the relevant programmes were no longer invariably relegated to minority viewing hours, but became mainstreamed into the more popular viewing times. This was definitely considered a sign of improvement. In fact, some politicians believed that already by mid-year a saturation point had been reached in the media.[22] Moreover, the strong media presence was certainly serviceable for pushing the issue of disability from the realm of social policy to that of high politics. Although the exposure was generous, it was also somewhat disproportional: official events and the conventional associations received the lion's share of the coverage, while emerging grassroots organizations remained ignored. The same applied to the portrayal of various types of disabilities: whereas the disabled population included a high proportion of women and older people and a wide range of physical, mental and developmental disabilities, official and public representations remained dominated by the young and middle-aged physically disabled men and by wheelchair and white-stick users in particular. "Hidden disabilities," i.e. those which are not immediately visible, such as deafness and mental illness, barely featured in the media.

As part of the official mid-year assessment, a confidential report was issued by Stephen Crampton, Secretary of the Committee to the Assistant Private Secretary of the Royal Prince of Wales. It addressed the "small but vocal" hostile element that opposed the IYDP before its outset primarily on three grounds: First, it was not sufficiently confrontational towards the government and as such it was "irrelevant." Second, based on the disparaging experiences drawn from the International Year of the Child (1979), many people questioned if the IYDP would have any impact at all. Third, some believed that even if the IYDP would yield some immediate results, in the longer run it would have no lasting value. As the author of the report noted, opponents in the second and third groups appeared to have been won over, but not those in the first: "Although critics of the first group remain, they are very few in number and are generally political extremists."[23]

The grassroots response

But who were these "political extremists" mentioned in the mid-year assessment? They entailed a number of groups and individuals who were unsatisfied with the official response and did not shy away from voicing their dissent. They believed that the IYDP certainly abounded in lip service and window dressing, but this merely concealed the intention to leave the status quo intact. These groups' voices became amplified and their activities gained extra impetus thanks to a number of developments on the international scene, in particular, the foundation of the world's first global cross-disability organization, Disabled People's International (DPI). DPI owes its existence to a scandal at the 1980 Winnipeg World Congress of Rehabilitation International, a conventional organization of medical and rehabilitation experts founded in 1922. The tension that emerged during this conference provides a good illustration of the changing perceptions. It was during that meeting that Swedish delegates recommended amending the organization's constitution in such a way that at least 50% of the delegates should be persons with disabilities. This amendment was rejected, much to the irritation of many participants who withdrew from the meeting. They organized an alternative one, at which they decided to form a separate world coalition of persons with disabilities.[24]

The formation of DPI did not in itself provide the pretext for the foundation of a new British organization in the same year, but it definitely lent credibility and legitimacy to a fledgling initiative: the establishment of the British Council of Organisations of Disabled People (BCODP), a national pan-disablement organization.[25] Its initiators remained thoroughly unimpressed with the IYDP:

> I suppose what really focused it for me was IYDP in 1981. I was very opposed to this and I went on the radio, the television, wrote articles in the *Guardian* – all over the place – saying what a rotten idea it was. We only seem to have international years for dogs, trees, children or disabled people – never for bank managers or university professors! The whole idea was bound to reinforce notions of dependency and stigmatise us further, rather than to help us – as its proponents were suggesting.[26]

Nevertheless, this frustration turned out to be a creative one because the masterminds of what soon became BCODP realized that what single-impairment groups could achieve was limited and that only a collective voice in the disability community would have the chance to convey an authoritative position. If the complete transformation of disabled people's lives was to be the aim, then the formation of a national organization was imperative. BCODP differed from existing organizations in that it did not cherish close links with politicians and did not accept the control of non-disabled experts. It is also true, however, that unlike the previous governments, Thatcher's government was no longer committed to corporatist negotiations and the influence that experts could exert on it was informal rather than direct.[27] Instead, BCODP sought to collaborate with the local authorities. Moreover, as we have seen, it did not shy away from confrontation.

One such clash occurred with the Snowdon Committee, which in the eyes of BCODP's leaders was coterminous with the traditional disability establishment. They thought of Lord Snowdon as someone who demonstrated interest in the lives of disabled people, but remained blissfully unaware of the agenda of the newly emerging disability movement. For BCODP to become eligible for funding, the precondition was to collaborate with the Snowdon Committee, or even to subordinate itself to it. As one of its leaders, Phillip Mason, later recalled: "Lord Snowdon was hysterical, they were trying to explain him that they were not opposed to his committee, only wanted disabled people to take control of it, but they were just adamant."[28] Mason contrasted the poverty of BCODP to the circumstances that he had experienced at a meeting of one of the most important traditional charities, the Leonard Cheshire Foundation: "It was full of these noble do-gooders, men, mainly elderly and mainly military. [...] The sherry was flowing, the room was full of smoke. The affluence that was exhibited was really, really disgusting."[29]

Another act of protest was expressed by Ian Dury (1942–2000), a British singer and leader of the punk-rock group Blockheads, who was paralysed as a result of contracting polio during the 1949 epidemics. As a prominent artist with a disability, Dury received countless letters from disabled people from all over the country and especially from those who lived in institutions and who shared their feelings of isolation and solitude with him. Dury's own contribution to the International Year was the song "Spasticus Ausisticus." He called it his own hymn, which was in fact made *against* the International Year, which, in his view, gave a false signal to people that in the year 1982 everything will be OK. As he put it: "I thought that it was disgusting, the Year of the Disabled." So, he added: "I wrote the record simply off the top of my head to tell'em to stick it up their aris."[30] Sending out a message to people "out there in the normal land," the title and lyrics of Dury's song reclaimed the word *spastic* from being an all-purpose derogatory term into one that expressed a distinct identity. It also mocked traditional charitable attitudes that portrayed disabled people as helpless, pitiable victims. Dury offered his song to the United Nations as his contribution to the International Year, but his gesture was unsurprisingly rejected. BBC also refused to play it with the excuse that it had a potentially insulting effect. Dury believed that if the subject matter of the song would have been different, it would have become an instant hit. As he explained: "Just as nobody bans handicapped people – just makes it difficult for them to function as normal people, the song was not banned, just was made impossible to function."[31]

It was not only the newly formed institutions that made their voices heard during the International Year, but also the already existing ones. UPIAS members noted the little publicity they received: "no accolades, no distribution of knighthood," but merely scraps from the table, a programme here, an interview there. They regretted that the "disability establishment" was co-opted to resist attempts at changing the status quo and that it could retain its grip on the media.[32] All in all, the leaders of UPIAS drew the ironic conclusion that the International Year, which its members renamed the Year of the Cabbage, reinforced the very attitudes and practices it was expected to change. UPIAS's fundamental departure from the traditional, charitable frameworks was also traceable in the different conceptual language that it employed. It addressed social segregation and oppression and focused on the *rights* of disabled people – or more precisely, the lack thereof:

> Predictably 1981 – the IYDP – deepened that already entrenched conditions which perpetuate the social oppression of physically impaired people.

> The year was ushered in by non-disabled people on our behalf and passed into history to fanfares orchestrated by the same elites [...] The status quo remained intact [...] We read of our nobility crawling out of the royal woodwork to preside over soggy garden parties designed to reinforce our position at the bottom of the social pile. Craftwork competitions were in greater than ever abundance. Arch-segregationists like Mr. Cheshire got their medals topped up for keeping cripples off the streets.[33]

The reference to arch-segregationist Mr. Cheshire was by no means coincidental: UPIAS was originally formed as a consumer group from the discontented residents of the so-called Leonard Cheshire homes; they were charitable nursing establishments of which the first was established in 1948 to find a place for war veteran, Leonard Cheshire. These institutions over time became eponymous with incarceration, where the main reason one ceased to be a service user was death. In 1972, Paul Haunt, a resident of the first Cheshire Home, Le Court, organized strikes and protest actions and sent a letter to *The Guardian* calling out to disabled people who found themselves subject to authoritarian and cruel regimes, something akin to the workhouse. As one analyst noted: "thousands of disabled people are simply surviving out of sight and out of mind in often inaccessible listed buildings situated at the end of a dirt track and/or a dual carriageway whist Local Authorities politely turn away from the truth that they are financing our incarceration."[34]

Initially, authorities were "in denial": they believed that a group of extremists was making noise and expected these radical voices would soon disappear. However, their resistance merely encouraged the protesters who reached the conclusion that the system cannot be changed from within, so they should themselves take initiatives if they wanted to get rid of the unnecessary and costly bureaucratic regulations. One milestone was reached in 1976, when a disabled couple, Maggie and Ken Davies, supported by UPIAS, succeeded in obtaining an accessible home to enable them to live there independently. This was nothing short of a sensation: both medical experts and social workers had insisted that their wish was entirely unrealistic and they would have no chance to succeed. The opposite turned out to be the case. Hence, UPIAS intensified its activities by initiating Project 81 with the aim to break the grip of the Leonard Cheshire Foundation. They planned to set up centres of integrated living which would be controlled and run by disabled people, with the long-term goal of the replacement of all segregated facilities with such arrangements.[35]

The right to work and independent living, and their neoliberal incarnations

As has been hinted earlier, at the official level, the overall impact of the International Year was evaluated in a cautious and somewhat self-exonerating way. For example, the chairman of the IYDP, Sir Christopher Aston, declared that the year could not be a magic wand and no one was foolish enough to claim that all problems could be solved.[36] Unsurprisingly, the disabled people's organizations were much more disapproving. The Disability Alliance produced a report which regretted the aforementioned reinterpretation of the International Year's aims of "full participation and equality" as "the promotion of greater integration and more participation of disabled people," for which the official excuse was that "the Year comes at a time when there are no resources available for significant improvement in benefits or services."[37] Furthermore, the report pointed to the discrepancies between the British realities and the international desiderata as outlined in international legal frameworks such as the United Nations' Declaration on the Rights of Disabled Persons (1975) and the European Parliament's resolution on the IYDP. The objectives in the international arena revolved around *rights*: the right to economic and social security and a decent level of employment; and the right to work and to live with family members and to participate in all social, creative and recreational activities. As we have seen, in the national context these desiderata were diluted in such a way that only the issues of attitudes and physical access were addressed: "as if when people with disabilities get inside buildings, they will automatically be integrated."[38]

The irony that the IYDP increased poverty and dependence for many people was not left unaddressed either. Personal social services were reduced, and the social security provision was no longer linked to inflation and was no longer in line with rise of prices or earnings.

This report also pointed out that low levels of income for disabled people were combined with extra expenses – such as additional consumption of food and heating, car for transport and artificial aids. But even sympathetic politicians were highly critical. For example, John Gorst, a Conservative member of the all-party Select Committee of Employment, noted the government got its priorities painfully wrong: "Cuts there have to be, but to choose to injure those who are already disabled seem to me to be a lack of feeling and lack of priorities – and to have done so during the year which was set aside for concentrating on the problems of the disabled shows astonishing insensitivity."[39]

The cuts were part of the wider ideology of the Thatcher government, which no longer accepted the core arguments about structural inequalities causing poverty. It was committed to reducing public expenditure, minimizing the role of the state and privatizing a whole range of services under the pretext of "independence." However, policy experts warned, "The pursuit of independence carries the considerable risk that, for little gain, the real strengths of the Welfare State will be lost."[40] The report issued by UPIAS concluded that the cuts of certain benefits and the removal of others led to a deterioration whereby the existing inadequate services became even more inadequate. It also regretted that "the prospect of the long-awaited non-statutory disability income looked further than ever."[41]

The Disability Alliance found it crucial that, in a society with a strong work ethic, the improvement opportunities be increased. But it concluded that the IYDP failed even on that account: "the hope that it would focus public attention on the widespread deprivation amongst people with disabilities and their need for income, employment and social services has not been fulfilled."[42] The rate of unemployment was at least double that of the non-disabled and even those who held employment worked for low pay and in poor conditions. A further critique of the Disability Alliance was that despite international recommendations, such as the ones by the European Parliament, in Britain the state failed to recognize that poverty constituted a defining experience for the majority of disabled people and likewise failed to introduce a disablement allowance and a quota system to help disabled people gain employment. At a more fundamental level, the Disability Alliance did not accept the state's artificial and false distinction between the social and economic fields and its prioritization of economic goals over the social ones by subordinating the needs of and rights of people with disabilities to economic demands. It believed that, quite the contrary, the economic policies should conform to the needs and rights of people with disabilities.[43]

The new measures criticized by the grassroots organizations had undoubtedly detrimental effects, but at least initially, they were not purposefully aimed at removing the existing frameworks of basic support. The Thatcher government did not deliberately target the "disability community": such a move could have proven counterproductive because the reputation loss would have been more detrimental than the financial gain.[44] Rather, the negative effects evolved, at least initially, as collateral damage arising from the general dynamics of the welfare retrenchment. However, in the late 1980s this started to change when the government decided to target "welfare dependency" and the (real or alleged) abuses of the welfare system. The policies of the welfare state, which had hitherto been expected to provide the solution to major economic and social problems, now became identified as the primary cause of those very problems.[45]

In determining the extent of its welfare provision, every state is confronted with a predicament, which Deborah Stone in her book *The Disabled State* (1994) phrased as the distributive dilemma: how to cater for the needs of those who have no access to the labour market without damaging the societal work ethic.[46] The government addressed this dilemma by reclassifying disability categories with the predetermined aim to restrict access to benefits and propel as many people as possible to employment. It redefined the concept of disability in terms of one's ability to perform paid work or not: those who were not able to work were labelled "sick," whereas the other group was expected to enter the workforce.[47] This new division recalled the old binary of the Poor Law between the "deserving" and the "undeserving" poor, and it removed some of the citizenship entitlements from the latter group.[48]

Although the government relied, to some extent, on the hegemonic power of medical experts, it retained the monopoly to reclassify the categories of working capacity. In doing so, it increased its reliance on means-testing with the excuse that this was necessary for concentrating assistance where it was most needed. But means-tested benefits are usually replete with ambiguous definitions that result in irrational and arbitrary decisions. Those who had lost their disability status as an outcome of this reassessment were expected to enter an employment market where even many able-bodied citizens had difficulties finding a job. If they fell out of the workforce, they experienced higher rates and longer periods of unemployment. Even when they were employed, they were subject to both "vertical" and "horizontal" segregation: they are overrepresented in less skilled and part-time, temporary work, and they also tend to be confined to specific types of work.[49] Without any legally binding expectations to accommodate special needs and enable workforce integration, employers relied on the "reserve army of labour" provided by disabled people only in times of labour shortages and/or as a way to control wages in times of growing demand for workers.[50] Those few who still managed to find a job had typically only very moderate forms of disability, and even they were employed in casualized, flexible forms. The impact of these new bureaucratic mechanisms was that many disabled people who had previously qualified for state disability entitlements were now propelled into disability workfare programmes. These programmes have been labelled as "disciplining regimes" because participation in them was a condition to maintain entitlements in their reduced form. The outcome of restratification was the emergence of a new group: people who were "living in-between," not being disabled seriously enough to deserve welfare provision, but not being able-bodied enough to get a chance at the job market.[51]

As these processes reveal, the disability movement's demand of the right to work was de-collectivized by the neoliberal state. It was reduced to merely being a means of self-sufficiency for the autonomous and competitive citizen. The dimension of social inclusion and contribution to a greater degree of equality was entirely ignored. Moreover, the disability movement envisioned participation with the necessary supporting mechanisms, another aspect that was thoroughly disregarded by the state. The consequence was that, paradoxically, the withdrawal of existing services and the lack of implementation of new support mechanisms often led to increased levels of poverty and marginalization rather than "independence."[52]

The concept of independent living and community care was first embraced by representatives of the disability movement and then by the neoliberal government. Ironically, while in the majority of cases, resistance to changing the status quo was justified by financial reasons on the part of the authorities, it was evident that the highly expensive institutional care entirely defied economic rationality. Hospitalization and/or residential care cost far more than allowing people to remain in their homes with adequate support, so, in fact, maintaining entirely unacceptable environments that deprived people of stimulation and affection cost the taxpayer dearly.[53] It is true that the notion of independent living and care in the community meant many things to many people:

> To the politician, 'community care' is a useful piece of rhetoric; to the sociologist, it is a stick to beat institutional care with; to the civil servant, it is a cheap alternative to institutional care which can be passed to the local authorities for action – or inaction; to the visionary, it is a dream of a new society in which people do really care; to social service departments, it is a nightmare of heightened public expectations and inadequate resources to meet them.[54]

In addition to these various approaches, the concept of independent living as envisaged by British representatives of the disability movement deviated from its original principles that were formulated in the United States in the 1970s. The rationale of independent-living centres in the United States drew strongly on the notions of consumerism, self-help, self-reliance and individual rights. To put it differently, it could be brought into alignment with neoliberal ideology and a market-oriented approach. By contrast, in Britain its initiators perceived independent living as an alternative model of self-organized welfare, which was expected to contribute to political autonomy and democratic participation and therefore did not fully embrace a market-based approach.[55] Nevertheless, it was a significant achievement of disability activists that the relevance of the concept gradually became indisputable even if its practical realization did not entirely follow the desired premises. Authorities were willing to support personal care and assistance with domestic chores but support for activities that would have facilitated social integration, such as hobbies or the cherishing of relationships were largely ignored. Another difference between the vision of the disability movement and the neoliberal state was the provision of care: representatives of the disability movement envisaged it in a formal contractual context, whereas the neoliberal preference was for informal care. A further step in the realization of a greater degree of independence was the idea of a personal budget and direct cash payment in lieu of social assistance which allowed disabled people to customize their needs for care. In this matter, disability activists succeeded in persuading the Conservative government that it was compatible with its agenda to promote market competition and personal choice. The year 1990 saw the passing of the NHS Community Care Act and 1996 the Direct Payment Act, and these gave greater role to the private and voluntary sectors in a quasi-market setting.

Epilogue

When the Thatcher government started to attack and, in many cases, reduce or abolish existing services, members of the disability movement were forced into a difficult position: instead of advocating the introduction of new services, they found themselves compelled to defend the legitimacy of the existing ones. This situation continued to persist even during tenure of New Labour governments, which further pursued the project of realigning the state, economy and society along the lines of the neoliberal agenda.[56] At the core of that agenda was market-based citizenship with the expectation that citizens should act in a "responsible" way while self-managing their lives. The concept of welfare-to-work, which implied work for those who can and security for those who cannot, likewise remained a central pillar.[57]

Whereas the International Year brought disappointment for many people, judged by its legacy in the longer term, the balance does not turn out to be entirely negative. For example, the International Year saw an attempt to introduce an anti-discrimination law, the Alf Morris Bill. While the attempt itself failed, the proposal provided the foundation for the Disability Discrimination Act (DDA) in 1995.[58] What was novel about this act is that it represented a new policy dimension by including a statutory right to challenge discrimination in the workplace. It is true that the original scope of this legislation was watered down in its final version: unlike in the case of comparable legislation on sex and race, discrimination was deemed illegal only if proven "unjustifiable" and the inclusion of the term "reasonable accommodation" removed the legislation's teeth by rendering guaranteed enforcement impossible. As disability activist Mike Oliver noted, the Tory leader William Hague regarded the DDA as one of his greatest successes, when in reality he had "turned the legislation into a pale shadow of what it should have been."[59] Another phenomenon which continued to characterize the post-1981 era was the tension between the agendas of traditional charities and the new disability organizations. To that end, Oliver regretted that the Spastic Society fiercely opposed the Disability Discrimination Act and only changed its attitude when its introduction became imminent.

In legislative terms, a landmark was reached in 2009 when Britain signed the United Nations' Convention on the Rights of Persons with Disabilities (CRPD). Yet, the trend that everyday practice continues to lag behind legislative norms has persisted: the pioneering human-rights-based approach failed to fulfil the expectations, all the more so because it promotes the importance of disability advocacy work and lobbying at the expense of service provision. Ironically, if they wished to be eligible for funding, even disabled people's organizations have been forced to accept these dynamics. Nonetheless, without satisfactory welfare services disabled people may feel that the expectation of independence is coterminous with their abandonment on the part of the state. The old warning that "invocations of self-help must bring a particular despair to those who would give anything to be able to help themselves"[60] remains valid, and the application of the human-rights-based model cannot succeed without first addressing the deficiencies of the welfare state that lie deep in its architecture. Ultimately, constant and often unqualified references to the notion of responsibility may provoke the question: what is the responsibility of *the state* towards its vulnerable citizens?

Notes

1 The author acknowledges the support of the ERC Consolidator Grant Rethinking Disability contract no. 648115 for writing this article.
2 Karen Soldatic and Helen Meekosha, "Disability and Neoliberal State Formations," in *Routledge Handbook of Disability Studies*, ed. Nick Watson, Alan Roulstone, and Carol Thomas (London and New York: Routledge, 2012), 207.
3 Among the two most recent seminal accounts are the doctoral thesis of Gareth Millward, "Invalid Definitions, Invalid Responses: Disability and the Welfare State, 1965–1995" (PhD thesis, London School of Hygiene and Tropical Medicine, 2013); Jameel Hampton, *Disability and the Welfare State in Britain: Changes in Perception and Policy 1948–1979* (Bristol: Policy Press 2016); Anne Borsay, *Disability and Social Policy in Britain since 1750: A History of Exclusion* (Basingstoke: Palgrave, 2004);

and Sonali Shah and Mark Priestley, *Disability and Social Change: Private Lives and Public Policies* (Bristol: Policy Press, 2011). The overview in this section draws on these works.
4 The material is held in the University of Liverpool Special Collections & Archives, under reference number GB 141 D383, and it contains 36 boxes; no online catalogue of these items is available at the moment. The records of the Secretariat, in addition to its own materials, also contain papers regarding the UN resolution and the IYDP working groups, as well as video and sound recordings, IYDP publicity, posters and press cuttings.
5 Disability Income Group's comment published in *The Times*, 1 February 1969, p. 2, as quoted in Millward, "Invalid Definitions, Invalid Responses," 285.
6 DIG Memorandum, as quoted in Millward, "Invalid Definitions, Invalid Responses," 73.
7 Irene Loach and Ruth Lister, "Second Class Disabled: A Report on the Non-Contributory Invalidity Pension for Married Women" (Equal Rights for Disabled Women Campaign: London, July 1978), 1, accessed 2 February 2019, https://disability-studies.leeds.ac.uk/wp-content/uploads/sites/40/library/lister-original-version.pdf.
8 Alan Walker and Peter Townsend, eds., *Disability in Britain: A Manifesto of Rights* (Oxford: Martin Robertson & Company, 1981), preface, ix.
9 Millward, "Invalid Definitions, Invalid Responses,"167.
10 Borsay, *Disability and Social Policy*, 201.
11 See Florence Sutcliffe-Braithwaite, "Neo-Liberalism and Morality in the Making of Thatcherite Social Policy," *The Historical Journal* 55, no. 2 (2012): 497–520.
12 Newsletter of the IYDP Secretariat (1981), 19, Archives of the International Secretariat, D 383/2/1/1.
13 Ibid., 5.
14 The full speech can be accessed online at www.royal.uk/christmas-broadcast-1981, accessed on 2 February 2019.
15 By the end of the International Year approximately 20 sizeable dossiers were filled with the correspondence of the Snowdon Committee, the majority of which included letters written by individuals. These dossiers are held under the classification D 383/2/2 in the Liverpool University Archives.
16 Archives of the International Secretariat, D 383/2/2/2.
17 A campaign in IYDP for a general disability income, brochure, 4, D 383/2/7/11.
18 Joint Project, All Party Disablement Group, House of Commons brochure, without page number, D 383/2/4/2.
19 "Motion: IYDP," *House of My Lords Parliamentary Debates. House of Lords Official Report* 416, no. 17 (14 January, 1981), 140, D.383/2/4/1.
20 Derek Kinrade, *Alf Morris: People's Parliamentarian – Scenes from the Life of Lord Morris of Manchester* (London: National Information Forum, 2007), 279.
21 Campaign for Disability Income, Minute Book of the IYDP Committee, 3, D383/2/1/11980/81.
22 "Motion: IYDP," *House of Lords Parliamentary Debates. House of Lords Official Report* 9, D.383/2/4/1.
23 Report produced on 16 July 1981, D 383/2/1/6.
24 Diane Driedger, *The Last Civil Rights Movement: Disabled People's International* (London: Hurst & Company, and New York: St Martin's Press, 1989), 36.
25 Jane Campbell and Mike Oliver, *Disability Politics: Understanding Our Past, Changing Our Future* (London and New York: Routledge, 1996), 84.
26 Ibid., 188–189.
27 Millward, "Invalid Definitions, Invalid Responses," 186.
28 Campbell and Oliver, *Disability Politics*, 82.
29 Ibid., 82.

30 Richard Balles, *Sex & Drugs & Rock 'n' Roll: The Life of Ian Dury* (London, New York, Sydney: Omnibus Press, 2011), 239. See also G.A. McKay, "'Crippled with Nerves': Popular Music and Polio, with Particular Reference to Ian Dury," *Popular Music*, 28. no 3 (2009): 341–365.
31 Balles, *Sex & Drugs & Rock 'n' Roll*, 240.
32 UPIAS – Union of Physically Impaired Against Segregation, *Disability Challenge* 2, December 1983, 5, accessed 2 February 2019, https://disability-studies.leeds.ac.uk/wp-content/uploads/sites/40/library/UPIAS-Disability-Challenge-2.pdf.
33 Ibid., 1.
34 " Laurence Clark, "Lenonard Cheshire vs. The Disabled Persons' Movement: A Review," Disability Studies virtual archives, accessed 2 February 2019, https://disability-studies.leeds.ac.uk/wp-content/uploads/sites/40/library/Clark-Laurence-leonard-cheshire.pdf.
35 UPIAS, *Disability Challenge*, 6–7.
36 "International Year of Disabled People: A Beginning Not an End" brochure, 46, D 383/2/1/1.
37 Alan Walker and Peter Townsend, *Disability in Britain: A Manifesto of Rights* (Oxford: Martin Robertson, 1981), 9.
38 Ibid., 15.
39 *The Guardian*, 30 January 1981, as cited in Walker and Townsend, *Disability in Britain*, 13.
40 Barbara Waine, *The Rhetoric of Independence? The Ideology and Practice of Social Policy in Thatcher's Britain* (New York and Oxford: Berg, 1991), 158.
41 UPIAS, *Disability Challenge*, 47.
42 Walker and Townsend, *Disability in Britain*, 5.
43 Ibid., 5.
44 Millward, "Invalid Definitions, Invalid Responses," 191.
45 Colin Barnes and Geof Mercer, *Exploring Disability* (Polity Press: Cambridge, 2010), 101.
46 Deborah A. Stone, *The Disabled State* (Philadelphia: Temple University Press, 1984).
47 Millward, "Invalid Definitions, Invalid Responses," 235–236.
48 Chris Grover and Karen Soldatic, "Neoliberal Restructuring, Disabled People and Social (In)Security in Australia and Britain." *Scandinavian Journal of Disability Research* 15, no. 3 (2013): 217.
49 Barnes and Mercer, *Exploring Disability*, 114.
50 C. Grover and L. Piggott, "Disabled People, the Reserve Army of Labour and Welfare Reform," *Disability and Society* 20, no. 7 (2005): 705–717.
51 Karen Soldatic and Helen Meekosha, "Disability and Neoliberal State Formations," in *Routledge Handbook of Disability Studies*, ed. Nick Watson, Alan Roulstone, and Carol Thomas (London and New York: Routledge, 2012), 202.
52 Ibid., 202.
53 Ibid., 214.
54 Jones K. Brown and J. Bradshaw, *Issues in Social Policy* (London: Routledge and Kegan Paul, 1978), 114.
55 Charlotte Pearson, "Independent Living," in *Routledge Handbook of Disability Studies*, ed. Nick Watson, Alan Roulstone, and Carol Thomas (London and New York: Routledge, 2012), 241.
56 For more on this, see Randall Owen and Sarah Parker Harris, "No Rights without Responsibilities: Disability Rights and Neoliberal Reform under New Labour," *Disability Studies Quarterly* 32, no. 3 (2012), accessed 2 February 2019, http://dsq-sds.org/article/view/3283.

57 For a more comprehensive account of this shift, see Bernhard Rieger, "Making Britain Work Again: Unemployment and the Remaking of British Social Policy in the Eighties," *The Historical Journal* 562, no. 133 (June 2018): 634–666.
58 Mike Oliver, "Rewriting History: The Case of the DDA 1995," *Disability & Society* 31, no. 7 (2016): 966–968.
59 John Pring, "Mike Oliver Delivers a Stringing Rebuke to 'Parasitic' Disability Charities," 30 November 2017, accessed 2 February 2019, https://ukdhm.org/one-of-the-key-figures-in-the-disabled-peoples-movement-has-come-out-of-retirement-to-deliver-a-stinging-rebuke-to-parasitic-disability-charities/.
60 Key Andrews and John Jacobs, *Punishing the Poor: Poverty under Thatcher* (London: Macmillan, 1990), 95.

8 Welfare: defended, questioned, complemented?

Belgian welfare arrangements in the 1970s–1980s from the perspective of disability organizations

Anaïs Van Ertvelde

Introduction[1]

Although much has been written about how welfare states have organized the care for marginalized groups, the degree of complexity that marks the relationships between these groups and the welfare state itself is rarely given a central role. The literature on evolving welfare systems tends to emphasize top-down policy changes as well as national perspectives.[2] This is part of a broader tendency: international entanglements are not really seen as being fully within the scope of research on the welfare state. As Kaufman notes in his article on the idea of social policies in Western societies: "the programmatic idea of the welfare state emerged on the transnational level as a result of the convergence of universalistic aims of the ILO and the doctrine of human rights conceived in a way that included social rights. However, for a long time, national welfare politics (as well as welfare state research) did not refer to these transnational legitimizations.[3] Although exceptionally, transnational historical perspectives on social policy have been proposed as alternatives to national welfare state models.[4] Marginalized groups, then, are portrayed as a concern for policymakers to respond to.[5] They are characterized as either the givers of care (i.e. women) or the recipients of care (i.e. people with disabilities), but seldom as both (i.e. women with disabilities).[6] In some cases they are included as actors working towards the expansion of social rights and the welfare system. However, these accounts are often used as a buttress for sweeping statements about the grand evolution of welfare arrangements. Such accounts, however useful in their own right, leave little room for local variations.[7] The intricate, sometimes even paradoxical, ways in which marginalized groups and their organizations thought of and interacted with welfare state systems remain out of reach.

Therefore I have chosen to explore Belgium's welfare state arrangements in a way that takes into account transnational entanglements, international legitimizations and a perspective from below. More specifically, I integrate the perspective of people with disabilities and their organizations. The choice to address the perspective of disability organizations was guided by the lack of existing Belgian welfare state literature that uses the interactions between disability organizations, policymakers and people with disabilities as a lens.[8] That disability can be a particularly illuminating lens with which to look at the welfare state was another motivating factor. Scholarly discussions have identified rising tensions between the different sorts of emancipatory claims made by marginalized groups. From the 1970s onwards, emancipatory claims based on distributive equality, often linked to the welfare state and to class struggles, are said to lose ground – perhaps too much ground – to emancipatory claims based on status equality, recognition, human rights and identity politics. Arguments on how these two sorts of emancipatory claims can be reconciled abound.[9] Disability, even though it is rarely framed as "a relevant form of social conflict,"[10] might just be a potent test case, since it is such a quintessentially hybrid category. Disability is clearly an issue of redistributive justice: without additional interventions the economic structure of the Western post-WWII society, in which the bodies of citizens are valued to the extent that they can be used in production processes, redistributes material resources away from people with disabilities. At the same time, disability is mired in questions of status equality. Disability organizations have been asking, not merely for material redistribution and welfare arrangements, but also for the recognition of disability as a positive identity, and the deconstruction of psycho-socio-cultural fears about the monstrous and the diseased that still have an impact on the status of people with disabilities in society.

In this chapter I will first introduce the necessary particularities of the Belgian welfare context, and then look into two turning points: after 1973 and after 1981. Both instances can shed light on the role developments at the international and transnational levels, and people with disabilities and their associations, have played in reshaping Belgium's welfarestate landscape during the 1970s and 1980s. This approach allows me to focus on the simultaneous but often paradoxical manners in which this reshaping took place: (1) by protesting the roll-back of the welfare state or even working towards its expansion; (2) by formulating a critique of the welfare state, its functioning and/or the effect it has on its citizens; and (3) by looking for (complementary) alternatives to welfare such as the development of disability rights.

The specificities of the Belgian welfare context

First, I shall take into account some of the specificities of the Belgian welfare system and the place facilities for persons with disabilities were assigned therein. The Belgian welfare system was based on a social insurance system, the so-called Bismarckian model, and a system of social assistance benefits. It became mandatory by law in 1944. Many social security institutions were run by societal organizations. Depending on the type of benefit or allowance, payments were to be made by trade unions or health insurance agencies, and not directly by the state itself.[11] Such trade unions and health insurance providers thus were important social players. They were part of a larger network of political, socio-cultural and economic organizations that all adhered to a particular ideological or religious pillar. This form of social structuring is called pillarization.[12]

The three main Belgian pillars – Catholic, socialist and liberal – were intertwined with the welfare state. Through the principle of subcontracting, the pillarized organizations could acquire government funding to create welfare facilities, grant citizens access to public goods and fund their own organizations: a generous expansion of the welfare state into parallel and competing channels was thus to the advantage of the different pillars.[13] With the Catholic Party in almost uninterrupted political power during a substantial part of Belgium's history, there was ample opportunity to create the ideal legislative and subsidiary circumstances for the Catholic pillar to flourish.[14] One of the other reasons for the predominance of the Catholic pillar over the socialist and liberal ones was its double power base. It was linked not only to the Catholic Party but also to the Church, which was backed up by a host of long-existing care institutions.[15]

Throughout *les trente glorieuses*, Belgium arrangements for persons with disabilities were firmly rooted in this pillarized welfare state. Where disability is concerned, the Belgian welfare system is made up of two parallel sets of arrangements, both of which have different historical track records.[16] The first set deals with mutual social insurances against sickness and invalidity, which originated in the second half of the nineteenth century and are paid out by the social partners mentioned earlier. The second set consists of social assistance and allowances for those people with disabilities, who could not fall back on social security schemes such as compensation payments for occupational accidents. These arrangements go back to a 1928 law that established the Fund for the Infirm and the Maimed whose financial payments were directly overseen by the state.[17] From the beginning, the law and the fund it had established were plagued by a precarious balancing act: providing costly allowances for people with disabilities as well as incentivizing their reintegration into the labour market. This last goal was to be reached through loans for the purchase of wheelchairs, prosthetics and adapted tools, as well as (re)training programmes.

In the course of the 1950s awareness grew that a new approach was needed to reach the goal of labour-market integration. Drawing on International Labour Organization (ILO) recommendations and examples from the UK and the US, additional ways of bringing about what was then called "social rehabilitation" were conceived. Aided by a steadily growing economy, laws on social rehabilitation and labour-market integration followed, including provisions for the establishment of sheltered workshops as was described in ILO Recommendation No. 99.[18] By 1963 a National Fund for the Social Rehabilitation of Disabled Persons was set up and new employment policies, like the highly contested quota, were brought to the fore.[19] From this period onwards policies regarding people with disabilities covered a continually expanding segment of the welfare state.[20] These developments proceeded under the watchful eye of the new pillarized disability organizations that emerged shortly after WWII. The Catholic Association for the Handicapped was the most important of these organizations, as it had close links to the Catholic health insurance fund, a network of local Catholic care institutions and more than 40,000 members.[21]

The Belgian welfare system in its entirety reached a culmination point in the early 1970s. Thereafter, when the oil crises and the economic downturn struck the country, an anti-welfare state discourse became popular and a transformation of the system was initiated. The economic malaise lingered on while the pillarized social organizations could not see eye to eye over possible solutions. For quite some time the federal government stuck with tried and tested Keynesian recipes and invested much off its energy in defederalization – the process by which powers of governance are transferred from the national level to the level of regions and communities. Only after the 1980 constitutional reform – which effectively lent more power to the regions and communities – did the Catholic-liberal federal government focus on the economic issues at stake and choose a change of direction, now favouring wage restraint and social spending cuts. The devaluation of the Belgian franc in 1982 became a symbol of the influx of a new sort of neoliberally influenced austerity policy.[22] By the end of the decade, the dreaded cutbacks in social spending and state provisions, however, remained limited. Austerity policy *à la Belgique* did not wish to reduce state bureaucracies to the same degree as its Anglo-American relatives did, and left core social security arrangements intact. However, the related idea of the citizen as a *homo economicus*, as someone who should be able to freely develop themselves without being too dependent on the state, did take hold.[23]

Where people with disabilities were concerned, contemporary authors pointed to a trend in social security and welfare towards more autonomy, personal responsibility and individualized approaches, and a move away from institutionalization and standardized care packages. At the time, sociologist Van Buggenhout even spoke of the 1980s as a period of a "true revolution" in social security measures and a change of mentality concerning the treatment of people with disabilities.[24] She pinpoints the changes in the way disability was defined by the end of the decade: less and less as a causal factor to be found in the body and more as a dynamic process linked to social integration.[25] According to Samoy, this decade was also the harbinger of an evolution that mixed exclusion policies based on allowances more and more with inclusion policies based on activation.[26] However, he remained critical of the way and degree to which these ideas were actually translated into policy and provisions, in particular in the first half of the 1980s. High unemployment rates pushed labour-market integration of people with disabilities off the list of priorities. At the start of the 1990s, the percentage of disabled people in the labour market was still very low at 30% – with numbers estimated to be even lower for women. At the same time that Belgium recorded these stagnating employment numbers, a new way of thinking about labour-market access was gaining ground: equal opportunities.[27]

How did these changes come about in a time of austerity politics, with which they – at first sight – seem to be at odds? The authors mentioned earlier point to several explanations for this phenomenon. First, Belgium's economic performance made a recovery in the second half of the 1980s. Then, a restructuration of care provisions for the disabled had to take place in any case. Important parts of the policy and provisions for people with disabilities were transferred from

Belgian welfare arrangements 141

the federal level to the regions in the defederalization process. Third, new social movements such as the women's movement had raised awareness of emancipation and participation as important values for marginalized groups. I will now look more closely at people with disabilities and their associations, and the impact of evolutions on the international level, to understand how the creation of welfare arrangements that allowed for more autonomy and individualization could coincide with a shift away from Keynesian policy recipes.

An uncertain change of heart – after 1973

Following the oil crisis of 1973, the global economic crisis hit Belgium: growth slowed, unemployment rates were on the rise and social expenditures followed suit, leading to deficits in state spending. The Keynesian state seemed unable to spend its way out of this particular crisis. The first attempts at state frugality were made by the Tindemans I government, which launched plans to reduce social security spending. These measures led to staunch resistance – the number of strikes rose by 47% in 1975–1976.[28] The rising unemployment rates and general atmosphere of economic crisis reinvigorated the new social movements. They started to resist the first attempts at rolling back welfare state schemes by rejecting austerity measurements. At the same time those new social movements were contributing to a welfare state critique in demonstrating a tendency

> towards questioning all forms of reproduction that had been incorporated by the welfare state in a process of planning and bureaucratic management: of the reproduction of the human species (ecological movement, anti-nuclear energy movement), of the reproduction of social living conditions (action groups around housing, transport and health) and of the reproduction of subjectivities (women's movement, youth movement).[29]

In this same vein welfare provisions for people with disabilities – mainly based on institutionalized care, allowances, vocational training and social rehabilitation – also came under scrutiny. Questions were raised about how effective welfare measurements were and how adequately they were organized, but also about their limited visions of what disability was and what the lives of disabled people could look like. Some of these queries pointed at possible organizational problems, which were fundamental to the particular ways in which the Belgian welfare state had developed. An example from an academic angle is the assessment made by Mia Bracke-Defever.[30] This lecturer in medical sociology points out several problem areas for Belgium. First, she noted the historically differing trajectories that led to two different sets of arrangements concerned with allowances and benefits. This two-tiered system produced unequal payouts. Persons with congenital disabilities would receive considerably lower benefits than persons with comparable disabilities caused by a workplace accident, mainly because of the latter's past contributions to the welfare state. Furthermore, Bracke-Defever pointed out that with regard to its care institutions, the Belgian setup can be seen as rather *laisser-faire*. It continues to emphasize private initiative, which in practice leads to a care landscape dominated by organizations run by the Catholic pillar.[31] Then, she characterized Belgium's disability policy as a piecemeal construction, spread out over different ministries and institutions, lacking a central agency or vision. Last, she criticized the welfare definitions of disability, which are, according to her, based on outdated medical notions that do not take into account individual variations or relational and situational factors. Bracke-Defever's critiques touch on how welfare arrangements should be organized to improve the quality of services. She discusses matters such as shortening waiting lists and increasing allowances. She also seems to indicate that a well-entrenched policy – one such as welfare arrangements for people with disabilities – is weighed down by its long history, by past public opinions that still linger and by the rigidity of existing institutions. These factors then render rethinking policy from scratch in an established domain such as welfare all the more challenging. But her remarks also seem to go a step further. Although not yet fully explicit in her formulations, I read her assessments as a sign of a developing awareness that welfare state arrangements can be a handmaiden of the status quo, especially when applied to minority groups. Allowances support a moderately comfortable level of survival in the margins of the existing social order, yet also maintain said margins. Rehabilitation gives the possibility to reintegrate into the mainstream social order but does not necessarily adapt this social order as such.

Similar concerns were voiced by people with disabilities themselves, often instigated by personal experiences with welfare bureaucracy and care institutions. In his 1978 memoirs *Handicap: Unexplained Ally* journalist and teacher Jean-Pierre Goetghebuer sets out the ways in which he creatively rearranged his life and personal ambitions after a spinal-cord injury.[32] The former prospective priest, who partially set aside his calling when he was immersed in the critical post-1968 atmosphere of an undisclosed Belgian student town, dedicates many paragraphs to a biting critique of the paternalistic manner in which he is treated both by Catholic charities and rehabilitation facilities. Yet he reserves an entire chapter for the tangle of unspoken administrative rules and obstacles he encounters when trying to secure employment as a secondary school teacher. He confronts a seemingly endless administrative confusion about whether a person using a wheelchair is even allowed to teach. In the end he decides to write to the Minister of National Education and to the chair of the Catholic education network to clear things up. The Minister of National Education personally tries to dissuade to dissuade him from teaching. The school buildings are inaccessible, he declares, and then there is the immaturity of secondary school students who cannot be trusted not to take advantage of a disabled person. The chair of the Catholic education network in turn sees no fundamental problems in employing a disabled teacher, but fears the verdict of the administrative health services. While there are no specific legal provisions prohibiting a disabled person from teaching, he explains, the physicians overseeing the health service can judge as they see fit. Precisely these inspections by health services had already eliminated Goetghebuer's confidence in the assessment system as a whole since he ended up with different invalidity rates on different occasions.[33] In this chapter Goetghebuer not only calls out the internal inconsistencies of this seemingly scientific metric system of access to welfare provisions, but also speaks of a bureaucratic marginalization, which, he adds, does nothing but discourage people with disabilities from taking part in everyday life.

At around the same time the workings of welfare state provisions for people with disabilities, as well as the power that those in charge wielded over disabled people's lives, were being examined and challenged, the existence of those very same provisions seemed to come under fire. The 1974–1975 economic crisis led to attempts at the federal/state level to implement budget cuts. The attempts to decrease social assistance evoked fierce resistance from the pillarized disability organizations, who saw the peril to their own established positions in the welfare state. The threat was that, for the first time in years, the situation of people with disabilities would deteriorate instead of improve. The taken-for-granted logic of incremental progress and ever-expanding social security measures might be overturned, and this seemed to make disability organizations more politically vigilant, if not downright combative.

Take the monthly magazine issued by the Catholic Association for the Handicapped. Whereas previous volumes of this magazine seemed more low key, concerned mainly with news from local sections, practical tips on excursions, aids or living arrangements, and entertainment such as crossword puzzles, the tone of the monthly becomes more political, confrontational even, in the course of 1974–1975.[34] "What do we expect from our new government!" a lead article from the June 1974 edition defiantly declares with its eye on the new Tindemans I government coalition.[35] A major cause for concern and discontent in those years was the revision of the allowance system for people with disabilities. The Catholic Association for the Handicapped perceived this revision as a major step backwards and a covert form of cuts in social assistance. The organization made this clear by organizing a protest in November 1974 in which sentiments like "back to the bottom" and "an allowance only suitable for vegetables to subsist on" dominated. The first issue of 1975 is a festive edition – marking the organization's thirtieth birthday – but also warns about more governmental savings at the expense of people with disabilities. It states outright that the organization is bracing itself for the upcoming fight to protect the achievements of the welfare system.[36] Especially precarious in this period was the situation of migrant workers trying to gain access to the welfare provisions for people with disabilities. In a 1975 ruling the European Court of Justice, basing its decision on the Treaty of the European Community and the fundamental freedom of movement set out therein, condemned the Belgian state for refusing to pay the customary allowances for disabled minors to a fifteen-year-old Italian boy whose parents had been working in Belgium since 1947.[37]

While the workings of welfare state provisions and their possible restricting effects on people with disabilities were scrutinized, and the rolling back of those same welfare state provisions was being called out, alternative ways of framing battles for social and economic justice were brought to the fore. Perhaps there were other –possibly complementary – frameworks that could be used to enable people with disabilities to live integrated and meaningful lives? Several historians of human rights have argued that human rights were developing into a more potent framework for emancipation from the second half of the 1970s onwards, much more so than in the post-WWII era of their initial conception.[38] Scholars like Sarah Snyder and Jean Helen Quataert take this a step further and argue that by the late 1970s an international human-rights movement – with the signing of the 1975 Helsinki Accords, President Carter's affiliation with human rights and Amnesty International winning the Nobel Peace Prize in 1977 – was not just underway but garnering full strength. Within this human-rights framework, unalienable rights for specific identity groups such as women and children – rights that were not *a priori* linked to the state but had a universal quality – were starting to get formulated in a complex interplay between international institutions, transnational organizations, national governments, and local activists.[39] The relationship between rights and welfare has been framed simultaneously as one of reaction and one of conformation. Human-rights historian Samuel Moyn has argued that "the notion that individuals have basic rights was shaped by the political economy," be that political economy one of state-regulated welfare capitalism or neoliberalism.[40] At the same time there is also a sense in his writings that in many countries the exclusionary mechanisms of the welfare state – he mentions the experiences of women in particular – were challenged in the 1970s and 1980s on the basis of this new set of rights, which were not so much being granted on the basis of national (welfare-)state membership as on the basis of group identity.

The idea that people with disabilities could be not only the worthy recipients of welfare state provisions but also the bearers of inalienable rights, such as the right to work or the right to health, was being formulated in an international and transnational manner as well. An example is the Belgian National Collective Action for the Handicapped, which grouped different disability organizations and had more than 100,000 members.[41] Collective Action drafted a proposal for a text, which would eventually become the UN Declaration on the Rights of Disabled Persons (1975).[42] Via local political connections the draft of Collective Action ended up on the desk of the Belgian foreign affairs minister, who then agreed to submit this project text to the United Nations. The proposal of Collective Action for a rights-based text for people with disabilities was itself influenced by internationally embedded organizations. Until that moment the notion of disability rights was virtually absent within Belgium's national welfare institutions. Collective Action drew immediate inspiration from the UN Declaration on the Rights of Mentally Retarded Persons (1971) and decided to adapt this earlier declaration to suit the needs of all persons with disabilities.[43] Interestingly enough, there is another layer to this process of formulating rights for persons with disabilities. The content of the 1971 UN Declaration on the Rights of Mentally Retarded Persons itself was based on a different text. The text – called the Declaration on the General and Special Rights of the Mentally Retarded – was issued, not by an international institution, but by a transnational organization for people with mental disabilities located in Brussels, a clear-cut example of the influence both national and international disability organizations had, not only on the formulation of disability rights, but on the conception of such a notion.[44]

The Belgian representation to the UN in New York worked very strategically, foreseeing and bypassing objections by the Soviet bloc, circumnavigating the conventional procedures and succeeding in getting the Declaration on the Rights of Disabled Persons approved by the General Assembly within the span of a year, to widespread acclaim.[45] In view of the 1971 and the 1975 UN declarations it seems logical that the formulation of rights for people with disabilities as part of a larger human-rights framework would then follow suit. In his doctoral dissertation on the internationalization of disability policies, Gildas Brégain agrees with this line of thinking, concluding that in the period 1967–1982 a series of international declarations and juridical instruments confirmed *les personnes handicapées comme des sujets de droits*.[46] The exact content of those disability rights, however, were not a given from the start. From the telegrams being sent back and forth between the Belgian foreign affairs minister and the Belgian representation at the UN it becomes clear that in the discussions leading up to the adoption of the declaration by the General Assembly of the UN, which exact rights were to be emphasized, and in particular whether socio-economic rights were to be included, was a matter of discussion and disagreement.[47]

A paradoxical state – after 1981

As a direct result of these evolutions the UN International Year of Disabled Persons (IYDP) was proclaimed in 1976. National governments would organize the International Year in their respective countries in 1981 to draw attention to persons with disabilities and the issues they experience.[48] Given the success of the 1975 declaration, the Belgian foreign affairs ministry saw a potential role for Belgium as a leader in international matters related to disability and had every intention of being strongly involved with the elaboration of the IYDP at the UN level.[49] The International Year and its follow-up, the World Programme of Action, put the emphasis on the involvement of disabled people's organizations, raised the issue of equal opportunities, and declared grand intentions not only for 1981 itself but also for the subsequent International Decade of Disabled Persons (1982–1993):

> The theme of IYDP was "full participation and equality", defined as the right of persons with disabilities to take part fully in the life and development of their societies, enjoy living conditions equal to those of other citizens, and have an equal share in improved conditions resulting from socio-economic development.
>
> Other objectives of the Year included: increasing public awareness; understanding and acceptance of persons who are disabled; and encouraging persons with disabilities to form organizations through which they can express their views and promote action to improve their situation.[50]

Despite these intentions the direct, short-term impact of the International Year at the Belgian national level seemed limited. It got buried by two major events: the Belgian state reform of 1980 and the incoming economic downturn of 1981. The economic downturn ushered in the political acceptance of neoliberal recovery policies. These policies would last throughout the 1980s although the limits to their success soon became clear: economic growth rebounded, but unemployment rates remained high and living standards fell.[51] With regard to policies on disability this translated throughout the 1980s into attempts along the lines of what Jamie Peck has called "the roll-back phase" of neoliberalism: characterized by attacks on allowances, Keynesian regulations, unions and planning institutions.[52] Only limited efforts were directed at the integration of people with disabilities into the general labour market. The idea of quotas, for instance, was laid to rest in response to a European Commission consultation. The roll-back logic was not all-encompassing, however. For example, sheltered workshops grew ever more popular as a relatively inexpensive solution to the problem of disabled people's employment.[53] In contrast with the lofty declaration of the International Year, the Belgian government's austerity measurements caused bad blood among disability organizations.

The Collective Action, which had composed the text for UN Declaration on the Rights of Disabled Persons a few years before, was not directly involved with the organization of the International Year. Rather, it acted as an outside voice of criticism. The discontent with the state of affairs culminated in two public moments of resistance. The first was a six-thousand-person strong public demonstration under the banner of *Jaar van de gehandicapten, is dat nu?* (Year of Disabled Persons, is it now?) in May 1981. The aim was to put pressure on the government to strive for more ambitious and concrete steps towards the integration of disabled people into Belgian society. Numerous participants expressed their doubts about the sincerity of the ambitious letters of intent produced for the International Year.

"The year of the disabled: a cherry on the cake? HUBERT: Do shut up about these years. They will not matter. Nothing but make-believe."[54]

The dissatisfaction with the International Year grew fiercely in the course of 1981, culminating in the autumn, as the Catholic minister of National Welfare and Public Health announced a another revision of the allowance system for people with disabilities that would affect people with disabilities negatively. Along with demonstrations, letter-writing actions and press conferences, the International Year became one of the tools at the disposal of disability organizations, a symbolic one. The International Year was deployed to protest against the reductions in national welfare stipulations for people with disabilities and give international legitimizations to the welfare demands of the Collective Action. "In our country the 'Year of the disabled' will go down in history as the year of budget cuts."[55]

The second event that cast a burden on the International Year was the Belgian state reform of 1980, which meant the onset of the slow process of defederalizing policy regarding people with disabilities. Matters of social security – and hence allowances for people with disabilities – remained a federal competence but "all matters related to the person" such as education and social housing were devolved to the community level. This led to major institutional changes in the way welfare arrangements for people with disabilities were organized that would take until the mid-1990s to be completed.[56] These institutional reforms created an opening to shake up entrenched welfare policies, but they did very little to undo the already fragmented nature of welfare disability policy. The consequences of these disruptions had already become clear during the International Year: the organizing committee had to be reorganized into a Dutch-speaking and a French-speaking committee, while the federal advisory council on disability – the organ that should have guaranteed the involvement of disability organizations – ceased functioning in the course of 1981.[57]

In response to the International Year, the European Commission (EC) came up with its first action programme, Social Integration of Disabled People – a Framework for Community Action (1982–1987). The title itself already speaks of a shift away from the former focus of the EC on rehabilitation to one that was more conscious of other means of social integration.[58] Another follow-up to the International Year was the 1982 UN World Programme of Action Concerning Disabled Persons. The programme consisted of two more traditional components – prevention and rehabilitation – but one part also spoke of the equalization of opportunities.[59]

And it is precisely this idea that seemed to come to fruition during the second half of the 1980s in Belgium. In 1985 Wivina De Meester took office as the first secretary of state to be explicitly charged with disability policies. For many years, De Meester had been involved with disability issues from a personal perspective. The politician was one of the co-founders of Monnikenheide: the first short-stay home for people with disabilities in Flanders that favoured small-scale activities and integration.[60] She shared her office with the very first secretary of state charged with emancipation policies: Miet Smet. This emancipation policy post had been explicitly pushed for by the Belgian women's movement and got a nudge in the right direction thanks to the influential UN Conference on Women, which took place in Nairobi in 1985.[61] Emancipation policies still focused mostly on women, but in the slipstream of these evolutions the idea of equal opportunities for different minority groups seems to have taken hold. By the beginning of the 1990s, when the ministers for equality policies started to take on their newly created posts at the level of the communities, people with disabilities were indisputably identified as the subjects of equal-opportunities policies. Legislative examples from abroad are also seen to have played a role in this, for example the Canadian Employment Equity Act.[62] The establishment of federal and regional equal-opportunity-policy competences also paved the way for opening a civil society that up until that moment had been claimed by pillarized organizations. From this period onwards organizations that were not linked to a particular religious or ideological pillar could now receive government funding, not on the basis of their attachment to welfare state provisions but solely on account of their campaigns for equal opportunities and rights.[63] The process of depillarization and secularization, which reached its zenith in the 1990s, only partially led to the dismantling of Catholic care institutions. This network of care organizations – whose Catholic religious character did substantially decrease – exists up to the present day.[64]

By the end of the 1980s and the beginning of the 1990s these evolutions were pushed further along by a new wave of disability groups. Among these groups was Independent Living Flanders, which drew inspiration from the international Independent Living movements. The roots of the Independent Living movement can be traced back to the U.S. Civil Rights movement and the fight for university accessibility for people with extensive disabilities in California in the 1960s, and reached Belgian disability activists through contacts in Sweden. Independent Living Flanders started to strive for the implementation of personal-assistance budgets (PABs), with which people with disabilities could organize their own individual care instead of being dependent on the care packages on offer. Care institutions should not hold the exclusive right to receive government subsidies, thus ultimately controlling what care looked like, was the line of thinking that Independent Living introduced. Disabled people should be able to autonomously organize their own lives and care options.[65] Comparable initiatives were doing the rounds within Elcker-Ik, a well-known organization for adult education that played a decisive role in the unfolding of the new social movements in Flanders. Their Working Group Disabled People, which started operation in the early 1970s, explicitly sought alternative ways of organizing disabled lives outside the solutions offered by the state but also outside of "the capitalist market." The working group on disability explored the idea of a social economy, and was involved with projects concerning integrated living, care reforms, accessible public transportation and sexuality.[66] Spurred on by transnational disability organizations, the concept of disability rights was further developed by international institutions as evidenced by the appointment of a UN rapporteur on disability and human rights and the "rights-inspired" UN Rules on the Equalization of Opportunities for Persons (1993).[67] However, at this time, no legally binding international rights framework was achieved.[68] In spite of this activity, at the Belgian policy level, disability rights were only rarely discussed. They were present in the expositions of disability groups such as AVERG (Active Defence of the Rights of the Disabled), which led the resistance against the budget cuts and price increases in residential and care institutions proposed by the first Flemish minister of well-being, Rika Steyaert, in the mid-1980s.[69] By the middle of the 1990s GRIP VZW – an organization that made disability rights its leitmotiv – came into existence. Policymakers on the federal and regional levels were slower to catch up. On the one hand, they were tempted by the rhetoric of rights, while, on the other, they were unsure about the impact of adopting a binding rights framework on some of the existing welfare state provisions for people with disabilities. Disability rights obtained a legally binding convention only in 2006 with the UN Convention on the Rights of Persons with Disabilities, which was signed by Belgium in 2009.[70]

In conclusion we can note that during the period 1973–1989 the Belgian government initiated the first attempts at weathering the economic downturn with neoliberal recipes that included the (covert) curtailing of social-assistance benefits. Where disability was concerned these neoliberal recipes played out in attempts to lower allowances for people with disabilities and save on health care expenditures. Policy implementations by no means followed an ideologically straight line. In the case of sheltered care, for instance, it seemed more advantageous to keep people with severe disabilities in state-sponsored institutions and out of the labour market – thus keeping them out of the unemployment rates. Further developments that aided the undermining of the caring state were the effects of the depillarization process that started to curb the power of the numerous pillarized assistance and care organizations at the heart of Belgian welfare state provisions, as well as the defederalization process. The latter reinforced the logic that state power could be shifted from the state, not only upwards to international organizations such as the UN, but also downwards to the local or regional level, or laterally to unelected bodies and civil society.[71] The turning points after 1973 and 1981 show that changes in the Belgian welfare landscape related to people with disabilities were influenced by the paradoxical ways in which citizens with disabilities, disabled people's organizations and academics interacted with governmental agencies responsible for organizing welfare provisions, and these tensions did not play out solely on the national level.

In the first instance, citizens with disabilities oftentimes rely on the different measures provided by the welfare state. Disabled citizens and their organizations, many of which were pillarized and thus invested in the welfare state themselves, come into conflict with governmental agencies when these cut social spending on disability, and they protest these decisions with a variety of tools, including public protests. Examples include the 1974 national protest of KVG against the allowance revisions for people with disabilities or the AVERG protests against Minister Steyaert's price increases in the care sector in the second half of the 1980s. In the struggle over legitimacy, different levels of government confront each other, for instance when Collective Action employed the 1981 UN International Year of Disabled Persons as a symbolically raised fist against national budget cuts in allowances for people with disabilities.

At the same time, people with disabilities, disability organizations and academics also made their own contributions towards a critique of both care and welfare provisions. They called into question the organizational functioning of the welfare state and raised the issue of what they perceived to be the stigmatizing, isolating and marginalizing effects of certain welfare interventions on people with disabilities. Such sentiments can be found in the memoirs of Jean-Pierre Ghoetgebuer, the analysis of sociologist Mia Bracke-Defever and in the statements of several disability organizations, which then tried to formulate alternative ways of framing battles for social justice for people with disabilities. We see this reflected in the Declaration on the Rights of Disabled Persons crafted by Collective Action and furthered by the Belgian representatives to the UN in 1975. This is also reflected in the shift from supply-driven welfare provisions to a demand-driven care market that would allow people with disabilities more choice and autonomy, as proposed by Independent Living Flanders from the end of the 1980s onwards, and in the establishment of government posts charged with the realization of an equal-opportunities policy during that same period of time.

In recent years the emancipatory potential of this new individualized approach in organizing care and welfare for people with disabilities has itself been called into question in public discussions.[72] This "socialization of care" is feared to entail an offloading of state responsibility onto the market and individual citizens. It has become a bone of contention that customized care might actually mean that people are left to fend for themselves. Determining who is accountable for care standards such as waiting times becomes more difficult, while labour-market participation can quickly turn from a right into a duty. In the 1970s and 1980s, disability organizations and academics voiced criticism of what they perceived to be the nanny state. The strategies they pursued in emphasizing autonomy, individuality and freedom of choices – even though they often also detailed a critique of the "capitalist" alternative – had the unforeseen effect of matching the neoliberal ethos.[73] This unlikely marriage was consolidated in its roll-out phase after the events of 1989, especially through the process of European integration.[74] Here the way was eased for a marketization logic to take hold in Belgian welfare arrangements for people with disabilities. A model of resolving the mounting tensions caused by the paradoxical moves of protesting welfare state cutbacks in the light of the fading star of Keynesian economics and fabricating a critique of the stifling workings of the pillarized welfare state was never fully realized.

Notes

1 The author acknowledges the support of the ERC Consolidator Grant "Rethinking Disability" contract no. 648115 for writing this article.
2 Franz-Xaver Kaufman, "The Idea of Social Policy in Western Societies: Origins and Diversity," *International Journal of Social Quality* 3, no. 2 (2013): 16–40.
3 Ibid., 26.
4 Pauli Kettunen and Klaus Petersen, eds., *Beyond Welfare State Models: Transnational Historical Perspectives on Social Policy* (Cheltenham: Edward Elgar, 2011).
5 Mark Priestley, "Disability," in *The Oxford Handbook of the Welfare State*, ed. Francis G. Castles, Stephan Leibfried, Jane Lewis, Herbert Obinger, and Christopher Pierson (Oxford: University Press, 2010), 406–420.
6 Monique Kremer, *How Welfare States Care: Culture, Gender and Parenting in Europe* (Amsterdam: Amsterdam University Press, 2007), 28–43; Julianne Ottmann, "Social Exclusion in the Welfare State: The Implications of Welfare Reforms for Social Solidarity and Social Citizenship," *Journal of Social Theory* 11, no. 1 (2010): 23–37.
7 Nancy Fraser, *Fortunes of Feminism: From State-Managed Capitalism to Neoliberal Crisis* (New York: Verso Books, 2013); Samuel Moyn, *Not Enough: Human Rights in an Unequal World* (Harvard University Press, 2018).
8 Guy Vanthemsche, Jean-Claude Burgelman, and Machteld De Metsenaere, *De tuin van heden: dertig jaar wetenschappelijk onderzoek over de hedendaagse Belgische samenleving* (Brussels: VUB Press, 2007); Dirk Luyten, Guy Vanthemsche, Machteld Demetsenaere, and Jean-Claude Burgelman, *Tussen staat en zuil: vijfendertig jaar Belgisch onderzoek over sociaal beleid* (Brussels: VUB Press, 2007). Two authors from outside the field of history who have paid a significant amount of attention to disability policies, social security and the labour market are Erik Samoy and Beatrice Van Buggenhout. Both researchers have occupied policy as well as academic positions

throughout their careers and were involved in academic research on disability issues regarding work or social welfare commissioned by policymakers operating at the Belgian, Flemish and even European levels. The r academic elaboration of the concept of disability is thus in a very straightforward way connected to the development of welfare state policies in Belgium.

9 Nancy Fraser and Axel Honneth, *Redistribution or Recognition? A Political-Philosophical Exchange* (New York: Verso Books, 2003).
10 Ibid., 119.
11 Herman Deleeck, "Belgium – Social Policy," in *Europe since 1945: An Encyclopedia*, vol. 1, ed. Bernard A. Cook (New York: Garland Publishing, 2001), 101–104.
12 Pillarization has been described as the compartmentalization of – extensive parts of – society into different parallel organizational complexes or pillars that are based on ideological or religious grounds and have a tendency towards self-sufficiency. This would then ideally lead to a situation in which individual citizens could be taken care of by organizations from their own pillar (such as but not limited to youth organizations, co-operatives, women's organizations, labour unions and health insurance agencies) and participate in services linked to their own pillar (like schools, health care facilities, libraries, and press) "from cradle to grave." See L. Vandenhove, "Ideologie en verzuiling in België," *Reflector* no. 3 (1986): 26–27; Hans Righart, *De katholieke zuil in Europa: een vergelijkend onderzoek naar het ontstaan van verzuiling onder katholieken in Oostenrijk, Zwitserland, België en Nederland* (Amsterdam: Boom Uitgeverij, 1986). For a more recent critical revision of the use of pillarization, see Peter van Dam, *Staat van Verzuiling. Over een Nederlandse mythe* (Amsterdam: Wereldbibliotheek, 2011).
13 Jaak Billiet, "Verzuiling, conflictregeling en politieke besluitvorming: ontwikkelingen in België," *Sociologische Gids* 38, no. 6 (1983): 429–446.
14 Jan-Frederik Abbeloos, "Een huis voor de zuil of van de jeugd? Analyse van de zuilgebonden coördinatie en legitimatie van de jeugdhuiswerking binnen de Belgische verzorgingsstaat voor de periode 1958–1973" (PhD diss., Universiteit Gent, 2003).
15 Staf Hellemans, "Verzuiling en ontzuiling van de katholieken in België en Nederland. Een historisch-sociologische vergelijking," *Sociologische Gids* 88, no. 1 (1988): 43–56.
16 This rather narrow definition of what welfare entails, focuses on social security, allowances, insurances, rehabilitation, and to a lesser extent care, but excludes special education which has its own significant history. See, for instance, Pieter Verstraete and Walter Hellinckx, *Met een handicap naar school: het ontstaan en de ontwikkeling van het onderwijs aan kinderen en jongeren met een handicap (1750–1970)* (Ieper: Stedelijke Musea, 2009).
17 An additional third track consisted of separate financial provisions for those who had been injured during war. This scheme was established shortly after WWI. Patricia Thornton and Neil Lunt, *Employment Policies for Disabled People in Eighteen Countries: A Review* (York: York University, 1997): 52–67.
18 Erik Samoy and Lina Waterplas, *Sheltered Employment in the European Community: Final Report Submitted to the Commission of the European Communities* (Leuven: Hoger Instituut voor de Arbeid, 1992), 47–48.
19 Erik Samoy, "Verleden, heden en toekomst van de arbeidsmarktintegratie van mensen met een handicap," in *Werk en Wereld in de Weegschaal. Confronterende visies op onderzoek en samenleving*, ed. Patrick Develtere and Ides Nicaise (Leuven: Lannoo Campus 2007), 162–168.
20 In summary, by the late 1960s the disability welfare state was carried out by the following core state institutions: Ministry of Social Welfare (disability allowances, 1928); National Fund for the Social Rehabilitation of Disabled Persons (vocational training, labour market reorientation, 1963); 'Fund 81' The Fund for Medical, Social and Educational Assistance to the Disabled (treatment, counselling, care facilities, 1967); National High Council for the Invalid (advisory council with members engaged in disability organiza-

tions or social-scientific activities regarding disability, 1967); Pillarized social partners (invalidity and sickness insurances, made mandatory, 1944); National Work for the War Invalids (invalidity pensions for civilians and soldiers, 1919).
21 E. Croux, "Het beeld van de fysiek gehandicapte bij de Katholieke Vereniging voor Gebrekkigen en Verminkten (1946 tot 1968): een kwantitatieve en kwalitatieve inhoudsanalyse, toegepast op de ledenbladen KVGV-berichten en KVGV-Benjamin," (PhD diss., KU Leuven, 1989).
22 Erik Buyst, "Belgium – Economy," in *Europe since 1945: An Encyclopedia*, ed. Bernard A. Cook (New York: Garland Publishing, 2013), 100–101.
23 Jonas Verplanken, "Het neoliberalisme in België. Invloed van het neoliberalisme op het Belgisch Sociaal Recht (1980–1987)," (PhD diss., Universiteit Gent, 2012), 124–128; Els Deweirdt, "Neoliberalisme in België (1980-1985)?" (PhD diss., Universiteit Gent, 2005), 162–164.
24 Beatrice Van Buggenhout, "Wetgeving in verband met gehandicapten," in *Ontwikkelingen van de sociale zekerheid, 1985–1991, wetgeving, rechtspraak*, ed. Dries Simoens (Brugge: Die Keure, 1991), 533–549.
25 Ibid., 534, 536.
26 Erik Samoy, "Ongeschikt of ongewenst? Een halve eeuw arbeidsmarktbeleid voor gehandicapten," (PhD diss., KU Leuven, 1998), 578–581, 610–612.
27 Ibid., 583.
28 Els Witte, Jan Craeybeckx, and Alain Meynen, *Politieke Geschiedenis van België* (Antwerpen: Standaard Uitgeverij, 2010), 339.
29 Ibid., 333. Translated by the author.
30 Mia Bracke-Defever, "Rehabilitation Policy in Belgium," in *Cross National Rehabilitation Policies: A Sociological Perspective*, ed. Gary L. Albrecht (London/Beverly Hills: Sage Publications, 1981), 205–222.
31 Ibid., 207.
32 Jean-Pierre Goetghebuer, *Handicap: een onverklaarbare bondgenoot. Profiel van een mens met hindernissen* (Tielt: Lannoo, 1978).
33 Ibid., 241–285.
34 *KVG Maandblad* 29–30 (1974–1975).
35 *KVG Maandblad* 29, no. 6 (June 1974): 3.
36 *KVG Maandblad* 30, no. 1 (January 1975): 81.
37 Disabled workers can benefit from this right which has been underpinned by a number of related rights: Article 2(1) of Regulation 1251/70, according to which workers who have been disabled can stay permanently in a member state; Article 7 of Regulation 1612/68, which gives migrant workers access to the same social and tax advantages; Article 12 of Regulation 1612/68, in which disabled children of migrant workers are given the same access to special education. See Lisa Waddington, "A European Right to Employment for Disabled People?" in *Human Rights and Disabled Persons: Essays and Relevant Human Rights Instruments*, ed. Theresa Degener and Yolan Koster-Dreese (Dordrecht and Boston: Martinus Nijhoff Publishers, 1995), 106–117; Judgment of the Court of 17 June 1975, *Mr. and Mrs. F. v Belgian State*. Reference for a preliminary ruling: Tribunal du travail de Nivelles. Case 7-75. ONU/Handicapés/4 Année Internationale Personnes Handicapés (AIPH), 18862, box 4. Newspaper clipping. Diplomatiek Archief, Brussels, Belgium.
38 Kenneth Cmiel, "The Recent History of Human Rights," *The American Historical Review* 109, no. 1 (2004): 117–135; Jan Eckel and Samuel Moyn, "The Return of the Prodigal: The 1970s as a Turning Point in Human Rights History," in *The Breakthrough: Human Rights in the 1970s*, ed. Jan Eckel and Samuel Moyn (Philadelphia: University of Pennsylvania Press, 2014), 1–15.
39 Sarah B. Snyder, *Human Rights Activism and the End of the Cold War: A Transnational History of the Helsinki Network* (New York: Cambridge University Press, 2011); Jean

Helen Quataert, *Advocating Dignity: Human Rights Mobilizations in Global Politics* (Philadelphia: University of Pennsylvania Press, 2009).
40 Moyn, *Not Enough*, 175.
41 The National Collective Action (Action Commune Nationale des Handicapés – Nationale Gemeenschappelijke Aktie voor Minder-Validen) consisted of at least the following organizations: Katholieke Vereniging Gehandicapten (Catholic Association for the Handicapped), Belgisch Blindenwezen (Belgian Body for the Blind), Belgische Vereniging voor Verlamden (Belgian Association for the Paralyzed), Vlaamse Federatie Gehandicaptenzorg (Flemish Federation of Care for the Disabled), Fédération Francophonee pour la promotion des Handicapés (French-speaking Federation for the Promotion of the Disabled), Vereniging van Vrienden voor Gehandicapte Kinderen en Militairen (Association of Friends of Disabled Children and Soldiers), Association Chrétienne des Invalides et Handicapés (Christian Association of the Invalids and the Handicapped). Droits de personnes handicapés: projet de déclaration 1975. ONU/Handicapés/4 Année Internationale Personnes Handicapés (AIPH), 18862, box 4, folder 6. Diplomatiek Archief, Brussels, Belgium.
42 UN A/RES/3447.
43 UN A/RES/26/2856.
44 The International League of Societies for the Mentally Handicapped (now Inclusion International) is an international umbrella organization founded in 1960, at that time consisting mostly of parent organizations. Their international headquarters were set up by Renee Portray, a Belgian doctor, lecturer on mental disabilities at the ULB, parent of a child with intellectual disabilities and secretary general of the league between 1963 and 1974. See Peter Mittler, *Making the Most of the United Nations* (Brussels: International League of Societies for Persons with a Mental Handicap, Brussels, 1992), 44.
45 Droits de personnes handicapés: projet de déclaration 1975. ONU/Handicapés/4 Année Internationale Personnes Handicapés (AIPH), 18862, box 4, folder 6. Diplomatiek Archief, Brussels, Belgium.
46 Gildas Brégain, "L'internationalisation imparfaite d'une modernité nord-atlantique: essai d'histoire croisée des politiques publiques du handicap en Argentine, au Brésil et en Espagne (1956–1982)," (PhD diss., Université Rennes 2; Universidade federal de Santa Catarina, 2014), 405.
47 Droits de personnes handicapés: projet de déclaration 1975 - correspondences. ONU/Handicapés/4 Année Internationale Personnes Handicapés (AIPH), 18862, box 4, folder 6. Diplomatiek Archief, Brussels, Belgium
48 UN A/RES/31/123.
49 Correspondence. Année Internationale Personnes Handicapés (AIPH), ONU/Handicapés/1, 18862, box 1. Diplomatiek Archief, Brussels, Belgium.
50 UN A/RES/31/123.
51 Witte, *Politieke Geschiedenis*, 308, 348–353.
52 Jamie Peck, *Constructions of Neoliberal Reason* (Oxford: Oxford University Press, 2010), 22–24.
53 Samoy, "Ongeschikt of Ongewenst," 440.
54 *KVG Maandblad* 36, no. 4 (April 1981): 92–93. Translated by the author from Dutch: *Het jaar van de gehandicapte: een klapper op de vuurpijl? HUBERT: Zwijg mij van die jaren. Die halen toch niets uit. Komedie tot en met.*
55 *KVG Maandblad*, 36, no. 11 (December 1981): 198. Translated by the author from Dutch: *Het "Jaar van de gehandicapte" zal in ons land de geschiedenis ingaan als het jaar van de besparingen.*
56 A simplified overview of the institutions charged with disability issues after the state reforms of 1980 and 1988: Ministry of Social Welfare (disability allowances); Four funds on the level of the communities and regions (established in the 1990s); National

High Council for the Disabled, as well as advisory bodies for the Walloon region, the Brussels region and the German-speaking community but not for Flanders.

57 Secretariaat Nationale Hoge Raad voor Personen met een Handicap, e-mail message to author, "Jaarverslagen 1979–1982," December 13, 2016.
58 Patrick Daunt, *Meeting Disability. A European Response* (London: Cassell, 1991), 13–14.
59 UN A/RES/37/52.
60 *Monnikenheide '40'* (Antwerpen: Vlaams Architectuur Instituut, 2013).
61 Romy Cockx, *Miet Smet. Drie decennia gelijkekansenbeleid* (Brussels: Instituut voor de gelijkheid van vrouwen en mannen/Archiefcentrum voor Vrouwengeschiedenis, 2009), 30, 60–67.
62 Samoy, "Ongeschikt of Ongewenst," 114–115.
63 Cockx, *Miet Smet,* 98–100.
64 Hellemans, "Verzuiling en ontzuiling," 43–56.
65 Aline Looten, "Een geschiedenis van het persoonlijk assistentiebudget in Vlaanderen 1987–2001" (MA diss., KU Leuven, 2013).
66 Walter Lotens, *Elcker-Ik. 45 jaar sociale actie* (Kalmthout: Pelckmans, 2015), 180.
67 Diane Driedger, *The Last Civil Rights Movement* (London: Hurst & Company; New York: St. Martin's Press, 1989). UN A/RES/48/96.
68 Gerard Quinn and Theresa Degener, *Human Rights and Disability: The Current Use and Future Potential of United Nations Human Rights Instruments in the Context of Disability* (New York and Geneva: United Nations, 2002).
69 Lotens, *Elcker-Ik,* 181–182.
70 UN HTSA/RES/61/106.
71 Lee Ann Banaszak, Karen Beckwith, and Dieter Rucht, "When Power Relocates: Interactive Changes in Women's Movements and States," in *Women's Movements Facing the Reconfigured State,* ed. Lee Ann Banaszak, Karen Beckwith, and Dieter Rucht (Cambridge: Cambridge University Press, 2003) 2, 7, 22–23.
72 Aurélie Decoene and Sander Vandecapelle, "Financiering gehandicaptenzorg: 'Van zorg op maat naar red uzelf'," *Knack,* 9 June 2016.
73 A development that has been described for other social movements as well: Fraser, *Fortunes of Feminism.*
74 William Outhwaite, *Europe since 1989: Transitions and Transformations* (London: Routledge, 2016), 41, 110–112.

9 A new inequality in the Danish welfare state

The development of immigration and integration policy in post-war Denmark

Heidi Vad Jønsson

Introduction

In 1964 Melvüt Kurt came to the small Danish city of Fredericia as one of the first Turkish guest workers in the 1960s. He was hired by the international company Constructors John Brown to join its team of welders along with a handful of other so-called guest workers. Melvüt Kurt came from Konya in Turkey and had arrived in Europe as a migrant worker in the early 1960s. His arrival in Denmark was due to classic push-and-pull factors. Denmark's economic growth and labour shortages were increasing the demand for labour and encouraging the opening of the Danish labour market to guest workers.[1] Melvüt Kurt had originally moved to Holland from Istanbul, but Denmark became his final destination. His skills were in demand, as he could perform a specialized welding technique required in the construction of the new oil refinery in Fredericia. His personal reasons for moving from Holland to Denmark were, as he explained when interviewed forty years later, mainly that wages were higher in Denmark than in other European countries and much higher than in Turkey. In addition, he had heard rumours of much better working conditions in Denmark. On arrival he entered the highly unionized Danish labour market in a period often described as the golden years of the welfare state.[2] Melvüt Kurt came to Denmark at a time when many Western European countries opened their labour markets and imported skilled and unskilled workers in order to meet the rising demand for labour in a post-war growth economy. When the oil crisis hit Denmark in the autumn of 1973 and a period of labour shortage was replaced by one of high unemployment, some guest workers left Denmark (and Europe). Melvüt Kurt chose to stay in Denmark. He had met his future wife, Henny, a few weeks after arriving in Fredericia, and he had strong ties to both Denmark and Turkey.[3] He became part of Danish society, part of the Danish population, but without Danish citizenship.

In the following years, guest workers became immigrants, and rising numbers of non-European migrants and refugees came to live transnational lives in the different European welfare states. In the Nordic countries the welfare state was founded on a universal principle of free and equal access regardless of tax contributions and labour market participation. The state played a key role in limiting inequalities, economic as well as social, and by the 1960s gender inequalities too. In the years to come immigration and integration became among the most heated and sensitive political issues in the Nordic and European welfare states. In Denmark the immigration issue has led to severe conflicts between and within the political parties. On the one hand, Denmark is counted among the universal welfare states, where state intervention is the means to limit various inequalities and plays a key role as caregiver in all aspects of life. On the other, Denmark has moved from being one of the most liberal to among the most restrictive immigration regimes. In addition, the debate on immigration in Denmark has appeared nationalistic. The welfare system is, as argued in this article, essential for understanding Danish immigration policy in the post-war period, since immigration was debated explicitly in the context of its consequences for the welfare system and the principles by which it was governed. Immigration and increased ethnic and cultural diversity gave rise to a new dilemma in the Nordic welfare states: If culture and ethnicity created new inequalities between so-called ethnic Danes and new Danes, how then should the system cope with this situation? Should immigrants integrate and assimilate, or could the traditionally homogenous Danish welfare system be maintained with a more diverse population?

This chapter explores how immigration became a new political issue in one of the Nordic welfare states: Denmark. More specifically, it seeks to answer two questions: To what extent and under what conditions were immigrants included in the welfare system, and how were immigration and immigrants' access to social security debated and politicized?[4]

Immigration and welfare research have traditionally been studied separately. However, in recent years there has been an increase in the number of publications that bridge the gap between welfare and migration research. Within migration research there is a long tradition of so-called IMER (immigration, migration, and ethnicity research), which includes studies of migration patterns, race and minority studies, as well as study of the politicization of migration, race and ethnicity. In studies concerning Denmark, an extensive number of debate-and-discourses analyses have shown a much more intense and polarized debate, especially following the increased number of spontaneous asylum seekers in the 1980s.[5] Other types of research include economic and demographic studies of the economic benefits and costs of immigration for the Danish welfare system. Whereas some researchers have argued that immigration from so-called non-Western countries became costly as immigration of asylum seekers rose in the 1980s,[6] others have argued that the very survival of the Danish welfare state and the Danish population has depended on immigration, owing to low birth rates and an ageing population.[7] Both debate and attitude studies as well as economic analysis identify the changing migration pattern of the 1980s as a crucial turning point. This is also the case in political science studies, which have shown how immigration became a hot political issue in the mid-1980s and by the 1990s had become an important factor in voting patterns. Whereas voters until the 1970s and 1980s had voted according to social class and tradition, issue-based voting grew thereafter until by the mid-1990s when immigration became one of the most important electoral issues in Danish politics.[8]

Historical institutional studies have shown how migrants' access to welfare benefits in Sweden changed from gradual inclusion in the 1970s to almost full inclusion in the 1980s.[9] As Diane Sainsbury has observed, "immigrants were formally incorporated into the welfare system on relatively equal terms with citizens by the early 1980s – and with little differentiation in social rights among entry categories."[10] The welfare reforms of the 1990s following the financial and economic crisis hit low-income groups harder than others and in turn had a negative effect on migrants' social rights: "the combined effect of retrenchment and the recession was a drop in the disposable income of foreign born during the decade [1990s], while that of Swedish born increased slightly."[11] As Sainsbury shows, the question of social rights is not merely linked to access in terms of eligibility, but also in terms of how welfare reforms affect different groups of residents. Sweden is often used as an archetypical case of a Scandinavian, universal, social-democratic welfare state, and with good reason; for example, Esping-Andersen in his seminal book *Three Worlds of Welfare Capitalism* uses Sweden as the "ideal case."[12] The question that arises, however, is whether Denmark follows the same pattern in terms of developments in migrants' social rights.

As Sainsbury has suggested, in order to understand issues around migration, including the politicization of immigration and the regulation of migrants' social rights, we need to look at the leading role played by institutional changes in welfare states. This does not mean that debates, discourses and attitudes have no effect. As Carly Schall has shown in her book *The Rise and Fall of the Miraculous Welfare Machine* (2016), Social Democrats were key agents in shaping perceptions of both the welfare state and migrants' access to welfare benefits. As Schall has argued, the idea of a homogenous population mattered for the construction of the Swedish welfare state because Social Democrats made it matter. The same is the case for discussions and regulations of migrants' access to welfare benefits in periods of both expansion and retrenchment. Hence, in order to understand how welfare states and their policymakers have reacted to immigration in the postwar period, both perceptions of immigration and welfare and also institutional changes in the welfare system should be included in the analysis of migrants' social rights. Social rights change, as do social policy ideas and perceptions of migrants' entitlement.

In the following section the historical development of immigration and the welfare state is outlined. There follows an analysis of the policy debate and institutional developments, and the chapter concludes with a discussion of the principal questions concerning the inclusion of immigrants in the welfare system and the politicization of the debate about their access to social security.

Immigration and welfare state development

Immigration to Denmark was not, of course, a new phenomenon in the 1960s. For centuries the Danish borders had been crossed by different groups of migrants,[13] some of whom became permanent immigrants (e.g. Moravian Brethren in Christiansfeld in the 1700s), whereas others were in Denmark for a limited time (e.g. travelling craftsmen or Russian Jews fleeing from the pogrom in the late nineteenth century). In the economic boom after World War II, Danish immigration followed the European tendency of increased mobility and labour importation, and in that same period the Danish welfare state expanded in terms of the areas covered by the state, the number of state personnel and the amount of public expenditure.[14] The Nordic welfare states were, with national variations, designed to cover their citizens socially and economically from cradle to grave with a comprehensive and integrated system of benefits and services founded on principles of social solidarity across social classes and between generations.[15] This system of high redistribution provided by the state and financed through taxes was later characterized as a universal system and a social-democratic welfare state model.[16]

When this system was at its peak in terms of coverage and generosity, the national, universal welfare state was confronted with a new wave of globalization, where goods, capital and people moved to a greater extent over larger distances. This so-called third period of globalization meant that the world seemed smaller, and that more and more people came to live transnational lives with families, friends and colleagues all over the globe. Increased mobility and immigration was gradually seen as a challenge for the national welfare system, which was designed and institutionalized in a national and Nordic context.[17] Class conflict had been limited by a welfare system that included all citizens in the "virtuous circles of solidarity."[18] The universal welfare system is a fine-meshed system of generous benefits and services "for everybody from everybody," as described by Richard Titmuss in 1967.[19] When facing a new, globalized world, the question "Who is everybody?" became much more significant. As the population became more mobile and diverse, new issues appeared.[20] Whereas the intention to limit class conflict had shaped welfare state developments in the first half of the twentieth century, new inequalities based on a combination of ethnicity, class, gender and citizenship provided a new challenge. As Stephen Castles has argued, nation states have in the age of modern migration attempted to reproduce and reinforce the imagined community of the nation as a reaction to a culturally and ethnically more diverse population.[21] Whether the national welfare system follows this tendency to reproduce and reinforce the existing system is a question to be addressed in this chapter, which is organized around a chronology of the welfare state based on welfare reforms and significant changes in the system and in socio-political thinking.

Labour immigration in the period of welfare expansion

In the years following World War II, Western economies experienced rapid growth, and by the 1950s Western Europe and the US had entered a period of economic boom. This was also the case in Denmark, where the economic growth period began in 1958, somewhat later than in Sweden. Unemployment fell and wages increased, and by the early 1960s Danish economists worried that increased economic growth would lead to production bottlenecks.[22] Hence, the question of how to increase the labour force entered Danish politics.

The labour minister expressed the problem clearly in a feature article in the Social Democratic newspaper *Aktuelt* in 1964: "everything would seem to indicate that for a long time to come Denmark will have a labour shortage problem. This can be resolved in two ways, either by limiting the scope of labour and production to the performance level of the existing workforce, or by producing additional labour."[23] The latter option was chosen, and hence the Danish labour market was liberalized and made more accessible to foreign labour. By the mid-1960s so-called guest workers from mainly Turkey, Yugoslavia and Pakistan had become part of the Danish workforce. These male industrial workers were expected to be in Denmark only temporarily and were to some extent an anomaly in the universal welfare system. In principle, guest workers with a valid work permit were not excluded from the welfare system and were covered to the same extent as Danish nationals, but with one exception: they could be deported if they needed social assistance for a longer period of time.[24] This question of limited (conditional) social rights was, however, considered less important than labour-market issues, and hence discussion of guest workers and the importing of foreign labour fell within the purview of the parties responsible for the labour market. The Danish system, where labour-market issues were (and are) regulated by collective bargaining between the LO (Labour Union) and DA (employers' union), meant that immigration issues in this period were regulated mainly in the political space of this cooperative system.

When importing labour was introduced as a possible solution to the labour shortage, LO and DASF[25] argued strenuously against this proposal and instead demanded that investment should be made in order to improve production machinery and thereby to limit the need for manual labour. Even though DASF and LO were highly critical, the labour movement accepted the importing of foreign labour as long as the new workers were organized in a union.[26] Importing guest workers, however, was not viewed uniformly within the labour movement, as we can see from Melvüt Kurt's arrival in Fredericia in 1965. The local Blacksmith Union demanded that recruitment of Turkish guest workers should take place only if no Danish (organized) welders were able to do the job. After a thorough investigation conducted by the union, the conclusion was reached that employment of Danish welders would not be sufficient to meet the needs of this extensive construction site. The local union therefore accepted that Melvüt Kurt and several other Turkish welders be hired. A year later the company announced a round of job cuts. In response the local Welders' Club suggested that the guest workers should lose their jobs before any Danish welders were fired. This suggestion was not acceptable in the eyes of the national Blacksmith Union. As union leader Hans Rasmussen pointed out: "I do not believe that we can take action against the Turks who have come here from far away. Moreover, we cannot find any fault with these people, neither as skilled workers nor as members of our trade union."[27] The logic and strategy of the union was to act against importing unorganized guest workers, but once a regulated importation had been accepted and the guest workers had become active members of the union, that they should be equally protected by the union.

For a short time the Danish labour force was supplemented by guest workers who were expected to be in Denmark only for a limited period. This temporality discourse, which dominated the debate, also meant that guest workers' social rights and access to welfare benefits beyond the benefits provided by the partially membership-sponsored "a-kasse" were of limited concern to policymakers and were therefore not politicized. This situation changed when the international oil crisis in 1973 put an abrupt end to a decade of economic growth.

Social rights in times of economic crisis

In the autumn of 1973 the Danish labour minister stopped the issuance of new labour permits, thereby introducing what became known as "the immigration-stop."[28] This regulation did not put an end to immigration to Denmark, but restricted it to a new type of immigration: family and marriage migration continued, but in a new economic context. Some of the male industrial workers, who had come to Denmark as guest workers, moved on as unemployment rose, whereas others stayed and changed their status from temporary guest worker to permanent immigrant. The economic recession had a negative effect on employment rates in general and hit guest workers harder than Danish workers, which meant that the issue of their social rights and access to welfare benefits became more relevant. In addition, the group of migrants had now changed from being mainly single male industrial workers to including their immigrant families. Thus immigration and immigrants now changed from being a labour-market issue to a socio-political one, and as a result migrants were perceived as a new social group. In that process the universal principle of the Danish welfare state framed the gradual politicization of immigration and immigrants. Access to social-assistance benefits was defined as a social right and had been since the social reform of 1933, but migrants' access to social benefits was conditional on their residence permit. In the case of long-term need for social benefits, migrants faced the risk of deportation.[29] Even though this deportation clause seems never to have been sanctioned, the issues arising from increased immigration made it clear that the universalistic principle of Danish welfare had potential limitations. Should migrants have full access to welfare benefits and be fully included in the circles of solidarity, or should newly arrived immigrants have limited access to the otherwise generous welfare state? If the welfare state was seen, as described by Richard Titmuss in the 1960s, as a system of social services for everybody from everybody, the definition of "everybody," e.g. the welfare citizens, became more pressing as the population became more diverse after a period of nation-building and welfare state development. This was particularly the case in the context of Social Democratic attempts to reduce inequality by means of high levels of redistribution through the state and welfare services in order to provided social protection and limit class conflict. The class compromise and the rise of Social Democracy as a people's party had played a significant part in this building of a welfare nation-state in the 1930s and in the post-war decades. The welfare state was the result of political compromises, which made the system robust and sustainable.[30] In Denmark, Social Democrats had played a large part in developing the universal welfare system, but the social policy had been institutionalized as a result of political compromises, and support for the system was high in the 1960s. This would change in the 1970s. The anti-system parties on the left were from 1972 counterbalanced by a new right-wing party, the Progress Party, that argued for abolition of what party founder Mogens Glistrup labelled welfare bureaucracy. In addition to political anti-welfare state movements, the economic recession brought the sustainability of the generous welfare state into question. Could this system, which was funded from taxes, survive in an economic crisis when, due to high unemployment, tax payments decreased and welfare expenditure rose?

In the midst of this emerging welfare crisis and severe economic recession, immigrants' access to the full welfare system became a more relevant topic. In order to address the question of access, a guest-worker consultant was employed in the Ministry of Social Affairs, and a committee was assigned the task of assessing guest workers' social conditions.[31] Migrants were in this period perceived as a group who had social problems, and the welfare system was expected to be able to solve these issues.[32] In 1976 bilateral agreements were made with Turkey and Yugoslavia which meant that immigrants from these countries gained full social rights in Denmark and in return Danish citizens with residence permits in the two countries were put on equal terms with Turkish and Yugoslavian nationals.[33] As stated in the Convention on Social Security between the Kingdom of Denmark and the Republic of Turkey: "affirming the principle that the nationals of one of the two countries should receive, under the social security legislation of the other, equal treatment with the nationals of the latter."[34] Since Turkish and Yugoslavian nationals were the two biggest groups of former guest workers in Denmark, this convention was an attempt to include migrants in the national social security system without changing the principles of the social legislation. This strategy had been used also in the 1940s and 1950s when the Nordic countries introduced social conventions expanding social rights to cover all Scandinavian citizens.[35] The social conventions with Turkey and Yugoslavia meant that Turks and Yugoslavs had full social rights in Denmark, but this did not put an end to the migration–welfare debate. On the contrary, by the end of the 1970s the left-wing parties argued in parliament that migrants continued to be a marginalized social group and that social rights included more than access to social-assistance benefits. The left-wing parties viewed migrants as a "new pariah caste" who should have equal access to society.[36] This position was shaped by a socialist and communist welfare critique that viewed the welfare state as an oppressive system that forced the working class to adapt to middle-class norms and values.[37] The socialist and communist parties therefore opposed the tendency of the welfare system to include migrants, e.g. through social conventions, and thereby reproduce the existing system, since the welfare state was seen as a way to oppress the working class. This gave rise to a debate in parliament, where the Social Democratic government, while recognizing that migrants should not become a new underclass, still maintained that problems pertaining to this particular group should be dealt with by the existing system. Immigrants were thus seen as a vulnerable group whose social conditions should be improved by extending social rights to all residents. This period can be characterized as a phase of social-rights expansion, where immigrants were viewed as a group who *had* social problems to be solved by the system and not, as we shall see later, as a group perceived as a socio-cultural problem *for* the system.

Thus in Denmark in the 1970s a new period began in various ways. The stable four-party system became destabilized as protest parties gained more votes. This was especially evident in the so-called earthquake election of 1973, when the old parties (the Social Democratic Party, the Liberals, the Social Liberals and the Conservatives) lost to new parties. This created an entirely new parliamentary situation which distinguished Denmark from Sweden, where the Social Democratic Party remained in office for decades. Furthermore, labour immigration into Sweden began earlier than in Denmark and was regulated to a greater extent via a new institution, the Immigration Agency, which regulated entrance and integration through language courses, housing, etc.[38] Thus the questions that Danish policymakers faced were similar to those in other universal welfare states, but the Danish debates were much more diffuse and policy development was less clear and less cohesive than in Sweden. The unstable parliamentary situation with several small parties and shifting minority governments, and the lack of clear policy development, marked by the absence of institutions such as the Migration Agency, would influence the Danish immigration and welfare debate and policy development in the following decades.[39]

Immigrants, refugees and the normative crisis of the welfare state

By the beginning of the 1980s the welfare system was being hotly debated, and both liberals and conservatives argued that a universal welfare state was economically unsustainable and more a part of the economic problem than the solution to the prolonged economic recession. Inspired by neoliberal trends in Thatcher's UK, including privatization and welfare state retrenchment, the neoliberal critique of a large state with high levels of redistribution and market regulation led to the so-called normative crisis of the welfare state.[40] The Danish economy suffered with high unemployment and increased public expenditure, and in 1982 the Social Democratic government eventually resigned.[41] The new government led by conservative prime minister Poul Schlüter pursued a balanced economy and focused on bringing down Denmark's international debt at the expense of employment, which meant that the 1980s was a period of high unemployment. Economic policy was one of the main issues in Danish politics in the 1970s and 1980s, but by the mid-1980s the immigration issue had gradually moved up the political agenda.

In 1982 a new Alien Act was presented in parliament and passed in 1983. This act, considered the world's most liberal Alien Act,[42] introduced a new distinction between temporary and permanent residence permits and clarified legal rights to residence permits in Denmark.[43] In addition, the act limited the ability to deport immigrants and refugees who had a permanent residence permit and needed more than temporary social assistance. This act was a turning point in immigrants' social rights, since access to social assistance was now defined as a social right for all citizens with a permanent residence permit regardless of their citizenship. A system of *ius sanguinis* was now institutionalized.[44] A year later, in 1984, Denmark, as well as other Western European countries, experienced a significant change in the refugee pattern, as groups of refugees applied for asylum at the Danish border; these were a new type of refugee labelled "spontaneous refugees." The rapid and uncontrollable increase in the number of asylum seekers caused a heated debate on immigration and refugees in Denmark from the mid-1980s. The question was whether the absolute number of asylum seekers posed a problem, and to what extent culture and religion should be seen as a threat or an enrichment to Danish culture. This period can therefore be categorized as a culturalization phase, when cultural encounters entered the immigration debate. If social problems were at the core of the debate in the 1970s, culture now became the main focus. This shift of focus was also found in the other Scandinavian countries, but the Danish parliamentary situation shaped the debates in Denmark, which were seen as more extreme than in neighbouring countries.

The new right-wing party, the Progress Party, argued strongly against immigration and viewed refugees as a cultural threat to the Danish nation-state. At the same time the party was highly critical of the social-democratic welfare system, which was viewed by the party leaders Mogens Glistrup and Pia Kjærsgaard as a system that limited personal freedom and enabled people to "sponge on society." In the eyes of the Progress Party immigrants should not have full social rights; on the contrary, the party proposed in Parliament that non-Danish nationals' access to social assistance should be annulled.[45] This suggestion was, of course, not passed, since the Progress Party was viewed as a radical right-wing party and not a "serious" political party; but the proposal meant that welfare nationalism had now entered the Danish immigration and immigrant-policy debate. Welfare nationalism became much more pronounced in European politics in the late 1990s and 2000s, especially among the new nationalist parties, but in Denmark such concepts as "convenience refugees" had become part of political discourse already by the mid-1980s. The term suggested that refugees fled from poverty and were therefore not to be considered as "real refugees."[46] The conservative-liberal government argued that immigration should be limited and also viewed increasing cultural diversity as a potential threat to the nation-state; but at the same time the conservatives were restrained by their coalition with the social liberals, who on immigration argued along the same lines as the left-wing Socialist Peoples Party and the Left Socialists. In spite of this intra-governmental conflict, immigration was still not the most important political topic in a period of unabated economic recession and crisis.[47] This changed a decade later.

The Danish political debate on immigration was in this period marked by significant disagreement: the left wing and the social liberals viewed immigration as a cultural enrichment, and the right wing took the opposite position. The Social Democrats – in opposition – were stuck in the middle and were divided on the immigration issue. Local Social Democrats argued for a more restrictive line and intensified focus on integration, whereas the parliamentary Social Democrats and the party leadership positioned themselves in opposition to the right-wing parties.[48] This was expressed by the party leader and former prime minister Anker Jørgensen: "All humans are equal. People should not fall into the abyss because they are old, unemployed, sick or because they are different than most people. It should not matter if you are black, white or red. Nor if you are man or woman."[49]

This was the fundamental principle of the Social Democrats, but as the immigration debate changed its focus from social issues to cultural matters, it became more difficult to maintain that immigrants' problems should be solved by the existing welfare system. By the late 1980s immigrants and refugees were increasingly viewed *as* a socio-cultural problem and not as a group *with* social problems. The immigration issue gave rise to profound disagreements and severe internal conflicts within the Danish Social Democratic Party, in contrast to their Swedish sister-party, which has a much more stable platform for policy development.[50]

In spite of the heated debate and significant conflicts that in 1985 had even led to violent attacks on a group of refugees who had been temporarily housed in the small city of Kalundborg, only minor institutional changes were introduced. The Alien Act passed in 1983 regulated immigration, and even though changes to this act had made Danish immigration policy more restrictive, the core principles of legal claims and full social rights for immigrants and refugees with a permanent residence permit were still maintained. In the sphere of the welfare state immigrant integration remained a local responsibility which municipalities should handle within the existing system.[51] Thus immigration was perceived as a cultural encounter and a possible threat to the nation state; and in addition welfare nationalism was a growing ideology supported by the anti-immigration language of the right-wing Progress Party. This party, which was very critical of the high level of redistribution, high taxes and bureaucracy of the welfare state, had in its anti-immigration rhetoric argued that access to this system should be limited to Danish citizens. Hence, the welfare-nationalist perspective gradually became part of the right wing, even in a period when right-wing parties were influenced by neoliberalism.[52]

Integration and welfare reforms

In 1993 a new Social Democratic government came into office as a consequence of the so-called Tamil case. The former minister of justice, Erik Ninn-Hansen, was found guilty first by a court investigation in January 1993 and later in a trial for high crimes and misdemeanours because he had overruled the right of a group of Tamil refugees' to family reunification. As a result of this case the conservative prime minister, Poul Schlüter, resigned. The new Social Democratic party leader, Poul Nyrup Rasmussen, now entered office as leader of a Social Democratic–Social Liberal government. In close alliance with the social liberals the Social Democratic prime minister reformed the Danish welfare state with a greater emphasis on active labour-market policy. The reforms of the welfare states in the 1990s have been called a second reinvention of the left, where old social-democratic parties acted under the influence of a soft variation of neoliberal thinking.[53] In the UK Tony Blair reinvented Labour, and in Denmark Poul Nyrup Rasmussen began a similar transformation of the Danish Social Democratic Party. One of the most debated reforms in this period was the social-policy reform which limited access to social assistance to seven and eventually four years. As a result of this change one could receive unemployment benefits for only four years. At the same time the welfare system was redesigned not only to provide social and economic security, but also to ensure that unemployed citizens were "activated" and always prepared to take a job.[54] This was a significant change in the welfare state, as the system designed to prevent people from "falling into the abyss" when unemployed now gained a new purpose: to ensure that all citizens who were able to work did indeed take a job. The main argument for introducing this employment line in Danish welfare policy was to avoid what was described as *clientalization*, which in this context meant welfare dependency. The dominant view at the time was that the fine-meshed welfare system that covered all aspects of life made vulnerable citizens too dependent on the system, a tendency that in the eyes of the Social Democrats and Social Liberals should be counteracted by employment and activation programmes provided by the service sector of the welfare state. Thus as a result of the welfare reforms of the 1990s the two pillars of this system became interconnected, with a stronger emphasis on the link between a high level of economic redistribution and services that included not only such traditional areas as childcare services and housing programmes, but also employment schemes and active integration.[55]

In this period of welfare reform immigration rose to the top of the political agenda. The discussions of the 1980s continued, and notions of welfare nationalism now entered the media debate and influenced mainstream political parties. In 1997 the Danish tabloid newspaper *Ekstrabladet* carried a series of feature articles in which immigrants' and refugees' access to social assistance was put up for debate. Under the headline "De fremmede" (the foreigners)[56] the newspaper showed that a male Somali refugee with two wives and several children had received over 600,000 kr.[57] in social assistance and indirect welfare benefits (e.g. housing support). This case gave rise to a profound discussion of migrants' access to welfare benefits as not only right-wing parties, which now also included the Danish People's Party (DPP),[58] but also municipal Social Democrats and eventually the Danish Social Democratic prime minister, Poul Nyrup Rasmussen, questioned and problematized free access to welfare for all citizens with a residence permit. In this public debate the welfare reforms, which had introduced a less generous welfare system for all, were contrasted with immigrants' and refugees' social services and benefits.[59] The DPP was highly critical and argued along the lines of pronounced welfare nationalism. The liberals and conservatives were also critical of the existing system, whereas the socialist parties took the opposite standpoint by arguing for free, equal and unconditional access to welfare for all citizens residing in Denmark, regardless of nationality. This discussion was seen by the government to indicate the need for reform. By 1997 immigration had become one of the hottest political issues in Danish politics. The immigration debate was impassioned, diverse and dominated by different definitions of the problem, which is why solutions were equally problematic. The Social Democratic government continued the process of welfare reform with a strong emphasis on employment. Its reform included an integration act, which required that all newcomers should participate in integration programmes for the first three years of their stay in Denmark. At the same time the new act introduced a new benefit: an introduction benefit, which was lower than the social-assistance benefit. This new and low introduction benefit was seen as highly problematic since immigrants and refugees would now be unable to receive full social assistance until they had completed the integration programme.[60] Integration also became a key requirement for obtaining a permanent residence permit. This reform was presented in Parliament in January 1998 and passed in June that same year, but only with a very narrow majority. This integration act not only required that newcomers (both refugees and immigrants) should participate in integration activities that would not only enable employment, but that also contained language and "Danish culture training." Newly arrived migrants were now obliged to show "knowledge of and respect for Danish values."[61] In effect, values – already a significant part of the immigration debate – were now considered a crucial condition for residence in Denmark and hence for accessing the Danish welfare state. This was the beginning of a new phase in Danish welfare and immigration policy, in which welfare nationalism, conditionality, a strong emphasis on values, and a new distinction between deserving and undeserving poor re-entered Danish welfare policy, and where residence, ethnicity, values, and ability to integrate became new dividing lines. In the 2000s this tendency was reinforced: access to social-assistance benefits has since 2002 required seven years of residence in Denmark, and access to cash benefits, *kontanthjælp*, has become conditional on a minimum of 220 hours of paid work per year. Thus the basic principle of social and economic security as an unconditional social right for all residents in Denmark has gradually been replaced by a system where citizens have to earn the right to welfare. In this period Danish immigration policy became increasingly restrictive, in sharp contrast to the more liberal immigration policy in Sweden.[62] From the beginning of the 1990s Swedish policymakers emphasized the importance of a liberal immigration policy, based on the idea that easy access to residence permits and citizenship combined with multicultural policies would create better conditions for immigrant integration.[63] This idea, which also shaped Dutch immigration and integration policy, was, as suggested earlier, not easily applied in a Danish context, where liberals and conservatives argued for a restrictive immigration policy, and broad coalition decisions on the immigration issue were unsuccessful. As a consequence Denmark moved in a more restrictive direction than Sweden in terms of immigration policy, and integration was by the late 1990s institutionalized as both a right and a mandatory duty for newly arrived immigrants and refugees.

After the introduction of the integration act and its enforced emphasis on employment and values, perceptions of the role of the welfare state gradually changed. Immigrants and refugees were now seen as a problematic social group whose access to welfare benefits and social rights required that they integrate to become "welfare citizens." In the purpose paragraphs of the first integration act integration measures were justified as enabling migrants to become self-supporting and less dependent on welfare benefits, but also as providing newly arrived immigrants and refugees with "knowledge and understanding of Danish values."[64] Whereas immigrants in the 1970s were defined as a group who *had* social problems, e.g. limited access to welfare benefits and services because of language barriers etc., immigrants and refugees were gradually redefined as a group who *were* a social problem and represented a cultural challenge to the nation state. In the 1990s integration became not only a question of access to welfare benefits, but also to a greater extent than previously a question of educating newly arrived immigrants and refugees with the purpose of transforming what were perceived as "un-integrated" migrants into new welfare citizens, using mandatory integration programmes as the main tool. To some extent the welfare system, like the nation-state, reproduced and reinforced the imagined community of the nation, and in this process the welfare state was an important identity marker. "Do your duties, claim your rights" became a slogan for the Social Democratic government as they stressed the symbiotic relationship between duties (e.g. to participate in society according to Danish values, to work and to pay taxes) and rights (e.g. access to language training, to education and to the labour market). In this process the identity politics of the welfare system became more pronounced. Access to welfare benefits had become a major aspect of welfare–migration discussions in the 1970s. In the 1980s the debate shifted focus from social policy to cultural encounters and conflicts. In the late 1990s social rights and cultural encounters and conflicts became the key aspects. Throughout this period the Social Democratic party played a leading role in welfare state transformation and in development of integration as the new welfare policy. However, it was a policy development process which took shape in a political climate dominated by increasingly right- and left-wing parties. The political climate seemed on the one had to play a significant role in transforming the welfare system, and on the other hand in identifying and politicising ethnicity as a new inequality, which in the early period (the 1970s and 1980s) gave rise to a demand for changes in the welfare system in order to make it more compatible with an increasingly multicultural population. While from the 1990s onwards ethnicity was still perceived as a factor that created inequalities in society, immigrants were to a greater extent assigned responsibility for overcoming those inequalities.

Conclusion

Perceptions of immigration, integration and the welfare system have changed dramatically over the decades analysed here. In the early years of modern migration, immigrants were gradually incorporated in the existing system, which was reproduced but not reformed. Universal access and coverage were the dominant principles, and in the 1970s policymakers attempted to include migrants in the Danish version of the *folkhem* (people's home) by focusing on social conventions. With the passing of a new Alien Act, deportation on account of a need for permanent social relief was abolished, and so the reform of 1983 became a turning point in the history of migrants' social rights. Immigrants and refugees were (almost) as well supported socially and economically as Danish nationals. From the mid-1980s welfare nationalism dominated the political debate, and by the mid-1990s migrants' access to social benefits was debated and questioned. The integration act of 1998 was a new turning point, as immigrants now had both the right and duty to become "welfare citizens" by participating in a three-year integration programme, which included not only employment schemes but also education in Danish values. Whereas the first period covered here can be characterized as welfare-system reproduction through social-rights expansion, the later decades are marked by a reinforcement of the national welfare system with special emphasis on norms and values. The same tendency can with some variation be identified in the other Scandinavian welfare states; but Danish Social Democrats operated in the context of a less stable parliamentary situation with narrow coalition minority governments, intra-party conflicts, and a growing anti-immigration and welfare-nationalist right wing. Hence, immigration and growing ethnic diversity were identified and politically negotiated in Denmark and in other universal welfare states as a new inequality which needed to be limited by the welfare state. Danish policy development, however, was not similar to, for example, that of Sweden, as the context for policy development differed significantly both in terms of welfare institutions (e.g. the absence of a Migration Agency in Denmark in the 1960s and 1970s) and in terms of the climate in which policy was debated. In Denmark immigration was a new, hot political issue that became part of an inter-party factional conflict between a strong multiculturalist left wing and an equally strong welfare-nationalist right wing. Thus significantly different political and institutional contexts had a decisive impact on the development of welfare policy.

Notes

1 Importing guest workers was, as explained further in this chapter, not accepted by all political parties. The Social Democratic Party was against importing unorganized labour, but it eventually accepted that this was required to maintain a high level of production. Henrik Zip Sane, *Billige og villige? Fremmedarbejdere i fædrelandet ca. 1800–1970* (Farum: Farums Arkiver og Museer, 2000).
2 See Jørn Henrik Petersen, Klaus Petersen, and Niels Finn Christiansen, eds., *Dansk velfærdshistorie*, vol. IV (Odense: Syddansk Universitetsforlag, 2013).
3 Heidi Vad Jønsson, *Indvandring i velfærdsstaten. 100 Danmarkshistorier* (Aarhus: Aarhus Universitetsforlag, 2018).
4 Daniel Béland has, among his long list of research publications, written several important pieces on ideational theory, which he links to institutional theory. See, for example, Daniel Béland and Robert H. Cox, eds., *Ideas and Politics in Social Science Research* (New York: Oxford University Press, 2011); Daniel Béland and André Lecours, *Nationalism and Social Policy: The Politics of Territorial Solidarity* (Oxford: Oxford University Press, 2008).
5 See, e.g., Lars Jørgensen, "Hvad sagde vi… om de andre?" (PhD thesis, Roskilde University, 2006); Lærke Klitgaard Holm, "Folketinget og Udlændingepolitikken – diskurser om naturaliserede, indvandrere og flygtninge 1973–2002" (PhD thesis, Aalborg University, 2006).

Inequality in the Danish welfare state 169

6 See, e.g., Gunnar Viby Mogensen, *Det danske velfærdssamfunds historie: Tiden efter 1970* (Copenhagen: Gyldendal, 2010).
7 See Hans Kornøe Rasmussen, *Den danske stamme. En befolkningshistorie* (Copenhagen: Politiken, 2008). The Danish welfare commission (2006) in its recommendations included both perspectives and argued that immigration of specific groups of migrant workers would be necessary to maintain a high level of welfare services. At the same time, the commission suggested that immigration of migrant workers (not including refugees) should be organized according to market-demand criteria. Velfærdskommissionen, *Fremtidens velfærd – vores valg (analyserapport januar 2006)* (København: Finansministeriet, 2006), accessed 19 May 2019, www.fm.dk/publikationer/velfaerdskommissionen/2008/rapporter-fra-velfaerdskommissionen/analyserapport.
8 Christoffer Green-Pedersen, *Partier i nye tider. Den politiske dagsorden i Danmark* (Aarhus: Aarhus Universitetsforlag, 2011); Jørgen Goul Andersen and Ole Borre, *Politisk forandring. Værdipolitik og nye skillelinjer ved folketingsvalget 2001* (Aarhus: Systime, 2003). See also The National Election Study, accessed 19 May 2019, www.valgprojektet.dk/pages/page.asp?pid=327&l=eng.
9 Research on immigration and the welfare state in Denmark includes various studies of integration-policy development. Heidi Vad Jønsson, *Fra lige muligheder til ret og pligt. Socialdemokratiets integrationspolitik i den modern velfærdsstats tidsalder* (Odense: Syddansk Universitetsforlag, 2018) argues that integration policy is a Social Democratic project that should be seen as a new pillar in the Danish welfare system, whereas Karen Nielsen Breidahl, "Når staten lærer: En historisk og komparativ analyse af statslig policy læring og betydningen heraf for udviklingen i den arbejdsmarkedsrettede del af indvandrerpolitikken i Sverige, Norge og Danmark fra 1970 til 2011" (PhD thesis, Aalborg University, 2012), has shown how the labour-market-oriented part of integration policy is the result of transnational learning between Scandinavian state officials.
10 Diane Sainsbury, *Welfare States and Immigrant Rights: The Politics of Inclusion and Exclusion* (Oxford: Oxford University Press, 2012), 87.
11 Ibid., 89.
12 Gøsta Esping-Anderson, *The Three Worlds of Welfare Capitalism* (Cambridge: Polity Press, 1990).
13 The term "migrant" is here used as an umbrella concept which includes all sub-categories, e.g. labour immigrants, immigrants, refugees, family migrants. See Stephen Castles, Hein de Hass, and Mark J. Miller, *The Age of Migration: International Population Movements in the Modern World*, 5th ed. (New York: Guilford Press, 2014). The term "migrant" is used in contemporary Danish politics to describe all types of immigrants except for refugees. Hence, sentences starting with "refugees and migrants" are often heard in political debates. The migrant category has, in a Danish context, changed from a broad term to a political label that suggests that migrants are a group of people who wish to enter Denmark to get access to the Danish welfare state. Hence, the migrant concept now has a negative connotation when used in the sphere of politics. It is important to note that the concept is used in this chapter as an analytical category and not as a politically biased concept.
14 See Castles et al., *The Age of Migration*, 102–146, for an overview of European immigration history. Danish welfare state history is analysed in Petersen et al., *Dansk velfærdshistorie* (2013 and 2014).
15 Niels Finn Christiansen and Klaus Petersen, "The Dynamics of Social Solidarity: The Danish Welfare State 1900–2000," *Scandinavian Journal of History* 26 (2001).
16 Esping-Andersen, *The Three Worlds of Welfare Capitalism*, has been paradigmatic in comparative welfare state research and the typologies of welfare regimes have been reproduced, though not without critique, in several volumes on welfare state research.

17 Mary Hilson, *The Nordic Model: Scandinavia since 1945* (Waterside: Reaktion Books, 2008); Niels Finn Christiansen, Klaus Petersen, Nils Edling, and Per Haave, *The Nordic Model of Welfare: A Historical Reappraisal* (Copenhagen: Museum Tusculanum, 2006).
18 Pauli Kettunen, "The Agent Called 'Society' in the Making and Challenging of the Nordic Welfare State" (paper presented at 34th Annual Social Science History Association (SSHA) Meeting: Agency and Action, Long Beach, California, 12–15 November 2009), accessed 19 May 2019, www.mv.helsinki.fi/ptkettun/kettunen-SSHA09.pdf.
19 Richard Titmuss, "Universalism versus Selection," in *The Welfare State Reader*, 2nd ed., ed. Christopher Pierson and Francis G. Castles, 40–48 (Cambridge: Polity Press, 2006).
20 Heidi Vad Jønsson, *Fra lige muligheder til ret og pligt. Socialdemokratiets integrationspolitik i den modern velfærdsstats tidsalder* (Odense: Syddansk Universitetsforlag, 2018).
21 Castles et al., *The Age of Migration*.
22 Hans Chr. Johansen, *Industriens vækst og vilkår 1870–1973. Dansk industri efter 1870 bind 1* (Odense: Odense Universitetsforlag, 1988), 267–269.
23 Hilmar Baunsgaard, "Udenlandsk arbejdskraft?" *Aktuelt* 29 June 1964. The translation is quoted from Heidi Vad Jønsson and Klaus Petersen, "From a Social Problem to a Cultural Challenge to the National Welfare State: Immigration and Integration Debates in Denmark 1970–2011," in *Citizenship and Identity in the Welfare State*, ed. Andrzej Marcin Suszycki and Ireneusz Pawel Karolewski (Baden-Baden: Nomos Verlagsgesellschaft, 2013), 168.
24 Karen Andersen, *Gæstearbejder - udlænding - indvandrer - dansker!: migration til Danmark i 1968-78* (Copenhagen: Gyldendal, 1979). For a detailed analysis of the institutional development, see Grete Brochmann and Anniken Hagelund, *Velferden grenser* (Oslo: Universitetsforlaget, 2010); Heidi Vad Jønsson and Klaus Petersen, "Danmark: den nationale velfærdsstat møder verden," in *Velferdens grenser*, ed. by Grete Brochmann and Anniken Hagelund (Oslo: Universitetsforlaget, 2010).
25 Dansk Arbejdsmands- og Specialarbejderforbund was the union for semi-skilled workers.
26 More details on labour importing and the reactions of the labour-market parties can be found in Henrik Zip Sane, *Billige og village? Fremmedarbejdere i fædrelandet ca. 1800-1970* (Farum: Farums Arkiver og Museer, 2000).
27 "Blacksmith foreman refuse to fire foreigners before Danes," Fredericia Dagblad, 27 October 1965. Quotation translated by Christian Damm Petersen.
28 Henrik Zip Sane, *Billige og village? Fremmedarbejdere i fædrelandet ca. 1800–1970* (Farum: Farums Arkiver og Museer, 2000).
29 Karen Andersen, *Gæstearbejder - udlænding - indvandrer - dansker!: migration til Danmark i 1968–78* (Copenhagen: Gyldendal, 1979).
30 Mary Hilson, *The Nordic Model: Scandinavia since 1945* (Waterside: Reaktion Books, 2008).
31 Hartmann, Fanny, *Betænkning om udenlandske arbejderes sociale og samfundsmæssige tilpasning her i landet* (Copenhagen: Socialministeriet, 1975).
32 Andersen, *Gæstearbejder*.
33 Lovtidende 1978, Tillæg C: 313–335.
34 Convention on Social Security between the Kingdom of Denmark and the Republic of Turkey, Lovtidende 1978, Tillæg C: 314. A similar convention was made with Yugoslavia.
35 Klaus Petersen, "Constructing Nordic Welfare? Nordic Social Political Cooperation 1919–1955," In *The Nordic Model of Welfare: A Historical Reappraisal*, ed. Niels Finn Christiansen, Klaus Petersen, Nils Edling, and Per Haave, 67–98 (Copenhagen: Museum Tusculanum Press, 2006).
36 See Beslutningsforslag 1979. Folketingstidende 1979/1980 pp.

37 See Jørn Henrik Petersen, Klaus Petersen, and Niels Finn Christiansen, *Dansk Velfærdshistorie*, vol. IV (2013) and vol. V (2014).
38 See Mats Wickström, *The Multicultural Moment: The History of the Idea and Politics of Multiculturalism in Sweden in Comparative, Transnational and Biographical Context, 1964–1975* (Aabo: Aabo Akademi University, 2015).
39 For a comparative study of immigration and welfare-policy development in the postwar period, see Grete Brochmann and Anniken Hagelund, *Immigration Policy and the Scandinavian Welfare State 1945–2010* (Basingstoke: Palgrave Macmillan, 2012).
40 Jørn Henrik Petersen, Klaus Petersen, and Niels Finn Christiansen, *Dansk Velfærdshistorie*, vol. IV (2013) and vol. V (2014) Odense: Syddansk Universitetsforlag, 2012.
41 Hans Chr. Johansen, *Industriens vækst og vilkår 1870–1973. Dansk industri efter 1870 bind 1* (Odense: Odense Universitetsforlag, 1988).
42 This labelling of the act as the world's most liberal was introduced in the Danish press after the new Alien Act was passed in Parliament and an increasing number of refugees came to Denmark and applied for asylum under the liberal conditions of the new act. See, for example, "Verdens bedste," *Berlingske Tidende*, 18 October 1984, 17.
43 This act has a mythical status among right-wing politicians, as it is viewed as the direct cause for the subsequent rise in the number of asylum seekers. Heidi Vad Jønsson, *Indvandring i velfærdsstaten. 100 Danmarkshistorier* (Aarhus: Aarhus Universitetsforlag, 2018).
44 Eva Ersbøll, *Dansk indfødsret i international og historisk belysning* (Copenhagen: Jurist- og Økonomforbundet, 2008).
45 Heidi Vad Jønsson, "Immigrations- og integrationspolitik," in *Dansk Velfærdshistorie. Bind 6,2. Hvor glider vi hen?* ed. Jørn Henrik Petersen, Klaus Petersen, and Niels Finn Christiansen (Odense: Syddansk Universitetsforlag, 2014), 861–996.
46 Bent Jensen, *De fremmede i dansk avisdeba: fra 1870'erne til 1990'erne* (Copenhagen: Spektrum, 2000).
47 Christoffer Green-Pedersen, *Partier i nye tider. Den politiske dagsorden i Danmark* (Aarhus: Aarhus Universitetsforlag, 2011).
48 See Heidi Vad Jønsson, *Fra lige muligheder til ret og pligt. Socialdemokratiets integrationspolitik i den modern velfærdsstats tidsalder* (Odense: Syddansk Universitetsforlag, 2018).
49 Anker Jørgensen, "Vi er ikke racister," I Ny Politik nr 11/12. Nytår 1985/86, 30.
50 See Carly Elizabeth Schall, *The Rise and Fall of the Miraculous Welfare Machine: Immigration and Social Democracy in Twentieth-Century Sweden* (Cornell: IRL Press, 2016); Wickström, *The Multicultural Moment*; Karin Borevi, "Sweden: The Flagship of Multiculturalism," in *Immigration Policy and the Scandinavian Welfare State 1945–2010*, ed. Grete Brochann and Anniken Hagelund (Basingstoke: Palgrave Macmillan, 2012).
51 Refugee integration was at the time managed by an NGO, *Danish Refugee Council*, for the first 24 months after a refugee was granted asylum in Denmark.
52 Niklas Olsen and Jacob Jensen, eds., "Theme Issue: Neoliberalisme," *Slagmark: Tidsskrift for Idéhistorie* (2016).
53 See Stephanie L. Mudge, *Leftism Reinvented: Western Parties from Socialism to Neoliberalism.* (Harvard: Harvard University Press, 2018). See also Geijs Schumacher, "Modernize or Die?: Social Democrats, Welfare State Retrenchment and the Choice between Office and Policy" (PhD thesis, Vrije Universiteit Amsterdam, 2012).
54 See Søren Kolstrup, *Den danske velfærdsmodel 1891-2011: sporskifter, motive, drivkræfter* (Frederiksberg: Frydenlund, 2015).
55 See Heidi Vad Jønsson, *Fra lige muligheder til ret og pligt. Socialdemokratiets integrationspolitik i den modern velfærdsstats tidsalder* (Odense: Syddansk Universitetsforlag, 2018).

56 This concept is somewhat difficult to translate into English, as it implies more than someone being of non-Danish nationality. To some extent this concept covers "the alienated foreigners."
57 This amount was close to a CEO's annual salary in the mid-1990s.
58 This party had been established in 1995 with Pia Kjærsgaard as leader. The party was a new construction in Danish politics as DPP was anti-immigration and pro-welfare, as opposed to the Progress Party, which had been anti-immigration and anti-welfare. The DPP posed an electoral threat to the Social Democratic Party as the new party argued along some of the same lines as core Social Democratic voters. See Christoffer Green-Pedersen, *Partier i nye tider. Den politiske dagsorden i Danmark* (Aarhus: Aarhus Universitetsforlag, 2011).
59 Jacob Gaarde Madsen, *Mediernes konstruktion af flygtninge- og indvandrerspørgsmålet* (Copenhagen: Magtudredningen, Politica, 2000).
60 Ruth Emerek, "Integration eller eksklusion?" AMID Working Paper Series, 2003, accessed 19 May 2019, http://vbn.aau.dk/files/17431483/AMID_wp_31; Lars Jørgensen, "Hvad sagde vi"; Holm, "Folketinget og Udlændingepolitikken."
61 Integrationloven, Folketingstidende 1998, Tillæg C.
62 Carly Elizabeth Schall, *The Rise and Fall of the Miraculous Welfare Machine: Immigration and Social Democracy in Twentieth-Century Sweden* (Cornell: IRL Press, 2016).
63 The effects of multicultural policies are highly debated. See, for example, Will Kymlicka *Multiculturalism: Success, Failure, and the Future* (Washington, DC: Migration Policy Institute, 2012), accessed 19 May 2019, www.humanityinaction.org/files/514-multiculturalism.pdf; Ruud Koopmans, *Assimilation oder Multikulturalismus?: Bedingungen gelungener Integration* (Berlin: LIT, 2017); Wickström, *The Multicultural Moment*.
64 Integrationloven, Folketingstidende 1998, Tillæg C.

Conclusion

Beyond citizenship and "responsibilization" in the exclusionary welfare state: realizing universal human rights through social resilience-building and interactional justice?

Veronika Flegar

Introduction[1]

The chapters in the volume reveal the changing social-welfare arrangements for different individuals and groups that are commonly labelled as vulnerable, marginalized or disadvantaged. The authors expose the centrality of legal and social citizenship for the provision of welfare state benefits. These accounts suggest fundamental normative conflicts in the rationale of Western liberal ideas of welfare and social inclusion.

Several authors relate these conflicts to the international sphere and expose the mutual influences and benefits of such an integrated account of national and international developments. Anäis Van Ertvelde, for instance, focuses on disability rights in the national context but simultaneously reveals how national actors such as "people with disabilities, disability organizations and academics" contributed to international developments for instance through their contributions to a disability rights declaration which was "furthered by the Belgian representatives to the UN in 1975."[2] Karim Fertikh most directly highlights these processes of mutual influence in his account of the development of the European Convention of the Social Security of Migrant Workers.[3]

In exposing these mutual influences, the chapters could be read as an implicit critique of the welfare state as failing to realize the universal human rights to social security and an adequate standard of living in Articles 22 and 25 of the Universal Declaration of Human Rights, and Articles 9 and 11 of the International Covenant on Economic, Social and Cultural Rights. This forms the starting point of this concluding chapter in which human rights are understood as legal rights codified in international law and justiciable in international courts, tribunals and human rights–monitoring mechanisms. The chapter seeks to highlight two central controversies in the relationship between the welfare state and marginalized groups: the legal citizenship–based exclusion from universal human rights and the increasing responsibilization of potential welfare beneficiaries. It highlights these conflicts in terms of their central threats for the realization of allegedly universal claims and suggests pragmatic policy alternatives that could contribute to mitigating the two controversies: resilience-building support for different types of structures and societal institutions, and an emphasis on interactional justice in individualized targeting mechanisms.

Unlike the previous chapters of this volume, this chapter does not, therefore, look into how specific actors use human rights language but, instead, uses human rights as the starting point of its normative argument: in ratifying international treaties, states have submitted themselves to international legal obligations they ought to fulfil. With this in mind, the chapter seeks to identify ways in which states can possibly do so without negating their general public interest to make effective use of limited resources and to direct governing efforts towards specific policy goals. In so doing, the chapter does not focus on the justiciability of human rights at the international level but merely seeks to identify pragmatic policy alternatives with these international legal obligations in mind.

Two normative eligibility conflicts in the realization of socio-economic human rights

Legal citizenship and the limits of universal human rights

According to the Universal Declaration of Human Rights and subsequent implementing treaties, human rights are universal in their personal scope and should therefore apply to every human being regardless of any citizenship-based considerations.[4] Eric Boot even holds that rather than this merely being a legal obligation, "many scholars today have come to refer to it [human rights] as the global moral *lingua franca*."[5] Yet, the previous chapters reveal how states frequently fail to realize these universal human rights when restricting the access of non-citizens to the welfare state. Heidi Vad Jønsson, for instance, explores the development of the immigration–welfare policy nexus in light of existing international social law. She concludes that during the first decades after the Second World War, universal access and coverage was the dominant welfare principle and resulted in attempts to include migrants in the Danish system. Yet, an important immigration reform in 1983, namely the abolition of the possibility to deport people on the basis of their need for permanent social assistance, resulted in a shift of these efforts. From then on, welfare nationalism led to migrants' welfare rights increasingly being questioned and being linked to a duty to adhere to Danish values and integrate into Danish society.[6]

Human rights literature suggests that such developments are due not only to economic pressures or nationalistic sentiments but also grounded in a peculiarity of international law: state sovereignty. State sovereignty allows countries to independently govern their internal affairs and to freely decide who is granted access to the political community and resources. On this basis, Saladin Mackled-García and Basik Cali point out that it can be justified to deny some rights to non-citizens because a state is a political community and as such "shapes itself democratically and develops its own terms of cooperation."[7] Thus, it becomes necessary to grant members of this community some rights not granted to non-members.[8] Hence, it has been argued that in the context of migration it is almost impossible to adopt a state sovereignty versus human rights argument because this ultimately boils down to the sovereign "right of any State to close its borders, to determine its own community and its own identity," thus winning the argument.[9] As Jack Donnelly holds, even where human rights are not realized, a state's "legitimacy in international law" is not lost and "sovereignty still ultimately trumps human rights."[10] At the same time, human rights essentially depend on the state for their implementation and could therefore not be realized without state sovereignty.

States have institutionalized this conflict between human rights and state sovereignty through formalizing the concept of citizenship as a means of inclusion and exclusion.[11] Conceptions of legal citizenship and migration status are commonly used to distinguish between a full state responsibility for the realization of the human rights of citizens and a diminished state responsibility for the realization of the human rights of non-citizens. Linda Bosniak suggests that citizenship therefore entails both "universalist and exclusionary commitments": it is universal on the inside as all citizens are commonly perceived as equal and entitled to the full realization of their human rights, and it is exclusive on the outside as non-citizens are usually perceived as (partially) excluded and subject to additional eligibility criteria in order to gain (partial) access.[12] The universalist commitments consequently apply only on the inside (the material rights domain), whereas legal citizenship–based exclusion dominates the outside (the border domain) of the political community.[13] Bosniak asserts that this balance, achieved through the "construct of citizenship," only works as long as there truly exists a separation between the inside and outside.[14] However, along lines similar to those in Vad Jønsson's account in this volume, Lieneke Slingenberg suggests that both spheres are increasingly mixed, which can lead to conflicts both at the border and within the state.[15] Recent EU policy efforts such as border controls and external processing centres for asylum seekers therefore seem to focus once more on the preliminary exclusion of non-citizens in the border domain.

The fundamental conflict between state sovereignty and human rights is no recent phenomenon. Hannah Arendt already observed in 1951 that human rights beyond sovereignty-protected citizenship rights are an illusion since, during the Second World War, "[t]he world found nothing sacred in the abstract nakedness of being human."[16] She explains her position by referring to Edmund Burke's *Reflections on the Revolution in France* (written in 1790) in which he prefers rights to originate "from within the nation" so concepts like "human race" or "the sovereign of the earth" become superfluous.[17] This, Arendt holds, suggests his preference for citizen rights above any human rights as the former are much more likely to be protected and enforced.[18] Hence, Arendt argues, once citizenship is lost and there is no state left to enforce any rights, the rights do not exist.[19] Both Arendt and Burke thus already seem to suggest that human rights are, in fact, only citizen rights which cannot exist beyond sovereign states and are thus not grounded in any common humanity but in a common nationality.

However, Arendt continues that citizen rights *cannot* be human rights because they do not arise from human embodiment. This position is grounded in the experiences of refugees and stateless persons after the Second World War. She finds that humanity easily equated people outside of the protection regime of a state as "savages" once someone was left with nothing else but human rights. Human rights beyond the state, she asserts, are thus commonly considered as something uncivilized. They remind us of the fact that we are human and cannot control every possible risk of suffering or deprivation.[20] She argues that the loss of citizen rights actually coincides with becoming a human being.[21] *Human* rights can thus only exist *beyond* citizenship and *citizen* rights cannot be human rights due to their intrinsic relationship to state sovereignty and citizenship rather than to a common human embodiment.

So, if human rights beyond the state cannot exist because they cannot be enforced yet human rights within the state cannot exist because they are not grounded in our human nature, then what exactly are we left with? Ayten Gundogdu argues that Arendt's criticism in this respect does not aim to abolish human rights but rather to reconceptualize them.[22] The next sections provide some starting points for such a reconceptualization.

Responsibilization and the end of unconditional welfare benefits

Universal human rights are generally perceived as unconditional and do not depend upon the meeting of certain responsibilities or obligations by individual actors wanting to claim these rights. This universality of human rights is put under pressure not only by the aforementioned legal citizenship and migration status–based exclusion. The chapters in this volume suggest that, while interpretations of the rights to social security and an adequate standard of living in international human rights law have expanded and concretized the scope of state obligations, this development is seldom matched by national welfare policies. As such, recent decades seem to have been marked by an increasing shift from universal welfare benefits towards the responsibilization and activation of citizens.

Monika Baár, for instance, reveals how in the 1980s the welfare provisions for disabled people were reshaped and increasingly emphasized independence, an objective which, she finds, was used to justify privatization, welfare spending cuts and an emphasis on citizens' own responsibility ("responsibilization").[23] As such, she finds that the right to work was increasingly understood as an obligation to work which, due to limited job opportunities for able-bodied as well as disabled citizens, resulted in "increased levels of poverty and marginalization rather than 'independence.'"[24] In relation to similar developments in Belgium, Van Ertvelde equally points to how activation policies in the form of "customized care" could leave people unassisted and turn labour-market participation "from a right into a duty."[25] While some of these developments might be understandable in light of limited resources and a desire to decrease dependency, these and other accounts in this volume simultaneously highlight the often counterproductive effects of such "activation" policies. As such, an increased emphasis on individual autonomy and the responsibilization of potential welfare beneficiaries often seems to aggravate rather than mitigate social exclusion. These findings fit into a broader body of social-policy literature which criticizes the increasing dismantling of universal welfare and solidarity ideas and emphasizes how "rights-based conceptions of citizenship are losing ground to obligation-centred notions."[26] Although developments differ across welfare states, this focus on duties rather than rights is, for instance, revealed in more conditions being attached to the eligibility for unemployment benefits and in financial means-tests becoming fundamental to social assistance schemes.[27]

This emphasis on individual responsibility and activation has led to narrower conceptions of social citizenship that question the extent to which a basic minimum standard of living is a citizenship right (let alone considering it to be a human right).[28] Some argue that the emphasis on individual responsibility and activation is "primarily coercive and disciplinary" in an attempt to curb perceived "social ills."[29] While, in some instances, such a coercive approach could be justified if it were to deliver the desired effects of actual participation and the realization of the human rights of marginalized individuals or groups, the chapters in this volume as well as other studies suggest that, hitherto, such responsibilization approaches have had limited success in this respect.[30] From a universal human rights perspective, these developments seem particularly concerning. They undermine the central and fundamentally unconditional idea of human rights as universal and inalienable entitlements by virtue of being human.

Nevertheless, ideas of activation and responsibilization might not necessarily be the source of all evil. Some authors, for instance, point to the fact that "all societies are systems of responsibilities" and that individual responsibility is a concept embraced by very diverse convictions of the political and ideological spectrum from "new right" to "care feminism."[31] Others assert that the increased emphasis on responsibility does not only mean that potential welfare beneficiaries are expected to act responsibly but that public service providers and even the private sector are equally undergoing responsibilization.[32] Again others argue that developments towards activation and responsibilization of potential welfare beneficiaries do not necessarily pose a threat to the realization of economic, social and cultural rights. After all, these rights have become increasingly institutionalized and "there is little evidence of reduced spending on social policy." Instead, these developments created "new choices about rights and protections for vulnerable populations."[33]

What is more, some authors even suggest that the emphasis on responsibility and human duties rather than human rights is crucial for the continued relevance and realization of human rights. These authors argue that, rather than diminishing the emphasis on responsibility, it is necessary to reconsider the content of this responsibility. Mounk, for instance, asserts that "it is high time to develop a positive account of responsibility: one that recognized the reasons why most people seek responsibility and actually helps them to live up to the responsibilities they embrace."[34] This reframing of responsibility might be worthwhile not only for national welfare debates, but, some argue, a shift towards such a reframed understanding of responsibility can also contribute to strengthening human rights altogether. Boot remarks in this respect that "rather than weakening or endangering human rights, a renewed emphasis on our duties will prove to *strengthen* human rights, particularly by preventing the proliferation of unclaimable rights."[35] Fineman equally calls for a reconceptualization of "the nature and scope of both individual and state responsibility."[36] Yet, when engaging in such a reconceptualization of responsibility one might want to keep in mind that shifts and diversifications in perceptions of individual responsibility do not necessarily imply different legal obligations for states. Even if one were to encourage individuals to take responsibility to contribute to the realization of universal human rights, it remains the state, not the individual, who has the legal obligation for this realization. States have signed and ratified international treaties and therefore remain the principal international legal personalities to be held accountable for any failure to abide by these treaties. Hence, shifting ideals about who should be taking whatever type of responsibility do not automatically imply any relief of the state's primary responsibility to fulfil their obligations under international law.

This section has suggested that an increased emphasis on responsibility is ambiguous, complex and not as black and white as is sometimes held by critiques of welfare responsibilization. Depending on how responsibility is framed, used and understood, it might entail not only problems but also provide opportunities for the realization of universal human rights. Without going into the philosophical debates about this point, there might just be a faint hint of a possibility that a different approach towards human rights, one that operates under a renewed emphasis on human duties and with a more complex understanding of different forms and functions of responsibility, might contribute to the reconceptualization of human rights which Arendt calls for. With this in mind, this chapter now proceeds to the more practical side of this argument and seeks to highlight two pragmatic policy alternatives, which might contribute to such a reconceptualization. The next sections seek to highlight two potential starting points for concrete policy measures that can contribute to mitigating the pressure upon universal human rights derived from both responsibility-oriented and sovereignty-based exclusion.

Two proposals for more inclusive social policy

The previous sections underlined how the intertwined rationales of sovereignty-based and responsibility-oriented exclusion continue to put the universal human rights ideal under pressure. These controversies seem to have been aggravated by recent developments such as the economic crisis, increasing migration and populism, and are unlikely to be reversed. The full realization of universal human rights and a return to universal welfare regimes thus seem rather far-fetched utopian ideas that are nice to keep in mind but unrealistic to implement in practice.

This raises the question of what, if any, politically and financially feasible alternative policy approaches can be found for the universal realization of socioeconomic human rights in Western welfare states. Answering this question in an increasingly complex social world requires some audacity. A variety of different approaches and ideas have been suggested. Rather than providing a comprehensive overview of all possible options, this section merely seeks to encourage further engagement with two proposals that, if integrated, could form part of a feasible mitigation mechanism for both of the aforementioned conflicts: (1) the resilience-focused strengthening of societal structures and community ties, and (2) the vulnerability-focused just administration of individualized eligibility assessments.[37] These suggestions should be understood as an invitation for a constructive dialogue on feasible mitigation mechanisms rather than as concrete implementation measures since, as the accounts in this volume also reveal, any specific policy is inherently context-dependent.

Resilience-focused strengthening of societal structures and community ties

Proponents of a reconsideration of the concept of responsibility in the context of human rights and social policy suggest that responsibility cannot be exclusively understood as linked to the individual but arises in a complex relationship of societal dependencies and structural factors that influence the outcome of individual actions.[38] As such, the extent to which allegedly responsible or irresponsible actions lead to a specific result depends, for instance, on the original biological and societal starting position of each individual and on a complex set of miscellaneous previous choices, opportunities and capacities throughout an individual's life course.[39] Moreover, the individual to be "activated" and "responsibilized" is "entangled within widespread ties, dependencies, and duties to others."[40] The policy subject is thus not an isolated human being but a socially and institutionally embedded person. This understanding provides opportunities for new policy foci since the shift away from state responsibility as the primary starting point provides room not only for an emphasis on individual responsibility but also for new collective endeavours on the basis of "new notions of 'community' and spaces for collective action and responsibility."[41]

Recent proposals along these lines commonly focus on the building of social resilience. In its broadest definition, resilience can be understood as "a positive, adaptive response to adversity."[42] Yet, like most social scientific concepts, resilience comes in a variety of different understandings, not all of which are equally useful for the realization of universal socio-economic human rights. Philippe Bourbeau, for instance, suggests that "although resilience may be in some instances a neoliberal device for governance, it has a wider range of meanings as well."[43] In order to limit the risk of social resilience becoming yet another responsibilization mechanism it is important to understand social resilience as a multi-layered concept.

In order to understand how such investments in social resilience could be strengthened so as to contribute to social inclusion and to the realization of universal socio-economic human rights, it seems important to be aware of the diverse social threads which embed individuals in society. In this respect, Serge Paugam provides a useful overview of four different but intertwined social bonds and their role for the protection, assistance and recognition of the individual.[44] These social bonds, he argues, "constitute the social fabric enveloping the individual."[45] The first bond he distinguishes is the bond between parents and children (the "Lineal bond"), which he characterizes along the lines of "intergenerational solidarity," "[c]lose protection" and "[a]ffective recognition." The second bond he highlights is the bond between partners, friends and selected acquaintances (the "Elective participation bond"), which is characterized by "the solidarity of elective acquaintances," "[c]lose protection" and affective or similarity-based recognition. Third, he exposes the bond between persons engaged in occupational life (the "Organic participation bond") as providing a "[s]table job," "[c]ontractualized protection" and "[r]ecognition through work and consequent social esteem." Last, he outlines the bond between members of a political community (the "Citizenship bond"), which is characterized by "[l]egal protection (civil, political and social rights) as per the principle of equality" and "[r]ecognition of the sovereign individual."[46]

Scholars focusing on social justice and substantive equality advance similar arguments. As such, Martha Fineman, for instance, asserts that "society's institutions interact in ways that actually provide (or fail to produce) social, political, and economic resilience" through conferring "privilege or disadvantage" in ways that determine the level to which an individual can participate in society and benefit from these institutions.[47] Allman equally holds that a "focus on structural inabilities allows for a more complex, multidimensional understanding of the interplay, overlap, and social distance between money, work, and belonging."[48]

These empirical and normative observations suggest that the state is indeed merely one of several societal elements that can provide protection, assistance and recognition. Yet, some would argue that citizenship constitutes the most fundamental of these bonds and therefore places a particular responsibility upon the state to facilitate and nurture all other bonds.[49] While this appears to be a normative rather than an evidence-based claim, the diversification of responsibility in recent years and the limited success in the activation of individuals certainly provides some grounds for considering whether and how the state can contribute to the strengthening of other social bonds. Policy interventions that seek to go beyond the (failed) responsibilization of allegedly autonomous individuals could seek to strengthen each of these four components. This does not necessarily suggest that active intervention by the state in these domains is desirable but firstly that the state has to create and foster an environment in which these bonds are protected and can flourish. This requires innovative forms of regulation and governance but can, depending on the specific context, also involve more active interventions. What exactly would be the most adequate approach requires further research and likely has to be decided on a case-by-case basis.

How exactly do these proposals contribute to mitigating the two aforementioned exclusion mechanisms? The preceding arguments seem to warrant the conclusion that a focus on social resilience-building can deepen our understanding of marginalization and disadvantage and, in so doing, can suggest alternative (and potentially more successful) pathways for activation policies. Analysing these contextual elements and facilitating changes in societal structures such as families, communities, organizations and state institutions in ways that can mitigate social exclusion could contribute to the actual success of activation policies, thereby listening to both demands for personal responsibility and demands for substantial equality. Here, the interests of the state as service provider and of the marginalized and/or disadvantaged as potential service beneficiaries seem largely aligned.

However, beyond the boundaries of citizenship, the benefit of social resilience-building becomes a murkier terrain. The primary state interest to determine membership in its political community remains fundamentally opposed to the realization of universal human rights. Nevertheless, a perspective that focuses on the building of social resilience can have two potential benefits for the realization of universal human rights. First, it opens up questions about the foundations for belonging in a political community. If, for instance, migrants are fully participating social citizens in ways that contribute to the strengthening of the political community's social resilience, it might no longer be justified to (partially) deny them the benefits of this political community. This might bring non-citizens at least one step closer to the realization of their universal human rights. Second, a resilient society with strong social bonds and informal networks can (and often already does) provide an alternative social safety net for those non-citizens without access to formal welfare benefits. Starting from the assumption that the primary goal is the realization of universal human rights regardless of whose responsibility this is or what politically or economically undesirable effects this could have, such an approach could thus potentially mitigate some of the exclusionary tendencies of legal citizenship and migration status.

Yet, even beyond these general considerations, a social-resilience-building approach also entails practical risks and potential pitfalls. Van Ertvelde in this volume, for instance, seems to refer to resilience-building elements of social policy when she speaks of the "socialization of care" and warns that this might result in "an offloading of state responsibility onto the market" and could "mean that people are left to fend for themselves."[50] Suzan Ilcan and Kiem Rygiel offer similar concerns in the context of resilience-focused humanitarian assistance since "[r]efugees are now expected not only to withstand adversity but also to thrive by becoming empowered and involved in the management of camp life."[51] Vasco Lub et al. equally highlight several *participatieparadoxen* (participatory paradoxes) through an example about persons with serious mental disabilities being placed within a community rather than in a separate institution.[52] They find that, despite intentions to the contrary, voluntary agencies are taken less seriously and are contacted less by the authorities, the freedom of movement of persons with serious mental disabilities is limited rather than expanded and assistance proves inadequate since potential beneficiaries are often not able to oversee their own problems or formulate their needs for assistance.[53] It seems that, under such circumstances, social resilience-building would not move much beyond the often ineffective responsibilization of welfare beneficiaries.

Another risk lies in the existing power imbalances in the different social structures at which resilience-building approaches are aimed. Bourbeau, for instance, suggests that resilience-building could come "at the expense of an analysis of the causes of inequality, injustice, power discrepancies, and vulnerability."[54] Gail Mason and Mariastella Pulvirenti similarly find that a "tension between individual and community needs" can lead to the "papering over" of community differences and issues such as domestic violence.[55] Undue attention to these power structures could hinder or even reverse any positive effects social-resilience-building approaches could have upon social inclusion and substantive equality.

Moreover, social-resilience-building approaches specifically aimed at encouraging citizens to participate more extensively in society by engaging with marginalized and/or disadvantaged individuals in their community and neighbourhood or as volunteers cannot only be ineffective but can even have counterproductive effects for society. A study on the Dutch *participatiesamenleving* (participatory society) reveals that this approach can lead to the state becoming the gatekeeper for what constitutes good social citizenship, which can lead to new forms of exclusion and a hollowed-out understanding of social citizenship as mere means to an end.[56] This risks "crowding out" the more critical and autonomous elements of social citizenship, which can result in "a waste of human and material resources and challenges the sustainability of democratic institutions over time."[57] There thus seems to be a very fine but blurry line between too much and too little steering in social-resilience-building approaches.

These observations suggest that adequate measures can be determined only context-specifically and through time and experience. This requires a careful evaluation of what is realistic and feasible, and the adequate preparation and capacity-building in communities and other social structures, as well as through attention to the interactional abilities of potential beneficiaries. Mason and Pulvirenti suggest that what is needed is "a model of resilience that moves beyond homogenous or normative understandings of community to recognize the unequal power relations that attach to different social roles within 'at-risk' or vulnerable populations."[58] In order to adopt such a more context-sensitive approach that takes into account power imbalances and the heterogeneity of individuals it is important not only to operate under a more nuanced understanding of communities but also to understand individuals as complex social beings with different basic needs, personal vulnerabilities and capacities.[59]

Hence, social-resilience-building efforts that were to focus solely on social structures and communities cannot be the only strategy to ensure social inclusion and mitigate the vulnerability of marginalized individuals or groups.[60] Rather, for such interventions to have the largest possible inclusionary impact *for individuals*, they should be informed by a deeper understanding of individuals and their social interaction. The complexity and heterogeneity of individuals means that there is no one-size-fits-all solution. One way in which this could be taken into account is by paying due regard to issues of recognition and intersectionality in the design and implementation of social-resilience-building programmes. In addition, it might be sensible to complement social resilience-building with (potentially activation-oriented) individual basic-assistance provisions on the basis of an interactionally just identification of a person's embodied and socially constituted vulnerabilities and capacities. The last point is elaborated upon in more detail in the next section.

Vulnerability-focused, individualized social service provision

The concept of vulnerability seems to be of fundamental relevance for understanding the mechanisms of inclusion and exclusion in relation to the marginalized or disadvantaged individual within society. Barbara Anna Misztal, for instance, asserts that some aspects of vulnerability are "inherent in the human condition" but that these aspects are reinforced or even initiated "by life in society" and that these aspects can increase inequalities.[61] She encourages "studying people's present relations with others, by exploring the risks people face and by examining the past forces and factors behind the formation of their personhood" in order "to develop the notion of vulnerability as a multidimensional and cumulative concept that refers to objective risks or deprivation and their subjective assessments by individuals."[62] Catriona Mackenzie equally holds that vulnerability is "both universal and context specific, both inherent to the human condition yet always already shaped by social and political relationships and institutions."[63] Hence, a vulnerability-informed starting position for social policy aims to do justice to both embodied and socially constituted vulnerabilities and capacities in order to better understand and mitigate marginalization and disadvantage.[64]

This starting position seems valuable for more effective welfare policies aimed at social inclusion and substantive equality since, as Catherine Elisabeth Brown elaborates, social-policy-related understandings of vulnerability comprise a contextual and behavioural component: vulnerability is "constructed and reaffirmed by broader social and economic systems and processes which influence the life of an individual" and can "subtly but pervasively serve wider policy mechanisms which establish what is appropriate and 'correct' behavior, and which subject people to sanctions should they fail to conform."[65] Knowledge about the effects of the norms and values which shape social-policy interventions can sharpen our understanding of the diverse factors which lead some policies to fail while others succeed. Where policy on social inclusion and substantial equality is concerned, this seems to require an inquiry into the underlying understanding of the individual in society and the weaknesses, risks, capacities, needs and, in essence, vulnerability involved.

Hence, focusing on a socio-psychologically informed understanding of vulnerability can help us (1) to better understand policy subjects so as to realize that even if it were possible to mitigate all societal factors, there are still personal embodied elements which make individuals different and form unique and differently challenging starting positions for a person's possibilities in society, and (2) to better understand policy effects so as to realize that it is not only the quantifiable effects or intentions of a policy that lead to a certain outcome but also the norms which underlie it and are communicated through it.

In more concrete terms, this means that individualized assistance is important. Although, in light of resource constraints, such individualized approaches might not always be feasible, they are crucial for complementing social-resilience-building approaches: the social inclusion of individuals cannot be achieved by one-size-fits-all approaches but require sufficient attention to individual differences and complexities. The combination of a possibility to approach public service providers individually in addition to assistance provided within the community is therefore pivotal to balance out potential power imbalances within communities and improve the access of individuals to services. Moreover, paying attention to and inventorying individual vulnerabilities and capacities allows a closer monitoring of the effects and impact of social resilience-building. Such inventories can reveal capacity gaps and needs for extra support for individuals whose lack of access might otherwise remain hidden – for instance because they might not be able to oversee their own situation or to adequately formulate their assistance needs. However, such individualized assistance does not come without pitfalls of its own, which is why it seems important to carefully consider the content and procedure of individualized service provision.

As regards the content of individualized service provision, vulnerability provides a useful consideration in not only focusing on dependencies but also on capacities that can foster (or limit) an individual's autonomous decision-making.[66] The Dutch Scientific Council for Government Policy (Wetenschappelijke Raad voor het Regeringsbeleid), for instance, emphasizes that more research is needed on the relationship between self-reliance and a person's mental state since previous literature suggests that stress, mental strain, and feelings of scarcity and poverty can have an effect on the extent to which a person is able to formulate goals for the future, to focus on these and to work towards them.[67] In more concrete terms, Trudie Knijn et al. equally suggest that "activation is most successful when the activation offers made to clients meet their needs, wishes and capacities" so as to transform assistance proposals "from 'an offer you can't refuse' into 'an offer you won't refuse.'"[68] Social scientific studies thus seem to suggest that attention to psychological effects, rather than merely to the material or embodied position of an individual in society, is important to ensure effective social policy. This also includes the comprehensive provision of services that not only includes "benefit payments and labour-market services (education and training, placement and job-search assistance) but also the provision of social services (child and elderly care, debt counselling, support for drug and alcohol abusers, disability assistance, housing provision, psychological and financial counselling)."[69] However, the complexity of these factors and services as well as their interplay calls for further research.

As far as procedural elements are concerned, the administratively just determination of eligibility and adequate assistance should take place on the basis of transparent and fair assessment mechanisms. A crucial consideration that seems of particular – and frequently neglected – relevance for marginalized and/or disadvantaged individuals is interactional justice.[70] The interaction between the service provider and the potential beneficiary usually involves vulnerability-related imbalances. As such, Mackenzie, for instance, asserts that "inequalities of power, dependency, capacity, or need render some agents vulnerable to harm or exploitation by others."[71] Vulnerability-focused approaches in the context of criminal proceedings provide additional guidance in this respect. Malini Laxminarayan, for instance, asserts that it is necessary to focus on a person's coping ability in order to ensure the proper treatment of a vulnerable individual.[72] Along these lines, interactional justice focuses on "treating people with respect and dignity" and, in so doing, "is more symbolic and psychological than tangible and material."[73] Awareness of vulnerability-related imbalances and due regard to them through interactional justice seems of crucial importance for the provision of services to persons who might face additional barriers in voicing their claims in conventional ways due to specific embodied, situational or social-structure-related vulnerabilities. This element should be taken into account in addition to prominently considered procedural- and distributive-justice guarantees in order to ensure transparent and fair assessment mechanisms of vulnerability, need and capacity in the context of social service provision.

This attention to the content and procedures of individualized service provision could mitigate the sovereignty versus universal human rights debate by strengthening a compassionate and human-dignity-based understanding of human rights as universal. It emphasizes that the realization of universal human rights is a complex process of a multitude of gradations rather than a question of either/or. This suggests that, from a vulnerability perspective, non-citizenship should not lead to the full exclusion from all rights or benefits of a political community but should be assessed on a case-by-case basis. This means that there should be room to grant pathways to citizenship for some individuals regardless of whether their initial step into the political community was lawful. While this does not (yet) realize the universal human rights ideal, it can at least be a step towards a more inclusive realization of human rights. This seems to also increasingly be propagated by the European human rights system. Non-citizens in precarious situations seem to increasingly be recognized as eligible for at least the provision of their basic needs such as food, shelter and basic health care.[74] Several of the judgments related to an adequate living standard and social assistance at the European Court of Human Rights and the European Committee of Social Rights seem to refer to vulnerability as one of the relevant considerations.[75] Vulnerability-related procedural guarantees in the context of migration are also increasingly considered – for instance in European asylum policies.[76] Although the vulnerability approach in these judgements is still evolving, it seems that the judicial bodies' understanding of vulnerability is not exclusively based on embodiment but also acknowledges the embedded, constructed and contextual nature of vulnerability.[77]

The attention to the content and procedures of individualized service provision along the lines of an understanding of the embodied and embedded nature of vulnerability could also mitigate the responsibilization debate. A thorough understanding of not only material but also psychological effects of individualized assistance as well as of potentially detrimental side effects is important for effective activation policies that contribute to social inclusion rather than to further exclusion. Beyond assessing eligibility, an interactionally just basic service provision that collects information on different individual trajectories can help to inform more effective policies in the future so as to allocate more adequate responsibilities and duties to the state, societal structures and the individual in ways that can actually improve substantive equality and social inclusion.

This section has sought to emphasize that there is no escape from individualized service provision. Yet, the determination of eligibility and adequate activation policies is largely context-dependent, and it is not the intention of this section to provide a definitive list of criteria. Rather, what this section sought to point out are the parameters that might be worthwhile considering when determining the content and procedure for assessing welfare-benefit eligibility.[78] While resilience-building seems potentially more sustainable in several respects, there are always people who fall between the cracks or whose situation is so specific that individualized professional assistance is required. Hence, while some might criticize individualized service provision as stigmatizing, neoliberal or simply ineffective, this chapter argues that there remains an added value to it that should not be overlooked. Despite its potential pitfalls, individualized service provision constitutes a crucial addition to social-resilience-building approaches. This is to say, the two approaches complement each other and vice versa: individualized service provision that aims at social inclusion and substantive equality cannot go without social resilience-building.

Conclusion

For the near future, issues of social inclusion and substantive equality will likely remain contentious policy terrains and continue to entail many unresolved challenges. It seems that we are still in an early stage of social-scientifically investigating, understanding and focusing on the connections and interplay between the vulnerabilities and capacities of individuals, society and the state and in an even earlier stage of integrating any such findings into policies. This chapter therefore merely intended to pinpoint a number of philosophical and practical elements that might be relevant to consider in the development of social-resilience-building approaches and individualized service provision aimed at social inclusion and substantive equality. It should be read as a modest attempt to provide some inspiration for policy and research, and an invitation to engage further with the benefits and pitfalls of such proposals.

The suggestions in this chapter cannot resolve the two fundamental conflicts identified in the beginning. However, the chapter sought to highlight how the proposals might be able to mitigate some of the consequences of these conflicts. Whether this is desirable essentially remains a value judgment that, at its core, questions the relevance of universal human rights ideals. This chapter suggests that, while defending the continued importance of universal human rights as a moral and legal framework, one should keep in mind that their realization is likely to remain a challenging and lengthy process that involves compromises, given resource constraints and political priorities. In light of this "reality check," shifting emphasis from entitlements to actual needs might not be completely undesirable.

Simultaneously, this should not result in losing sight of the internationally well-established primary responsibility of states for the realization of universal human rights (for its citizens and beyond). Hence, normatively speaking, the special responsibility of the state towards its citizens should always remain the starting point in a welfare state that desires to adhere to its international legal obligations. A variety of points can be brought forward to support this claim, but, in legal terms, the most obvious one is that states commit themselves to the realization of universal human rights through the ratification of international treaties. Thus, although their responsibility might not always be enforceable in practice, acquitting states of their special and primary responsibility for the realization of universal human rights would likely be detrimental to the international order as we know it.

To conclude, this chapter seeks to encourage readers to build on and critically engage with the normative and practical problems and suggestions highlighted in this chapter since there is no simple solution to social inclusion. Yet, rather than seeing this as a bleak outlook, we should be motivated to continuously challenge and reassess existing ideas. As the historian Arthur M. Schlesinger Jr. (sometimes labelled "the spokesman for post-war liberalism"[79]) noted: "all important problems are insoluble: that is why they are important. The good comes from the continuing struggle to try and solve them, not from the vain hope of their solution."[80]

Notes

1 The arguments in this article are based on Veronika Flegar's PhD research at the University of Groningen.
2 Van Ertvelde, Chapter 8, this volume. The author acknowledges the support of the ERC Consolidator Grant Rethinking Disability under grant agreement number 648115.
3 Fertikh, Chapter 2, this volume.
4 The chapter does not delve into discussions of universality since they have become increasingly outdated. Compare, e.g., Eric R. Boot, *Human Duties and the Limits of Human Rights Discourse* (Cham: Springer, 2017), 26.
5 Boot, *Human Duties*, 3.
6 Vad Jønsson, Chapter 9, this volume.
7 Saladin Meckled-García and Basak Cali, "Lost in Translation: the Human Rights Ideal and International Human Rights Law," in *The Legalization of Human Rights: Multidisciplinary Perspectives on Human Rights and Human Rights Law*, ed. Saladin Meckled-García and Basak Cali (New York: Routledge, 2006), 18.
8 Ibid.
9 Catherine Dauvergne, "Irregular Migration, State Sovereignty and the Rule of Law," in *Research Handbook on International Law and Migration*, ed. Vincent Chetail and Céline Bauloz (Cheltenham: Edward Elgar Publishing, 2014), 90.
10 Jack Donnelly, "The Relative Universality of Human Rights," *Human Rights Quarterly* 29, no. 2 (May 2007): 289.
11 Linda Bosniak, *The Citizen and the Alien: Dilemmas of Contemporary Membership* (Princeton: Princeton University Press, 2006), 4.
12 Ibid.
13 Lieneke Slingenberg, *The Reception of Asylum Seekers under International Law: Between Sovereignty and Equality* (Oxford: Hart Publishing, 2014), 5–8.
14 Bosniak, *The Citizen and the Alien*, 4.
15 Slingenberg, *The Reception of Asylum Seekers*, 5–8.
16 Hannah Arendt, *The Origins of Totalitarianism* (Cleveland: Meridian Books, 1951), 299. Although Arendt more prominently refers to civil and political rights, it is now commonly acknowledged that these rights cannot be realized without economic, social

and cultural rights. It is for this reason that this chapter does not disentangle Arendt's conception of human rights in any more depth. For an interesting article on this issue, see, e.g., Natalie Oman, "Hannah Arendt's 'Right to Have Rights': A Philosophical Context for Human Security," *Journal of Human Rights* 9, no. 3 (2010): 279–302.
17 Arendt, *The Origins of Totalitarianism*, 299.
18 Ibid.
19 Ibid.
20 Ibid., 299–301.
21 Ibid., 302.
22 Ayten Gündogdu, *Rightlessness in an Age of Rights: Hannah Arendt and the Contemporary Struggles of Migrants* (Oxford: Oxford University Press, 2015), 28, 54.
23 Baár, Chapter 7, this volume.
24 Ibid.
25 Van Ertvelde, Chapter 8, this volume.
26 Sylvia Fuller, Paul Kershaw, and Jane Pulkingham, "Constructing 'Active Citizenship': Single Mothers, Welfare, and the Logics of Voluntarism," *Citizenship Studies* 12, no. 2 (2008): 157. Compare also, e.g., Jane Jenson and Ron Levi, "Narratives and Regimes of Social and Human Rights: The Jack Pines of the Neoliberal Era," in *Social Resilience in the Neo-Liberal Era*, ed. Peter A. Hall and Michèle Lamont (New York: Cambridge University Press, 2013), 76; and Susanna Trnka and Catherine Trundle, "Competing Responsibilities: Moving Beyond Neoliberal Responsibilisation," *Anthropological Forum* 24, no. 2 (2014): 138.
27 Hakan Johansson, "Placing the Individual 'At the Forefront': Beck and Individual Approaches in Activation," in *Making It Personal: Individualising Activation Services in the EU*, ed. Rik van Berkel and Ben Valkenburg (Bristol: The Policy Press, 2007): 70.
28 Fuller et al., "Constructing 'Active Citizenship,'" 168.
29 Ibid., 160.
30 This volume. Compare also Bruno Parlier and Claude Martin, eds., *Reforming the Bismarckian Welfare Systems* (Malden: Blackwell Publishing, 2008).
31 Trnka and Trundle, "Competing Responsibilities," 137, 141; Fuller et al., "Constructing 'Active Citizenship,'" 157.
32 Rasmus Hoffmann Birk, "Making Responsible Residents: On 'Responsibilization' within Local Community Work in Marginalized Residential Areas in Denmark," *The Sociological Review* 66, no. 3 (2018): 608.
33 Jenson and Levi, "Narratives and Regimes," 71.
34 Yasha Mounk, *The Age of Responsibility: Luck, Choice and the Welfare State* (Cambridge: Harvard University Press, 2017), 145.
35 Boot, *Human Duties*, 5–6.
36 Martha A. Fineman, "Equality, Autonomy and the Vulnerable Subject in Law and Politics," in *Vulnerability: Reflections on a New Ethical Foundation for Law and Politics*, ed. Martha A. Fineman and Anna Grear (Farnham: Ashgate, 2013), 25.
37 Proposals such as a basic income or different variants to this as well as more specific policy issues are therefore deliberately excluded from this discussion.
38 Compare, e.g., Mounk, *The Age of Responsibility*, 172.
39 Mounk, *The Age of Responsibility*, 11.
40 Trnka and Trundle, "Competing Responsibilities," 139.
41 Ibid., 140.
42 Robert J. Chaskin. "Resilience, Community, and Resilient Communities: Conditioning Contexts and Collective Action," *Child Care in Practice* 14, no. 1 (January 2008) 66.
43 Phillippe Bourbeau, "Resilience and International Politics: Premises, Debates, Agenda," *International Studies Review* 17 (2015): 374.
44 Serge Paugam, "Poverty and Attachment Regimes in Modern Societies," in *Soziale Bildungsarbeit - Europäische Debatten und Projekte*, ed. Joachim Schroeder, Louis Henri Seukwa, and Ulrike Voigtsberger (Wiesbaden: Springer, 2017), 24. Compare also Brigit Obrist, Constanze Pfeiffer, and Robert Henley, "Multi-Layered Social

Conclusion 189

Resilience: A New Approach in Mitigation Research," *Progress in Development Studies* 10, no. 4 (2010): 287; and Chaskin, "Resilience, Community, and Resilient Communities," 72–73.
45 Paugam, "Poverty and Attachment Regimes," 24.
46 Ibid., 13.
47 Fineman, "Equality, Autonomy and the Vulnerable Subject," 24.
48 Dan Allman, "The Sociology of Social Inclusion " *SAGE Open* (January–March 2013): 11. Compare also Sandra Fredman, "Redistribution and Recognition: Reconciling Inequalities," *South African Journal on Human Rights* 23 (2014): 227.
49 Compare, e.g., Fineman and Grear, *Vulnerability*.
50 Van Ertvelde, Chapter 8, this volume.
51 Suzan Ilcan and Kim Rygiel, "'Resiliency Humanitarianism': Responsibilizing Refugees through Humanitarian Emergency Governance in the Camp," *International Political Sociology* 9 (2015): 334.
52 Vasco Lub, Liesbeth Schotanus, and Matthijs Uyterlinde, "Als 'meedoen' een dogma wordt. De participatieparadoxen van de Wmo,' in *Brave burgers gezocht: De grenzen van de activerende overheid,* ed. Imrat Verhoeven and Marcel Ham (Amsterdam: Uitgeverij Van Gennep, 2010), 26.
53 Ibid.
54 Bourbeau, "Resilience and International Politics," 388.
55 Gail Mason and Mariastella Pulvirenti, 'Former Refugees and Community Resilience: 'Papering Over' Domestic Violence," *British Journal of Criminology* 53 (2013): 411.
56 Imrat Verhoeven and Marcel Ham, "De overheid op zoek naar brave burgers," in *Brave burgers gezocht: De grenzen van de activerende overheid,* ed. Imrat Verhoeven and Marcel Ham (Amsterdam: Uitgeverij Van Gennep, 2010), 15.
57 Ibid.
58 Mason and Pulvirenti, "Former Refugees and Community Resilience," 412.
59 Compare, e.g., Catriona Mackenzie, Wendy Rogers, and Susan Dodds, *Vulnerability: New Essays in Ethics and Feminist Philosophy* (Oxford: Oxford University Press, 2014); and Barbara Anna Misztal, *The Challenges of Vulnerability: In Search of Strategies for a Less Vulnerable Social Life* (London: Palgrave Macmillan, 2011).
60 Bourbeau, "Resilience and International Politics," 388.
61 Barbara Anna Misztal, *The Challenges of Vulnerability: In Search of Strategies for a Less Vulnerable Social Life* (London: Palgrave Macmillan, 2011), 46.
62 Ibid., 45–46.
63 Catriona Mackenzie, "The Importance of Relational Autonomy and Capabilities for an Ethics of Vulnerability," in *Vulnerability: New Essays in Ethics and Feminist Philosophy,* ed. Catriona Mackenzie, Wendy Rogers, and Susan Dodds (Oxford: Oxford University Press, 2014), 56–57.
64 Compare, e.g., Mackenzie, "The Importance of Relational Autonomy," 7; and Fineman and Grear, *Vulnerability*.
65 Catherine Elizabeth Brown, "The Concept of Vulnerability and Its Use in the Care and Control of Young People," (PhD diss., University of Leeds, 2013), 33.
66 Mackenzie, "The Importance of Relational Autonomy," 56–57.
67 Wetenschappelijke Raad voor het Regeringsbeleid, *Weten is nog geen doen: Een realistisch perspectief op redzaamheid* (Den Haag: Wetenschappelijke Raad voor het Regeringsbeleid, 2017), 101–102.
68 Trudie Knijn, Claude Martin, and Jane Millar, "Activation as a Common Framework for Social Policies towards Lone Parents," in *Reforming the Bismarckian Welfare Systems,* ed. Bruno Parlier and Claude Martin (Malden: Blackwell Publishing, 2008), 112.
69 Martin Heidenreich and Patrizia Aurich-Beerheide, "European Worlds of Inclusive Activation: The Organisational Challenges of Coordinated Service Provision," *International Journal of Social Welfare* 23 (2014): 20.

70 Robert Folger, "Distributive and Procedural Justice: Multifaceted Meanings and Interrelations," *Social Justice Research* 9, no. 4 (1996): 395–416.
71 Mackenzie, "The Importance of Relational Autonomy," 6.
72 Malini Laxminarayan, "Interactional Justice, Coping and the Legal System: Needs of Vulnerable Victims," *International Review of Victimology* 19, no. 2 (2013): 145.
73 Folger, "Distributive and Procedural Justice," 412, 418.
74 Compare, e.g., Gijsbert Vonk, "Migration, Social Security and the Law: Some European Dilemmas," *European Journal of Social Security* 3/4 (2002): 315–332.
75 Compare, e.g., the judgements by the European Court of Human Rights in *MSS v Belgium and Greece* and *Tarakhel v Switzerland*, and the judgements by the European Committee of Social Rights in *DCI v Belgium* and *CEC v the Netherlands*.
76 Compare, e.g., Veronika Flegar and Marie-Noelle Veys, "De Europese verplichting voor procedurele waarborgen in de asielprocedure en de Nederlandse implementatie vanuit kwetsbaarheidsperspectief," *Journaal Vreemdelingenrecht* 11, no. 2 (2017): 28–49.
77 Compare, e.g., Veronika Flegar, "Vulnerability and the Principle of Non-Refoulement in the European Court of Human Rights: Towards an Increased Scope of Protection for Persons Fleeing from Extreme Poverty?" *Contemporary Readings in Law and Social Justice* 8, no. 2 (2016), 148–169; and Alexandra Timmer, "A Quiet Revolution: Vulnerability in the European Court of Human Rights," in *Vulnerability: Reflections on a New Ethical Foundation for Law and Politics*, ed. Martha A. Fineman and Anna Grear (Farnham: Ashgate, 2013), pp. 147–170.
78 Compare, e.g., Brown, "The Concept of Vulnerability," 33.
79 Douglas Martin, "Arthur Schlesinger, Historian of Power, Dies at 89," *The New York Times*, 1 March 2007.
80 Arthur Schlesinger, *The Vital Center: The Politics of Freedom* (Boston: Houghton Mifflin, 1949), 254, as cited in Chaskin, "Resilience, Community, and Resilient Communities," 72–73.

Index

Page numbers in **bold** reference tables.

1975 Helsinki Accords 144

ACIR 61–62
ADA (Americans with Disabilities Act) 75
Agricultural Committee 21
agriculture, social policy 20–2
Albright, Paul 59
Alfred, John 59
Alien Act (1983) (Denmark) 162, 164
Allied Control Commission 107
All-Party Disablement Group 124
Americans with Disabilities Act (ADA) 75
Arendt, Hannah 175–176
Argentina: professional integration of disabled 63; promotion of vocational rehabilitation 60–62
Armstrong-Jones, Antony 123–124
Article 29 52–53
assistance 103–104
Aston, Christopher 128
Atlantic Charter motto 103
AVERG (Active Defence of the Rights of the Disabled) 148
awareness of disabled persons, IYDP (International Year of Disabled Persons) 71–72

BCODP (British Council of Organisations of Disabled People) 126–127
Belgian National Collective Action for the Handicapped 144
Belgian welfare system 138–141; after 1973 141–145; after 1981 145–149; socialization of care 150
Bennett, Arthur 50, 58
Bertrand, Alfred 13, 15, 17, 19
Beveridge Plan 103

Beveridge, William 83
Beyen, Johan 15
Birkelbach, Willi 13, 17–18, 21
Blacksmith Union (Denmark) 159
Blair, Tony 165
Boct, Eric 174, 177
Bosniak, Linda 175
Bourbeau, Philippe 179
Bourgeois, Leon 110
Bracke-Defever, Mia 141–142, 149
Brazil: professional integration of disabled 63; promotion of vocational rehabilitation 60–62
Briggs, Asa 85–86
Britain: employment 129–131; grassroots response to IYDP 125–128; IYDP (International Year of Disabled Persons) 119–120, 122–125; right to work and independent living 128–132; welfare state and disabled persons 120–122; *see also* United Kingdom
British Council of Organisations of Disabled People (BCODP) 126–127
British Disability Discrimination Act (1995) 76
Brown, Catherine Elisabeth 183
Buggenhout, Van 140
Burke, Edmund 175
Burke, Roland 38
Buset, Max 14

Cailliau, Michel "Charette" 105
Cali, Basik 174
Campbell, Ian 59
CAP (Common Agricultural Policy) 19
Carloni, Carlo 36, 43
Carter, Jimmy 144

Index

Casanova, Laurent 114
Castle, Barbara 121
Castles, Stephen 31, 158
Catholic Association for the Handicapped, Belgium 139, 143
Catholic Party, Belgian welfare system 139
Cazenave, Noel A. 95
CCNR (Central Commission for the Navigation on the Rhine River) 34
Centro de rehabilitación profesional ACIR 62
Cheshire, Leonard 128
Cheshire homes 128
Cibeira, Jose 60
citizenship, legal citizenship and limits of universal human rights 174–176
"civilian disability" 121
clientalization 165
Cloward, Richard A. 86
CNRL (Comisión nacional de rehabilitación del lisiado) 61–62
"coal crisis" (1958) 19
Collective Action (Belgium) 146
"collective morality" 113
Comité Français de Libération nationale (France) 105
Commissariat des prisonniers, déportés, réfugiés (CPDR) 104–106
Common Agricultural Policy (CAP) 19
Common Assembly 10, 16; occupational safety 17
Common Market 14–15
Community Action Programmes for Disabled People 72
'community care,' Britain 131–132
compulsory employment of disabled workers 53
Conseil National de la Resistance, France 105
"considerable burden," disabled persons 70–71
convenience refugees, Denmark 163
Convention on Social Security 161
Convention on the Rights of Persons with Disabilities (CRPD) 77, 133
Convention on the Social Security of Migrant Workers 31–32
Cooper, Norman Edward 50
Coppé, Albert 11
costs of social security 42–43
Council of Europe 36
CPDR (Commissariat des prisonniers, déportés, réfugiés) 104–106
Crampton, Stephen 125

CRPD (Convention on the Rights of Persons with Disabilities) 77, 133
Cruz, Santa 57
Cuoco, Ubiracy Torres 64

DA (Disability Alliance) 121, 129
DA (employers' union) 159
Danish People's Party (DPP) 165
Danish Social Democratic Party 165
D'Aragona Commission 103
DASF, Denmark 159
Davies, Ken 128
Davies, Maggie 128
Declaration on the General and Special Rights of the Mentally Retarded 144
Declaration on the Rights of Disabled Persons (1975, UN) 144–145
Declaration on the Rights of Mentally Retarded Persons (1971, UN) 144
Dedieu, Jean 37
De Gaulle, Charles 105
Degener, Theresia 75
Delors, Jacques 24
De Meester, Wivina 147
Denmark 155–156; immigration 155–158; integration and welfare reforms 164–167; normative crisis of the welfare state 162–164; social rights in economic crisis 160–162; welfare expansion 158–160
Department of Social and Health Services (DSHS) 92
Deveali, Dr. 64
DIG (Disablement Income Group) 121
Dijsselbloem, Jeroen 1
Direct Payment Act (1996), Britain 132
disability 2
disability activists 72–74
Disability Alliance (DA) 121, 129
Disability Archive UK 120
disability rights 75, 76, 148
Disabled People International (DPI) 72–74, 126
"Disabled People's Parliament Resolution to support the UN Standard Rules" 74
disabled persons: "considerable burden" 70–71; welfare state and, Britain 120–122
Disabled Persons Act (1981) 124
Disabled Persons (Employment) Act, UK 55
Disablement Income Group (DIG) 121
"disciplining regimes" 131
"distributive dilemma" 2

Dobbernack, Wilhelm 38
Donnelly, Jack 175
Doublet, Jacques 36–37, 39–40, 42
DPI (Disabled People International) 72–74, 126
DPP (Danish People's Party) 165
DSHS (Department of Social and Health Services) 92
du Boisson, Megan 121
Durand, Paul 37
Duranti, Marco 3, 10
Dury, Ian 127
Dutch Scientific Council for Government Policy 184

early European communities 9
EC (European Commission), Social Integration of Disabled People (1982–1987) 147
ECHR (European Convention on Human Rights) 10
Economic and Social Committee 10
economic crisis, social rights (Denmark) 160–162
economic development 86
ECSC (European Coal and Steel Community) 10, 36; mine safety 16–18; social policy 13–16
EEC (European Economic Community) 10, 36; European Convention of the Social Security of Migrant Workers 32, 34; social security 37
Ekstrabladet 165
Elcker-Ik 148
"Elective participation bond" 180
emancipation policies 147
"embedded liberalism" 9
employment: Belgium 140; for disabled persons (Britain) 129–131; sheltered employment 55; women 23
end of unconditional welfare benefits, responsibilization 176–178
entrepreneurs, internationalized social security 35–38
equal-wages clause 23
Ernst, Charles F. 92–94
Esping-Andersen, Gosta 157
ethnicity, Denmark 166–167
EU (European Union) 70
"Eur'able" 75
European Center for Social Security 42
European Coal and Steel Community (ECSC) 10, 13
European Code of Social Security (1964) 34

European Commission (EC), Social Integration of Disabled People (1982–1987) 147
European Convention, national social security organizations 38–43
European Convention of the Social Security of Migrant Workers 29–31, 34, 36, 43–44
European Convention on Human Rights (ECHR) 10
European Council, disability recommendations 71–72
European Disability Forum 76
European Economic Community (EEC) 10
European integration 23–25; promoting workers' welfare (1953–1955) 11–15
European Investment Bank 10
"Europeanization" of social policies 30
European Miners' Statute 19–20
European Movement, "Social Conference" 37
European Parliament 10
European Pillar of Social Rights 24
European "relaunch" (1955–1957), lobbying for supranational social policies 15–18
"European rescue" 19
European Social Fund 10, 20, 25
European social model 69
European Social Security Fund 39
experts in vocational rehabilitation, selective placement 58–60

family allowances 39–40
"farm-income parity" 21
farms, employment 21
"favourite creditors of the Nation" 114
federalism 82, 88–92
Federal Republic of Germany, combining with national interests and individual rights 39
female employment 23
Ferrera, Maurizio 30
Fineman, Martha 178, 180
Finet, Paul 17
Finkelstein, Vic 122
Framework Equal Treatment Directive (2000) 76
France 102–103; Conseil National de la Resistance 105; CPDR (Commissariat des prisonniers, déportés, réfugiés) 104–6; health insurance systems 113; MPDR, transformation of 113–114; populationists 40; repatriation 104–106; social security 40–43; social services 110–113

Frenay, Henri 105, 107, 111
fund for the Infirm and the Maimed, Belgium 139

Gailly, Arthur 19, 23
Gasparotto, Luigi 111–112
Gazier, Albert 40
gender inequality 25
general welfare 83–84
Ghoetgebuer, Jean-Pierre 149
G.I. Bill, United States 109–110
Gilens, Martin 87–88
Giubonni, Stefano 23
Glistenti, Giuseppe 39
Glistrup, Mogens 161, 163
Goetghebuer, Jean-Pierre 142–143
Gorst, John 129
grassroots response to IYDP, Britain 125–128
"grey materials" 120
GRIP VZW 148
guest workers, Denmark 159
Gupta, Akhil 94

Hallsworth, Simon 86
Hampton, Jameel 120
harmonization 39
Harris, José 83
Haunt, Paul 128
health insurance systems, post-war period 112–114
HELIOS 72–73
HELIOS II 72–75
Heyer, Katharina 75
hidden disabilities 125
hidden welfare state 87
High Authority, social policy 12
High Authority and European Commission 10
housing 40
Howard, Christopher 87
Hulek, Aleksander 57
human rights 9–10, 72–73, 144; universal human rights *see* universal human rights
Human Rights and Disability (1991) 75
Humphreys, John 59–61, 63
Hunt, Paul 122
Hurst, Rachel 74

ILO (International Labour Organization) 9, 10, 30; European social model 69; injured veterans 49–50; social security 33–37; vocational integration for the disabled 51–58; vocational integration for the disabled, Latin America 58–65
IMER (immigration, migration, and ethnicity research) 156
immigration (Denmark) 155–157; development of welfare state 157–158; normative crisis of the welfare state 162–164; welfare expansion 158–160; welfare reform 164–167
immigration (Sweden) 166
immigration, migration, and ethnicity research (IMER) 156
"immigration stop," Denmark 160
inclusion of disability, age, and sexual orientation 77
inclusive social policy 178–179; resilience-focused strengthening of societal structures and community ties 179–182; vulnerability-focused, individualized social service provision 183–186
income for disabled persons, Britain 129
independent living, Britain 128–132
Independent Living Flanders 148
individualized solution of placement, vocational integration for the disabled 55–56
individual rights, combining with national interests 38–43
inequality 2–3
injured veterans, ILO (International Labour Organization) 49–50
INR (Instituto nacional de rehabilitación del Lisiado) 61–62
institutionalization of self-advocates 72–74
insurance 103–104
integration (Denmark), welfare reform 164–167
"intergenerational solidarity" 180
International Day of Disabled Persons 74
International Decade of Disabled Persons (1982–1993) 145
internationalization of social security 31–35; entrepreneurs 35–38
International Labour Organization *see* ILO (International Labour Organization)
International Social Security Agency (ISSA) 43
International Social Security Association 41
International Society for Labour and Social Security Law 43

International Year of Disabled Persons (IYDP) 70–72; Belgium 145–146; Britain 119–120, 122–129
ISSA (International Social Security Agency) 43
Italian New Deal 113
Italy 102–103; MAPB (Ministry of Post-War Assistance) 108–110, 114; post-war assistance 107–110; social services 111–113
IYDP (International Year of Disabled Persons) 70–72; Belgium 145–146; Britain 119–120, 122–129

Jantz, Kurt 36, 39
Jønsson, Heidi Vad 174
Jørgensen, Anker 164

Kaufman, Franz-Xaver 137
Kayser, Armand 36–38, 41
Keynesian welfare state 86
Kjærsgaard, Pia 163
Knijn, Trudie 184
Knudsen, Ann-Christina L. 19
Kott, Sandrine 69, 81, 85
Krier, Antoine 20
Kurt, Melvüt 155, 159

labour immigration (Denmark), welfare expansion 158–160
labour shortages, Denmark 159
Ladies' Committee of the Help Action Research for the Crippled Child 124
Laroque, Pierre 34–35, 37, 103
Latin America (1955–1970s), vocational integration for the disabled 58–65
Laxminarayan, Malini 184
Lea, John 86
legal citizenship and limits of universal human rights 174–176
legitimacy, building for European integration by promoting workers' welfare (1953–1955) 11–15
lens of inequality 2–3
Leonard Cheshire Foundation 127–128
liberal legalities, vocational integration for the disabled 56–58
"Lineal bond" 179–180
LO (Labour Union), Denmark 159
lobbying for supranational social policies during European "relaunch" (1955–1957) 15–18

Lub, Vasco 181
Lussu, Emilio 108, 111
Lyman, R. 58

Maastricht Treaty 76
Mabbett, Deborah 77
Mackenzie, Catriona 183
Mackled-Garcia, Saladin 174
Maier, Charles 9
Mansholt, Sicco 21
MAPB (Ministry of Post-War Assistance), Italy 108–114
marginal groups 1–2
Marinova, Vera 50
Marshall, T.H. 85, 103
Mason, Gail 181, 182
Mason, Phillip 127
maternity benefits 39–40
Mencap 121
migrants: Convention on the Social Security of Migrant Workers 31–32; European Convention of the Social Security of Migrant Workers 29–30; *see also* immigrants
Mills, Charles 89
Milward, Gareth 120
Milward, Alan 9, 19
Mind 121
"Miners' Statute" 17, 20
mine safety 16–18
Ministry of Post-War Assistance (MAPB), Italy 108–110
Misztal, Barbara Anna 183
Monnet, Jean 11
Monnikenheide 147
Moore, Berit 121
Moreira, Godoy 61
Moreno, Héctor Ruiz 63–64
Morris, Alf 124
Morse, David 50
Motz, Roger 16
Mounk, Yasha 177
Moyn, Samuel 144
MPDR, France 106–107, 111–114
Müller, Kurt 64
Mutter, André 18

Naficy, Mr. 52–53
naming the welfare state 82–84
National Association for Mental Health (Mind) 121
National Association of Parents of Backward Children (Mencap) 121

Index

National Fund for the Social Rehabilitation of Disabled Persons (Belgium) 139
"national interests" 38–43
nationality principle 39
national social security organizations, European Convention 38–43
Nederhorst, Gerard 12–15, 19–21, 23
Neocleous 86
neoliberal crises, phantom welfare state 92–94
neoliberalism, "roll-back phase" 146
neoliberal principles 92–93
neoliberal turn 119
Neubeck, Kenneth J. 95
New Deal (US) 82–84
NHS Community Care Act (1990), Britain 132
Ninn-Hansen, Erik 164
Niwa, Isamu 50
Normand, Roger 10
normative crisis of the welfare state, Denmark 162–164

Obinger, Herbert 88
occupational safety 16–17
Oliver, Mike 76
Olson, Joel 91
Olzendam, Roderic 93
"original constitutional compromise" 23

PABs (personal-assistance budgets) 148
Parodi, Alexandre 103
participatieparadoxen 181
participatiesamenleving (participatory society) 182
Partito d'Azione 108
Paugam, Serge 179
Peck, Jamie 146
personal-assistance budgets (PABs) 148
perspectival perception, United States 88–92
Petrilli, Giuseppe 24
phantom lives, United States 94–96
phantom pains, United States 88–92
phantom welfare state 81–82; neoliberal crises 92–94; racial contracts 89–92; *see also* United States
Philip, André 105
Phillips, Norman 60–61, 64
pillarization, Belgian welfare system 138–139, 151n12
Piven, Frances Fox 86
"politics of productivity" 9, 12
Polizeistaat 86

populationists 40
Probst, Maria 23
post-war assistance 102–103; France, social services 110–113
post-war period: "Europeanization" of social policies 30; France 104–107, 110–113; health insurance systems 112–113; Italy 107–113; social security 32–35; social services 110–113
Priestley, Mark 76
Prince Charles, IYDP (International Year of Disabled Persons) 123
Probst, Maria 21
professional insertion, socialization of local actors to liberal standards on 62–65
professional integration of disabled, Latin America (1955–1970s) 63–65
programmatic parameters, welfare state 87–88
Progress Party (Denmark) 161, 163
project 81 128
promoting workers' welfare (1953–1955) 11–15
promotion of vocational rehabilitation, Latin America (1955–1970s) 60–62
public charity, Italy 108–109
Pulvirenti, Mariastella 181, 182

Quataert, Jean Helen 144
Queen Elizabeth, IYDP (International Year of Disabled Persons) 123
quota systems, vocational integration for the disabled 52–54

racial contracts, phantom welfare state (US) 89–92
racism, phantom welfare state (US) 95–96
Rasmussen, Hans 159
Rasmussen, Poul Nyrup 164–165
Recommendation No. 99 52–55, 57, 65
recommendations on disability, European Council 71–72
refugee crisis 1
refugees: Denmark, normative crisis of the welfare state 162–164; France 105–107; Italy 109
rehabilitation, UNRRA (United Nations Relief and Rehabilitation Administration) 109
rehabilitation institutes, Latin America (1955–1970s) 60–62
rehabilitation of disabled citizens, ILO (International Labour Organization) 50

rejection of proposals for vocational rehabilitation, socialist countries 51–52
repatriation, France 104–106
resilience-focused strengthening of societal structures and community ties 179–182
responsibilization and the end of unconditional welfare benefits 176–178
right to work, Britain 128–132
Roberts, Dorothy E. 81, 88
"roll-back phase" of neoliberalism 146
Roosevelt, Franklin Delano 82–84
Rouault, Georges-Yves 59–61, 63
Ruggie, John 9

Saarland 33
Sacco, Italo Mario 12
Sainsbury, Diane 157
Samoy, Erik 140
Sandri, Lionello Levi 24
"sanitary cordon" 107
Schall, Carly 157
Scharpf, Fritz 24
Schierup, Carl Ulrich 31
Schlüter, Poul 162, 164
SDSS (State Department of Social Security) 94
second injury funds 63
selective placement, Latin America (1955–1970s) 60–62
self-advocates 72–74
sheltered employment 55
Slater, Mr. 53
Slingenberg, Lieneke 175
Smet, Miet 147
Snowdon, Lord 123–124, 126–127
Snowdon Committee 123, 126
Snyder, Sarah 144
Social Affairs Committee 10–15; expansion of welfare vision (1958–1962) 19–23
Social Affairs Committee of the Common Assembly 10
social citizenship 85–86
Social Committee of the European Parliamentary Assembly 10
social concept 85
"Social Conference," European Movement 37
social control 86
Social Democracy (Denmark) 160–161
Social Democratic Party (Denmark) 162–163
Social Democrats (Denmark) 164
Social Democrats (Sweden) 157
social dumping 39
"Social Europe," 24
social exclusion 77
social inclusion 25
social insurances 29, 32
Social Integration of Disabled People (1982–1987), European Commission (EC) 147
socialist countries, rejection of proposals for vocational rehabilitation 51–52
socialization of care, Belgium 150
socialization of local actors to liberal standards on, professional insertion 62–65
social policy 10, 12–15; agriculture 20–22; inclusive social policy *see* inclusive social policy
social prestige 36
social progress 36
social rehabilitation, Belgium 139
social reintegration, MPDR 112
social-resilience-building approaches 182
social rights 31, 103; during economic crisis (Denmark) 160–162
social security 103; international framing of 32–35; internationalization 31
Social Security Act (1935) 82
"Social Security Provision for Chronically Sick and Disabled People" 121
social service programmes, Washington State (US) **90–91**
social services: France 110–113; Italy 111–113
social service state 83, 85
socio-economic human rights: legal citizenship and limits of universal human rights 174–176; responsibilization and the end of unconditional welfare benefits 176–178
solidarism 111
Spaak Committee 15
Spastics Society 121
"Spasticus Ausisticus" (Dury) 127
"spontaneous refugees," Denmark 163
Spyropoulos, Georges 37
Standard Rules on the Equalization of Opportunities for Disabled Persons (1993) 73
State Department of Social Security 94
Steyaert, Rika 148
Stone, Deborah 130
Storch, Anton 20

Studer, Brigitte 31
subnational welfare states 88–89
supranational social policies, European "relaunch" (1955–1957) 15–18
SUSERPS 61
Sweden 157; immigration 166

Tamil case, Denmark 164–167
territoriality 42
Thatcher, Margaret 119, 122
Titmuss, Richard 81, 158
Tixier, Adrien 49
transnational categories of an international social right 41
transnational social policy 29
Treaties of Rome (1957) 10, 15, 39
Treaty of Amsterdam (1997) 76
Treaty of Paris (1951) 10
Tremezzo conference 113
Troclet, Léon-Éli 32, 35
Turkey, Convention on Social Security 161
typologies 4

unemployment, Italy 109
UNESCAP (United Nations Economic and Social Commission for Asia and the Pacific) 73
Union of the Physically Impaired Against Segregation (UPIAS) 122, 127
United Kingdom (UK): Disabled Persons (Employment) Act 55; self-advocates 76
United Nations (UN): CRPD (Convention on the Rights of Persons with Disabilities) 133; Declaration of Human Rights 9–10; Declaration on the Rights of Disabled Persons (1975) 144–145; Declaration on the Rights of Mentally Retarded Persons (1971) 144; Economic and Social Commission for Asia and the Pacific (UNESCAP) 73; Human Rights and Disability (1991) 75; IYDP (International Year of Disabled Persons) 70–72; Relief and Rehabilitation Administration (UNRRA) 104
United States (US): Americans with Disabilities Act (ADA) 75; compulsory employment of disabled workers 53; G.I. Bill 109–110; meaning of welfare state 84–87; New Deal 82–84; perspectival perception and phantom pains 88–92; phantom lives 94–96; programmatic parameters for welfare state 87–88; racial contracts and white democracy 89–92; subnational welfare states 88–89
universal human rights: legal citizenship and 174–176; responsibilization and the end of unconditional welfare benefits 176–178
universal welfare system 158
UNRRA (United Nations Relief and Rehabilitation Administration) 104; rehabilitation 109
UPIAS (Union of the Physically Impaired Against Segregation) 122, 127
US G.I. Bill 109–110

Valeri, Gino Andrés 65
Verschueren, Nicolas 20
Vichy regime 105–106; social services 110–111
vocational integration for the disabled: ILO (International Labour Organization) 51–58; Latin America (1955–1970s) 58–65; liberal legalities 56–58
vocational rehabilitation 49–51
Vocational Rehabilitation (Disabled) Recommendation (No.99) 50
Vredeling, Henk 21, 23
vulnerability-focused, individualized social service provision 183–186

Waddington, Lisa 77
Ward, Deborah E. 89
Washington State (US): social service programmes **90–91**; subnational welfare states 88–89
welfare, term used by FDR 83
welfare bureaucracy 161
welfare citizens, Denmark 166–168
welfare nationalism, Denmark 165
welfare racism 95
welfare reforms, Denmark 164–167
welfare state 3, 30; Britain, disabled persons and 120–122; Denmark, immigration and 157–158; naming 82–84; phantom welfare state 81–82; programmatic parameters 87–88; United States, meaning of 84–87
welfare vision, Social Affairs Committee 19–23
Western European Union 36
white democracy, phantom welfare state (US) 89–92

white supremacy, phantom welfare state 95–96
Wincott, Daniel 82, 85
Winnipeg World Congress of Rehabilitation International (1980) 126
Winstanley, Lord 124
women, employment 23
Working Group Disabled People 148

World Council of Disabled People International 73
World Programme of Action 145

Yugoslavia, Convention on Social Security 161

Zaidi, Sarah 10

Printed in the United States
By Bookmasters